Partnering
with Families
for Student Success

Partnering with **Families** for **Student Success**

24 SCENARIOS
FOR PROBLEM SOLVING
WITH PARENTS

Patricia A. Edwards
Rand J. Spiro
Lisa M. Domke
Ann M. Castle
Kristen L. White
Marliese R. Peltier
Tracy H. Donohue

Foreword by Joyce L. Epstein

TEACHERS COLLEGE PRESS
TEACHERS COLLEGE | COLUMBIA UNIVERSITY
NEW YORK AND LONDON

Published by Teachers College Press, 1234 Amsterdam Avenue, New York, NY 10027

Copyright © 2019 by Teachers College, Columbia University

Cover photos courtesy of arinahabich, FG Trade, FatCamera, CREATISTA, monkeybusinessimages, ti-ja, and Steve Debenport, all via iStock by Getty Images.

Library of Congress Cataloging-in-Publication Data is available at loc.gov.

ISBN 978-0-8077-6117-5 (paper)
ISBN 978-0-8077-7760-2 (ebook)

Printed on acid-free paper
Manufactured in the United States of America

26 25 24 23 22 21 20 19   8 7 6 5 4 3 2 1

Contents

Foreword

A while ago, a popular commercial aimed at helping smokers to break the habit concluded, "Every great why needs a great how." This catchy phrase captures the goals of this book by Professor Patricia A. Edwards and her colleagues. Everyone—teachers, parents, administrators, and students— knows *why* family engagement is important. Decades of studies confirm that students do better in school if their parents are involved in their education.

What has been missing from the repertoires of many educators are strategies for *how to* move from confirmed findings to regular and universal teaching practice. There are two major elements in comprehensive programs of family and community engagement: (1) whole-school organization and (2) individual teacher initiatives.

Whole-school organization. At Johns Hopkins University, the National Network of Partnership Schools (NNPS) invites districts, schools, organizations, and state departments of education to join researchers and other educators to use evidence-based approaches to organize, implement, evaluate, and continually improve programs of school, family, and community partnerships. NNPS provides publications, training, tools, and ongoing services to enable educators to engage all families—not just those easy to reach— as partners in their children's education (Epstein et al., 2019). With "nested leadership," district leaders for partnerships guide and support their schools' Action Teams for Partnerships (ATPs) to set goals, write plans, and implement family and community engagement activities that engage all families, create a welcoming climate, and improve students' academic and behavioral outcomes. In this way, family and community engagement is understood as an essential and sustainable component of good school organization.

Individual teacher initiatives. Every teacher is an active participant in a school's partnership program. Presently, most colleges in this and other countries fail to prepare future teachers to connect and communicate with students' families (Epstein, 2011; Willemse et al., 2018). In this book, Professor Edwards and her colleagues contribute to this critical agenda with 24 modules that guide future teachers to work with the highly diverse families and students they will meet in their schools and classrooms from the first day of their professional careers to the last.

Everyone loves stories—especially stories of difficult challenges and successful solutions. The 24 stories in this book will help future teachers envision their work through the experiences of others. Each module presents a challenge, requires deep thinking, elicits creative solutions, and shares successful strategies that should increase teachers' skills and confidence in communicating creatively and caringly with all students' parents and other caregivers.

The activities in each module ask future teachers to think about how each partner—student, parent/caregiver, and teacher—feels about their power, prestige, position, and resources in causing and in solving the featured communication challenge. At the end of each module, the authors "rebuild" the case and report one or more strategies for solving the initial problem. All of the solutions demonstrate how teachers and parents accomplish more to help students succeed in school by working together than by avoiding, dismissing, or dissing each other.

For example, Module 4: Caregivers with Complex Job Situations, guides a discussion of a challenge that all teachers face: having students whose parents are employed and/or have more than one job. These realities affect parents' availability to attend meetings and events at the school building during the day and/or evening. They require individual teachers and the school as an organization to consider other options using new technologies, creative scheduling, and alternative designs for engagement at school, at home, and in the community.

Similarly, all future teachers need to explore Module 6: Caregivers Who Speak Limited or No English—a near-certainty in every teacher's experience (Hutchins, et al., 2012). The case study guides teachers to improve connections by activating translators and interpreters among district staff, teachers, parents and volunteers, high school and other students, and Google Translate.

The authors offer good advice throughout the book: *Never give up* in trying new ways to connect with every student's family; *remain professional* by barring negative labels and demeaning discussions about parents who are not yet good partners; and *consider each situation*, because the modules are not "recipes" to cook up in all instances. Rather, the examples aim to encourage creative thinking and responsive solutions for each emerging challenge.

This book is a trove of treasured stories about *how* to communicate with diverse families to support student success in school. Teachers will keep this reference handy because they *will* meet similar challenges. The message is clear: Family and community engagement should be part of teacher education because it is part of every teacher's professional work.

—Joyce L. Epstein, Ph.D.
Johns Hopkins University
Center on School, Family, and Community Partnerships

REFERENCES

Epstein, J. L. (2011). *School, family, and community partnerships: Preparing educators and improving schools* (2nd ed.). New York: Westview Press/Taylor and Francis.

Epstein, J. L., Sanders, M. G., Sheldon, S. B., Simon, B. S., Salinas, K. C., Jansorn, N. R., . . . Williams, K. J. (2019). *School, family, and community partnerships: Your handbook for action* (4th ed.). Thousand Oaks, CA: Corwin Press.

Hutchins, D. J., Greenfeld, M. D., Epstein, J. L., Sanders, M. G., & Galindo, C. L. (2012). *Multicultural partnerships: Involve all families.* New York, NY: Taylor and Francis.

Willemse, T. M., Thompson, I., Mutton, T., & Vanderlinde, R. (2018). Preparing pre-service teachers for family-school partnerships. *Journal of Education for Teaching, 44* (Issue 3), 251–412.

Acknowledgments

A book of this magnitude owes very much to very many. Pat wants to begin by thanking her six brilliant co-authors, Rand J. Spiro, Lisa M. Domke, Ann M. Castle, Kristen L. White, Marliese R. Peltier, and Tracy H. Donohue, for their excellent work and support. Pat thanks Rand for sharing with us how his Cognitive Flexibility Theory can help teachers build a repertoire of flexible responses to the many variations of caregiver situations that will arise. Pat thanks her other five co-authors (Lisa, Ann, Kristen, Marliese, and Tracy) for their willingness to work on this book project while they were either taking their comprehensive exam, writing a dissertation, or going on job interviews. Pat appreciates their attention to detail and their work ethic. Without their diligence, hard work, and several late nights and early mornings, Pat would not have been able to meet the deadline. Her coauthors had an unbelievable amount of last-minute changes, and Pat appreciates their flexibility very much. It's that kind of flexibility and dedication that helped to not only launch this book on time, but with a wonderful result.

We cannot express our gratitude and appreciation in strong enough terms for the unimaginable grace and patience combined with astounding insight, expertise, and thoughtful questions offered throughout this process by our editor, Jean Ward. What an exceptional editor she is. Our book is much stronger because of her.

We thank John Bylander, our production editor, who was heroic in not only clearing up our words, but also in keeping us honest when we drifted off course. He was patient, tireless, and meticulous as we polished everything up to get it ready for final production. We thank Nancy Power for her awesome promotional statement about our book and Joy Mizan for giving us fantastic strategies to promote our book.

We would like to say a special "thank you" to Joyce L. Epstein for so graciously agreeing to write the Foreword and building the case for why our book will improve and enhance school, family, and community partnerships. We thank Elfrieda "Freddy" Hiebert for her praise of our book and for encouraging our readers to apply our process of exploring perspectives, getting on the same page, listening to expand perspectives, fixing it, and rebuilding.

We owe so much to our family and friends who have supported us. We feel fortunate that they listened with genuine interest and insight to all our work stories. For these reasons and more, we want say a big "thank you" to our family and friends, because their love, patience, encouragement, and good humor keep us going.

CHAPTER 1

The Importance of Family–School Partnerships

"When schools, families, and community groups work together to support learning, children tend to do better in school, stay in school longer, and like school more." That's the conclusion of *A New Wave of Evidence*, a report by Henderson and Mapp (2002, p. 7) from the Southwest Educational Development Laboratory. The report, a synthesis of research on parent involvement over the past decade, also found that regardless of family income or background, students with involved parents are more likely to

- earn higher grades and test scores, and enroll in higher-level programs;
- be promoted, pass their classes, and earn credits;
- attend school regularly;
- have better social skills, show improved behavior, and adapt well to school; and
- graduate and go on to postsecondary education (see Henderson & Mapp, 2002).

Therefore, involving parents and families in their children's education is important, and the concept of family–school partnerships seems relatively simple. It is about a seemingly plausible idea: that teachers should encourage all families to become involved in their children's education and that teachers should reach out to families in new and different ways.

This idea has heavily influenced educational reform over the past decade, and it lies at the center of most school-restructuring initiatives (Edwards, 2004, 2016; Epstein, 2011). As with most complex reforms, though, it is difficult to decipher exactly what advocates of school restructuring want by way of family involvement. Unfortunately, many advocates of restructuring seem to believe that by acknowledging they want families involved in the business of the schools, teachers and administrators will restructure how they think about family involvement, which will in turn increase the overall participation of families and subsequently lead to improved performance of students. Unfortunately, this is not a reality in most schools.

We believe, like Epstein (1987), that while "parent involvement is on everyone's list of practices to make schools more effective, to help families create more positive learning environments, to reduce the risk of student failure, and to increase student success" (p. 4), that involvement does not automatically occur. Epstein correctly notes that "parent involvement is everybody's job but nobody's job until a structure is put in place to support it" (p. 10). Therefore, it comes as no surprise that there is little real parent involvement in schools given the lack of infrastructure to foster and support it. Merely stating a desire for family involvement is not enough; the extent of the responsibility has to be accepted by parents, teachers, the school, and the community. Epstein emphasizes that:

> Parent involvement is not the parents' responsibility alone. Nor is it the school's or teachers' or community educators' responsibility alone. All groups need to work together for a *sustained period of time* to develop programs that will increase parents' understanding of the schools and their ability to assist their children, and that will promote student success and reduce failure at every grade level (p. 10).

As we explain below, one of our goals in developing our parent involvement modules is to seriously address the notion of parents and teachers working together and create a structure for family involvement in grades kindergarten through 8. Given the importance of family involvement and the time it takes to develop family–school partnerships, we advocate for helping teachers develop knowledge, competencies, and confidence in this area during their teacher preparation programs.

PARENT INVOLVEMENT AND TEACHER PREPARATION PROGRAMS: WHY HAVE TEACHER EDUCATORS BEEN SLOW TO RESPOND?

There is broad consensus on the importance of the family's role in education (e.g., Edwards, 2004, 2016; Epstein, 1987, 2011; Henderson & Mapp, 2002), and there are several documented examples of teacher educators preparing teachers to work with parents (e.g., D'Haem & Griswold, 2017; Epstein & Sanders, 2006; Garibaldi, 1992; Hiatt-Michael, 2006; Hoover-Dempsey, Walker, Jones, & Reed, 2002; Levine, 2006; Patte, 2011; Safran, 1974; Williams, 1992). While teacher educators may agree that parents are important participants in the educational process, teacher educators too often "believe that the knowledge, skills, and attitudes for working with parents flow naturally from the teaching experience. Yet, teachers in classrooms are frequently just as uncomfortable dealing with families as are the teacher educators who trained them" (Kochan & Mullins, 1992, p. 272). Not only are many teachers uncomfortable dealing with families, but teacher educators have similarly voiced their discomfort with preparing prospective teachers to work with families. Epstein and Sanders (2006) surveyed administrators in 161 teacher preparation programs and reported that although respondents agreed that involving families was important, few believed that graduating teacher candidates were fully prepared to do so. The lack of documented examples of teacher educators preparing teachers to work with parents is particularly alarming when the research literature has repeatedly highlighted the fact that parents are their child's first teacher, and teachers are children's second teacher (Edwards, 2016; Epstein, 2011).

As we describe in more detail below in our discussion of our goals for this book, the modules we have developed are an attempt to remedy this disparity and to provide prospective as well as practicing teachers with recommendations for dealing with the many diverse situations they may encounter regarding relations with parents, families, and other caregivers.

Receiving instruction, support, and guidance related to working with families and other caregivers is especially important when students and their caregivers come from different cultural, economic, and/or linguistic backgrounds from their teachers. Researchers have noted concerns about prospective teachers' lack of preparation to teach diverse learners and appreciate the impact of the relationships between these caregivers and schools (e.g., Cazden & Mehan, 1989; D'Haem & Griswold, 2017; Delpit, 2006; Florio-Ruane, 1994; McDiarmid & Price, 1993; Paine, 1988; Epstein & Sanders, 2006; Shartrand, Weiss, Kreider, & Lopez, 1997). For example, Epstein and Sanders (2006) suggested that many educators have inadequate understanding to effectively create partnerships in inner cities that differ from the communities in which they live. While prospective teachers may feel that issues of socioeconomic status, ethnicity, or language would not affect their relationships with families/caregivers (e.g., Foster & Loven, 1992), Lareau (1989) has noted that inequalities in caregivers' resources and dispositions—for example, education, occupational status, or income—critically affected levels of parent/caregiver involvement, regardless of caregivers' aspirations for their children.

Therefore, not only must teachers develop skills in working with families in general, but findings from Foster and Loven (1992) and Lareau (1989) also point to the need for all teachers, prospective and practicing, to learn how to work with culturally different students and families. One reason such training is needed is that the culture of poor, minority, and immigrant students might conflict with the middle-class educational vision that a primarily White, middle-class, K–12 teaching staff brings to the classroom and school environment (McDiarmid & Price, 1993; Paine, 1988). A lack of shared background frequently makes it difficult for instructors to connect subject matter to the lives of their students, which may prevent these students' parents/caregivers from becoming involved in school affairs. They might become discouraged and dissatisfied with teachers' inability to successfully teach their children. Unfortunately, this often leads to an unraveling of the relationship between home and school. Because of this miscommunication, children are caught in the crossfire and ultimately suffer academically.

OUR GOALS FOR THIS BOOK

Given the need to prepare teachers to work with families and learn to build bridges across socioeconomic, ethnic, linguistic, and other divides, we have written this book to support prospective teachers, practicing teachers, and teacher educators. We have developed a series of caregiver-involvement modules to provide teachers with strategies to use when confronting challenging situations and, more importantly, to broaden teachers' perspectives on caregivers* so that teachers can identify and attempt to address the underlying needs and situational factors affecting caregivers' actions instead of finding deficits in the caregivers (and students) themselves.

Dealing with difference is never easy, whether it involves differences in race, class, ethnicity, language, worldviews, or roles (e.g., parents and teachers). With these modules, we wanted to explore many ways in which teachers might encounter differences or difficulties with caregivers so that teachers can explore the implications of the situations in safe spaces and reflect on possible solutions before they must make in-the-moment decisions. Because each situation is different, we use Cognitive Flexibility Theory as the underlying theory of these modules. Cognitive Flexibility Theory is necessary when each individual case differs from every other case and we cannot rely on a set of prescriptive behaviors that will work in every situation. Instead of relying on a "template," teachers employ cognitive flexibility by using their prior knowledge and experiences acquired over different times and integrating those with information from the specific case (Spiro, 2015). See Chapter 3 for further information on Cognitive Flexibility Theory.

We realize that teacher preparation programs cannot prepare teachers for every situation, so our goal is to help teachers critically evaluate situations and develop reflective habits because those skills transcend specific situations. In Chapter 2, we introduce the format of the modules. We have also created a table in which we present an overview of the module topics and how they connect to the Interstate New Teacher Assessment and

---

*In the modules, we generally use "caregiver" instead of "parent" or "family" because "caregiver" can refer to anyone actively involved in raising and educating a child and is thus more inclusive and reflective of the diversity of students' home situations.

Support Consortium (InTASC) standards (Council of Chief State School Officers, 2013). This table can be found online at www.tcpress.com.

REFERENCES

Cazden, C. B., & Mehan, H. (1989). Principles from sociology and anthropology: Context, code, classroom and culture. In M. Reynolds (Ed.), *Knowledge base for the beginning teacher* (pp. 47–57). New York, NY: Pergamon.

Council of Chief State School Officers. (2013). *InTASC model core teaching standards and learning progressions for teachers 1.0: A resource for ongoing teacher development.* Washington, DC: Author.

Delpit, L. (2006). *Other people's children: Cultural conflict in the classroom* (2nd ed.). New York, NY: The New Press.

D'Haem, J., & Griswold, P. (2017). Teacher educators' and student teachers' beliefs about preparation for working with families including those from diverse socio-economic and cultural backgrounds. *Education and Urban Society, 49*(1), 81–109.

Edwards, P. A. (2004). *Children's literacy development: Making it happen through school, family, and community involvement.* Boston, MA: Allyn & Bacon.

Edwards, P. A. (2016). *New ways to engage parents: Strategies and tools for teachers and leaders, K–12.* New York, NY: Teachers College Press.

Epstein, J. L. (1987). Parent involvement: State education agencies should lead the way. *Community Education Journal, 14*(4), 4–10.

Epstein, J. L. (2011). *School, family, and community partnerships: Preparing educators and improving schools* (2nd ed.). Boulder, CO: Westview Press.

Epstein, J. L., & Sanders, M. G. (2006). Prospects for change: Preparing educators for school, family, and community partnerships. *Peabody Journal of Education, 81*(2), 81–120.

Evans, D., & Nelson, D. (1992). The curriculum of aspiring teachers: Not a question of either/or. In L. Kaplan (Ed.), *Education and the family* (pp. 230–242). Boston, MA: Allyn and Bacon.

Florio-Ruane, S. (1994). The future teachers' autobiography club: Preparing educators to support literacy learning in culturally diverse classrooms. *English Education, 26*(1), 52–66.

Foster, J. E., & Loven, R. G. (1992). The need and directions for parent involvement in the '90s: Undergraduate perspectives and expectations. *The Journal of the Association of Teacher Educators, 14*(3), 13–18.

Foy, S., Freeland, R., Miles, A., Rogers, K. B., & Smith-Lovin, L. (2014). Emotions and affect as source, outcome and resistance to inequality. In J. D. McLeod, E. J. Lawler, & M. Schwalbe (Eds.), *Handbook of the social psychology of inequality* (pp. 295–324). Dordrecht, Netherlands: Springer.

Garibaldi, A. M. (1992). Preparing teachers for culturally diverse classrooms. In M. E. Dilworth (Ed.), *Diversity in teacher education: New directions* (pp. 23–39). San Francisco, CA: Jossey-Bass.

Henderson, A., T., & Mapp, K. L. (2002). *A new wave of evidence: The impact of school, family, and community connections on student achievement.* Austin, TX:

Southwest Educational Development Laboratory. Retrieved from www.sedl.org
/connections/resources/evidence.pdf

Hiatt-Michael, D. (2006). Reflections and directions on research related to fami-
ly-community involvement in schooling. *The School Community Journal, 16*(1),
7–30.

Holm, G., & Johnson, L. N. (1994). Shaping cultural partnerships: The readiness of
preservice teachers to teach in culturally diverse classrooms. In M. J. O'Hair
& S. J. Odell (Eds.), *Partnerships in education: Teacher education yearbook II* (pp.
85–101). Fort Worth, TX: Harcourt Brace Jovanovich College Publishers.

Hoover-Dempsey, K., Walker, J., Jones, K., & Reed, R. (2002). Teachers involving
parents (TIP): Results of an in-service teacher education program for enhancing
parental involvement. *Teaching and Teacher Education, 18*(7), 843–867.

Kochan, F., & Mullins, B. K. (1992). Teacher education: Linking universities, schools,
and families for the twenty-first century. In L. Kaplan (Ed.), *Education and the
family* (pp. 266–272). Boston, MA: Allyn and Bacon.

Lareau, A. (1989). *Home advantage: Social class and parental intervention in elementary
education.* New York, NY: Falmer Press.

Levine, A. (2006). *Educating school teachers.* Retrieved from www.edschools.org/pdf/
Educating_Teachers_Report.pdf

McDiarmid, G. W., & Price, J. (1993). Preparing teachers for diversity: A study of
student teachers in a multicultural program. In M. J. O'Hair & S. J. Odell (Eds.),
Diversity in teaching: Teacher education yearbook I (pp. 31–59). Fort Worth, TX:
Harcourt Brace Jovanovich College Publishers.

Paine, L. (1988, April). *Orientations toward diversity: What do prospective teachers bring?*
Paper presented at the annual American Educational Research Association
meeting, New Orleans, LA.

Patte, M. (2011). Examining preservice teachers' knowledge and competencies in
establishing family–school partnerships. *The School Community Journal, 21*(2),
143–159.

Safran, D. (1974). *Preparing teachers for parent involvement.* Orinda, CA: Center for the
Study of Parent Involvement.

Shartrand, A. M., Weiss, H. B., Kreider, H. M., & Lopez, M. E. (1997). *New skills
for new schools: Preparing teachers in family involvement.* Cambridge, MA: Harvard
University Press.

Spiro, R. J. (2015). Cognitive flexibility theory. In J. M. Spector (Ed.), *The SAGE
encyclopedia of educational technology* (pp. 111–115). Thousand Oaks, CA: SAGE.

Williams, D. L., Jr. (1992). Parental involvement in teacher preparation: Challenges
to teacher education. In L. Kaplan (Ed.), *Education and the family* (pp. 243–254).
Boston, MA: Allyn and Bacon.

CHAPTER 2

Tools to Deepen Understanding and Develop Solutions

Exploring the Module Format

In this chapter we describe the six sections of each module: (1) Case Scenario, (2) Exploring Current Perspectives, (3) Getting on the Same Page, (4) Listening to Expand Perspectives, (5) Fixing It, and (6) Rebuilding the Case. In some of the sections, we ask teachers to engage in organized reflective tasks. These tasks contain prompts and activity templates to help readers think through the obvious—and not-so-obvious—underlying needs of caregivers, teachers, and students, and to develop solutions to specific scenarios in order to prepare them to encounter similar situations. The tasks and guidance for thinking about them can be found in the appendixes and also online at www.tcpress.com. To further facilitate readers' comfort in using these tools, examples of completed tasks are provided for the following modules: Module 4: Caregivers with Complex Job Situations, Module 15: Advocating for a Neurodiversity Paradigm, and Module 18: Caregivers with Frequent Concerns.

SECTION 1: CASE SCENARIO

Each module begins with a case scenario that introduces a situation teachers may face when working with caregivers. Teachers will explore their reaction to the situation and revisit it throughout the module as they analyze the situation and potential solutions.

In these case scenarios, we have tried to represent typical situations in which teachers find themselves (including those in which we have found ourselves). It is not our intention to reinforce stereotypes, and we realize that family structures take many forms, including stay-at-home dads, a mom and a dad, two moms/dads, single-parent households, grandparents raising children, foster parents, and others—all of which we could not represent in every module.

SECTION 2: EXPLORING CURRENT PERSPECTIVES

Following the case scenario, readers will explore their current perspectives by engaging in tasks to reflect on their initial reactions (see Appendix A). Tasks include the completion of worksheet templates that teachers will use to identify caregiver needs and concerns. They will then be asked to probe deeper to analyze the issues underlying the caregivers' actions in the case scenario.

In our work with caregivers and schools, in the roles of teachers, school professionals, researchers, teacher educators, and caregivers ourselves, we have found that usually even in the most challenging interactions between caregivers and teachers, all parties want what is best for the child. However, sometimes it can be difficult to determine the cause of a caregiver's anger or withdrawal. These emotions are often responses to perceived inequities (Foy, Freeland, Miles, Rogers, & Smith-Lovin, 2014), perhaps stemming from feeling that their child's needs (or their own needs) have not been met, or that their power, prestige, positioning, and/or access has been threatened. Because these concepts are central to determining and understanding caregivers' reactions, we use these concepts as part of the framework of each module and explain and define them here:

- **Power:** Because parents/caregivers are their children's first teachers and because they have ultimate responsibility for their children, it is important that caregivers have some control as to what happens to their children. When people lose control or power over a situation, they often feel fear and anxiety (Foy et al., 2014).
- **Prestige:** Prestige involves a person's status and often relates to the power they have. Loss of status is related to negative emotions that depend on how people attribute the source of the loss. If they blame themselves for the loss of prestige, they may feel shame, embarrassment, sadness, or depression. If they blame others for their loss of prestige, they may feel anger (Foy et al., 2014).
- **Positioning:** The ways in which children and caregivers are positioned influence their reactions. For example, if teachers and schools position caregivers as knowledgeable, that gives them power and validates their role in their children's lives at school. If teachers and schools position caregivers as deficient, absent, or unimportant, caregivers are marginalized, and they may lash out in order to regain power.
- **Access:** In our context, access involves the ability to obtain and use resources necessary for living and learning. Being able to access resources affects people's status and their feelings of power/control over their needs and lives.

These concepts are interrelated in that power is similar to prestige, and positioning and access can convey power and prestige. All four concepts relate to Maslow's (1943) Hierarchy of Needs, which we have used as another part of our framework for the modules (see Figure 2.1). Only by moving beyond outward emotions and identifying caregivers' underlying needs can teachers and schools work with caregivers and find meaningful solutions that benefit all parties.

Focusing on caregivers' underlying needs and ways in which they may perceive actions of teachers and schools as threatening their power, prestige, positioning, and/or access moves teachers out of a pattern of feeling threatened by caregivers, blaming them, and/or dismissing them as being overly emotional or irrational. When teachers take these negative stances, nothing can be accomplished because the relationship turns into an opposition of us versus them. Instead, we advocate that teachers take an asset-based perspective by focusing on positive aspects and/or contributions. With an asset-based perspective, teachers look for ways in which caregivers can contribute to their children's learning and identify the needs and threats that underlie their behaviors so that all parties can work together to find solutions. To find these solutions, teachers must be armed with information. The more they know about their students, their caregivers, and their caregivers' situations, the less likely they are to jump to conclusions that limit students' and caregivers' potential. Information is power. And it is important to remember that no solution should put all responsibility on the caregivers. The teacher/school must have specified steps to help solve the problem. After all, it is the teacher's job to help students, and the only way that can be accomplished is by working *with* caregivers, not in opposition to them.

Figure 2.1. Maslow's (1943) Hierarchy of Needs

**Self-
Actualization
Needs**
(achieve potential,
self-fulfillment)

Esteem Needs
(achievement, adequacy,
independence, reputation, recognition)

Love/Affection and Belongingness Needs

Safety Needs
(security, health and wellness, knowing what to expect)

Physiological Needs (food, water, sleep)

SECTION 3: GETTING ON THE SAME PAGE

After reading the initial case scenario, reflecting on it, and probing deeper to consider caregivers' needs and issues of power, prestige, positioning, and access, we provide background information about the topic. We refer to the work of researchers and practitioners to help readers "get on the same page" and to provide various perspectives to inform teachers' understanding of the issues happening in the scenario. As noted in the previous section, knowledge is power, and the more information teachers have about their caregivers and situations, the better they will be able to evaluate the situation and work toward resolution.

SECTION 4: LISTENING TO EXPAND PERSPECTIVES

Armed with background information about the topic, readers will engage with tasks (see Appendix B) that will help them to revisit the case scenario and explore the ways in which needs, power, prestige, positioning, and access are at play in the case scenario as they listen to expand their perspectives. The tasks include worksheet templates to help teachers organize their analysis.

SECTION 5: FIXING IT

Next, we provide some possible solutions for "fixing" the interaction depicted in the case scenario, but we stress that they are *possible* solutions. No single solution works in every case. Rather, as we described in Chapter 1, our goal is twofold: (1) to use Cognitive Flexibility Theory to help teachers be reflective and (2) to foster in them the ability to analyze caregivers' needs using an asset-based perspective. These skills transcend situations. As teachers analyze suggestions that could help "solve" the case, they will complete tasks (see Appendix C) to determine a plan of action. We have adapted the ABC (antecedent-behavior-consequence) model of behavior analysis (Pierce & Cheney, 2013) as a framework to support analysis of the case studies. While the ABC model is traditionally associated with the field of behavioral analysis, we feel the model affords teachers a way to identify the complexity of interactions that influence events presented in the case scenarios. We have adapted the model to consider factors both environmental and socioemotional that affect the identified behavior. In sum, we use the ABC model to help understand complex relationships among individuals, environmental factors, and identified behaviors so that supportive responses can be developed.

SECTION 6: REBUILDING THE CASE

Finally, after presenting several possible solutions, we "rebuild the case" by showing how at least one of the possible solutions could change the situation. We then ask readers to reflect on the changes in the situation after implementing a solution and to explore what could be done further.

REFERENCES

Maslow, A. H. (1943). A theory of human motivation. *Psychology Review, 50*(4), 370–396.
Pierce, W. D., & Cheney, C. D. (2013). *Behavioral analysis and learning* (5th ed.). New York: Psychology Press.

CHAPTER 3

Preparing Teachers for Interactions with Parents

Some Thoughts on Using Case Modules from the Perspective of Cognitive Flexibility Theory

It has long been understood that any area of teacher preparation will face the challenge of complexity and novelty (Ball & Lampert, 1999; Grossman, 1992; J. Shulman, 1992; L. Shulman, 1992; Sykes & Bird, 1992). Individual cases of teacher preparation in the classroom—or outside of it, as in the modules in this volume—will include many facets that have to be juggled. Across cases, there will be extensive variation from one case to the next, even for cases classified as being of the same type. Put those two characteristics together—individual case richness and irregularity across cases of the same purported type—and the result is a pervasive cognitive demand for dealing with real-world complexity and at least partly novel situations. The usual remedy for such ill-structured complexity is to provide generic advice that is a poor match for many new cases or to just leave things to be learned over time from experience. Unfortunately, the rule of thumb is that it takes roughly 10 years of experience in any real-world domain of practice to attain a reasonable degree of expertise(e.g., Ericsson, 2006).

Cognitive Flexibility Theory(CFT) addresses the aforementioned kinds of difficulties in learning for knowledge application in real-world contexts (Spiro, 2015; Spiro, Coulson, Feltovich, & Anderson, 1988; Spiro & DeSchryver, 2009; Spiro, Feltovich, Jacobson, & Coulson, 1992; Spiro & Jehng, 1990). CFT is a longstanding approach to accelerated learning for application in complex and ill-structured domains. It has been applied to a variety of domains, including professional cognition in such domains as medicine (Feltovich, Spiro, & Coulson, 1989, 1997), law (Feltovich, Spiro, & Coulson, 1995), teaching reading (e.g., Palincsar et al., 2007; Spiro, 2002; Spiro, Klautke, & Johnson, 2015 Spiro, Morsink, & Forsyth, 2012), and new forms of assessment for 21st-century skills (Spiro, Klautke, Cheng, & Gaunt, 2017).

In this book appear a large number of cases of teacher–parent interaction and partnership, a domain that is classically complex and ill-structured, as previously described. These rich accounts are an important step in CFT-type learning: In a complex, ill-structured domain (ISD), one must learn *in* the individual case because if one could generalize *across* cases (examples, occurrences, events), it would not be an ISD. The learning is *in* the cases in an ISD.

Situations that arise in real-world teaching can be quite complex, and the scenarios in this book reflect that complexity, presenting plentiful detail for each case. Having this kind of multifaceted complexity represented so well within these modules will not only help teachers resist a mindset to oversimplify their understanding of new cases they face (in interacting and partnering with parents, but also in all teaching if the more general lessons found here are applied), a crucial problem in teacher preparation; it will also better prepare them to find appropriate precedents to put together in assembling a response to new cases they encounter that is tailored to the novel aspects of the case. The rest of this chapter will be devoted to expanding on the ways that the modules in this volume can be used to foster flexibly adaptive practice.

IMPLICATIONS OF COGNITIVE FLEXIBILITY THEORY FOR USING THE PARENT–TEACHER INTERACTION MODULES

In this section we will discuss some ways that CFT can be applied with these modules. First, though, it is worth pointing out again that the built-in features of these extraordinary modules already present much of the complexity that is needed for adaptive practice. Also, the last section of each module discusses possible contextual variations that would have impact on the case scenario at the center of the module. Features like the latter two, case complexity and context-dependence (as well as others in the modules that could be mentioned, such as the opportunity for guided, active reflection), help to instill an appropriate epistemic mindset or worldview (Spiro, Feltovich, & Coulson, 1996), ways of thinking appropriate for case-based learning and for eventually dealing with newly encountered real-world cases in professional practice.

That said, what follows are some additional considerations that CFT would recommend keeping in mind in using these modules and extending their applicability even further.

Don't treat the modules as prototypes or templates. One thing that makes a domain ill-structured is that you cannot usually apply *intact* cases as prototypes—in ISDs, there is simply too much case-to-case variation, nonscriptedness, and irregular patterns of deviation from the routine. Just as one cannot rely on generic schemas or templates in ISDs, one must also avoid another kind of overly reductive overgeneralization that would limit the applicability of learned cases and produce maladaptive oversimplifications in applying the cases: It is important not to treat a case as a template itself. CFT calls this "reduction to prototype." Using an abstract schema or a prototype case as a basis for future performance would be nice—if it worked. We would be able to prepare teachers for the messiness of practice much more easily if that were so. Unfortunately, as we have described above, new cases are too often unlike some abstract pre-stored pattern, and the same goes for a pre-stored case that would be used across a variety of new situations. That is why it is so helpful to see case variants presented in the modules. Not only does this provide more kinds of additional case information to draw on to guide responses to cases encountered later, but it helps to reinforce the essential "one size does *not* fit all" cognitive mindset.

Whether it is a conceptual schema or a prototype case, in the messy real world of ISDs like this one, *parts* of concepts and cases will be drawn on and combined in formulating a response to new cases—what makes these domains ill-structured is that *intact* conceptual and case structures do not generalize and thus, as we will discuss below, response to new cases will require *assembling* a "schema of the moment" to fit the needs of the situation at hand. The modules in this volume help teachers to resist the tendency to overextend prototypes to a wide range of new cases.

Pay attention to context and variation across contexts. An important feature of ISDs is that cases occur in rich contexts, and key concepts and prescribed actions vary as a function of context. As you can see in the final section of every module, such contextual variation is clearly addressed. A good exercise is to now imagine other kinds of contextual variation that would matter, and what effects such changes would have.

Another thing to do is see how the same contextual features (e.g., language abilities of a parent, or ways of dealing with the key concept of "positioning") vary as a function of different case contexts in which the concept occurs. These kinds of concepts do not have a *fixed* meaning as one might find in a dictionary. One of the first learning steps in any CFT-based learning environment is a "conceptual variability" search, so that learners can see a variety of case examples that illustrate a given concept, revealing the family resemblance across uses of the same concept, but also lots of variations as a function of the different situations to which they are applied. They thus get the idea immediately that one must *tailor* the meaning of concepts to their case contexts. For example, in a CFT-based hypertext learning environment for teaching reciprocal teaching (Palincsar et al., 2007), teachers assigned to address a problem in applying reciprocal teaching in a particular reading comprehension instruction situation typically first wanted a definition of the key concept of "scaffolding"; however, after seeing various actual video scenes of reciprocal teaching in which scaffolding played somewhat varying roles, they quickly realized that scaffolding is a family resemblance concept that does not have a strict definition that can guide practice. Instead they started looking in the CFT-based video-case library (Spiro, Collins, & Ramchandran, 2007) for case situations that were similar to their assigned problem in which scaffolding came into play. The same idea would apply here to the concepts that run through these modules.

Look for connections across modules using common themes. In an ISD, new cases are often hybrids, pertinent to more than one higher-order conceptual category. The ideal of compartmentalization of key ideas does not work in ISDs. So a useful thing to do is to look for common ideas and occurrences *across* cases and note them when they are found. Power, prestige, positioning, and access are, of course, common themes running through the cases. Other conceptual themes are discernible as well.

These conceptual themes are the basis for forming networks of connections, along multiple dimensions, which will greatly increase the adaptive flexibility of one's knowledge, fostering the ability to construct the kinds of "schemas of the moment" that have to be tailored to particular situations and problems (a crucial aspect of CFT that will be described below).

Look for ways concepts combine in context. Influential factors like power, prestige, positioning, and access (as well as lower-level concepts and context descriptors found in the modules) interact in contexts of application. These concept combinations are as meaning-altering as the variation in individual concepts discussed earlier. The combination of interacting concepts forms a kind of "ecology" for understanding a case in which the whole is greater than the sum of the parts (Spiro et al., 1992, Spiro & Jehng, 1990).

Also, as in earlier sections, there is a benefit here of practicing patterns for knowledge combination. Concepts will have to be combined in new contexts, so this becomes a kind of preparation for that situational assembly of knowledge.

Practice assembling "schemas of the moment" for newly encountered cases. CFT was developed as a reaction to schema theories (e.g., Anderson, Spiro, & Anderson, 1978; Rumelhart, 1980; Rumelhart & Ortony, 1977), which seemed too often to rely on an assumption of well-structured orderliness. In early CFT papers (e.g., Spiro et al., 1988; Spiro & Myers, 1984; Spiro, Vispoel, Schmitz, Samarapungavan, & Boerger, 1987), it was argued that one cannot have a prepackaged schema in memory that can be retrieved for every situation encountered. The world just is not that orderly, especially domains of professional practice like teaching. Instead of instantiating a retrieved schema or template, a key process in CFT is situ-ation-sensitive construction or assembly of what we call a "schema of the moment." If you do not already have a schema, then you have to build one for the situation at hand out of aspects of prior knowledge and experience (Spiro et al., 1992; Spiro & Jehng, 1990).

One can practice that situation-sensitive assembly of schemas of the moment for new cases using the modules in this book. For example, imag-ine some *new* scenario, or even better, think about one from your own experience. Try to find one that you find especially difficult and complex. How does that case involve *facets* of *multiple modules* in this volume, and how can those facets be put together to form a candidate solution to the problem you have posed? Or try the exercise of putting together the topics from two or more modules and see if you can imagine a case that would combine module features in that way.

Beyond the traditional casebook. The overall picture that can be gleaned from the modules' construction and from the additional CFT-based suggestions found in this chapter is something quite different from a tra-ditional casebook for professionals. In the latter, cases are nested under concepts, with the concept having primacy. A case is an example of a par-ticular concept. In an ISD, this structure must be flipped. Cases are central (because of the case-to-case variation that characterizes ISDs), and con-cepts are easily shown to wind through cases in varying combinations. The modules in this volume are ready to be used in this new kind of casebook way, and thus can help to build the special epistemic mindset we have been discussing.

A note on case-based hypertext learning environments for teacher preparation. CFT has usually employed *hypertext* learning environments be-cause of their inherent affordances for flexible and adaptive rearrangement of case information in varying contexts and for different purposes (e.g., Jacobson & Spiro, 1995; Spiro et al., 2006; Spiro, Collins, & Ramchandran, 2007; Spiro, Collins, & Thota, 2003; Spiro & Jehng, 1990). All of the raw materials for starting to build such a case-based learning environment can be found in the modules that follow. Creating such a computer-supported case-based learning environment would be a natural next step to build upon this extraordinary collection of cases and supporting materials that address a crucial set of skills that teachers must master.

REFERENCES

Anderson, R. C., Spiro, R. J., & Anderson, M. C. (1978). Schemata as scaffolding for the representation of information in discourse. *American Educational Research Journal, 15*, 433–440.

Ball, D. M., & Lampert, M. (1999). Multiples of evidence, time, and perspective. In E. C. Lagemann & L. S. Shulman (Eds.), *Issues in education research: Problems and possibilities*. San Francisco, CA: Jossey-Bass.

Ericsson, K. A. (2006). The influence of experience and deliberate practice on the development of superior expert performance. In K. A. Ericsson et al. (Eds.), *The Cambridge handbook of expertise and expert performance* (pp. 683–704). Cambridge, UK: Cambridge University Press.

Feltovich, P. J., Spiro, R. J., & Coulson, R. L. (1989). The nature of conceptual understanding in biomedicine: The deep structure of complex ideas and the development of misconceptions. In D. Evans & V. Patel (Eds.), *The cognitive sciences in medicine* (pp. 113–172). Cambridge, MA: M.I.T. Press.

Feltovich, P. J, Spiro, R. J., & Coulson, R. L. (1997). Issues of expert flexibility in contexts characterized by complexity and change. In P. J. Feltovich, K. M. Ford, & R. R. Hoffman (Eds.), *Expertise in context: Human and machine*. Cambridge, MA: MIT Press.

Feltovich, P. J., Spiro, R. J., Coulson, R. L., & Myers-Kelson, A. (1995). The reductive bias and the crisis of text (in the law). *Journal of Contemporary Legal Issues, 6*(1), 187–212.

Grossman, P. (1992). Teaching and learning with cases: Unanswered questions. In J. Shulman (Ed.), *Case methods in teacher education*. New York, NY: Teachers College Press.

Jacobson, M. J., & Spiro, R. J. (1995). Hypertext learning environments, cognitive flexibility, and the transfer of complex knowledge: An empirical investigation. *Journal of Educational Computing Research, 12*, 301–333.

Palincsar, A. P., Spiro, R. J., Kucan, L., Magnusson, S. J., Collins, B. P., Hapgood, S., Ramchandran, A., & DeFrance, N. (2007). Designing a hypertext environment to support comprehension instruction. In D. McNamara (Ed.), *Reading comprehension strategies: Theory, interventions, and technologies* (pp. 441–462). Mahwah, NJ: Lawrence Erlbaum.

Rumelhart, D. E. (1980). Schemata: The building blocks of cognition. In, R. J. Spiro, B. C. Bruce, & W. F. Brewer, *Theoretical Issues in Reading Comprehension* (pp. 33–58). Hillsdale, NY: Lawrence Erlbaum Associates.

Rumelhart, D. E., & Ortony, A. (1977). The representation of knowledge in memory. In R. C. Anderson, R. J. Spiro, & W. E. Montague (Eds.), *Schooling and the acquisition of knowledge* (pp. 99–136). Hillsdale, NY: Lawrence Erlbaum Associates.

Shulman, J. (1992).Teacher-written case with commentaries: A teacher-research collaboration. In J. Shulman (Ed.), *Case methods in teacher education* (pp. 131–152). New York, NY: Teachers College Press.

Shulman, L. (1992). Toward a pedagogy of cases. In J. Shulman (Ed.), *Case methods in teacher education* (pp. 1–30). New York, NY: Teachers College Press.

Spiro, R. (2004). Principled pluralism for adaptive flexibility in teaching and learning to read. In R. B. Ruddell & N. J. Unrau (Eds.), *Theoretical models and processes of reading* (5th ed., pp. 654–659). Newark, DE: International Reading Association.

Spiro, R. J. (2015). Cognitive flexibility theory. In J. M. Spector (Ed). *Encyclopedia of educational technology* (pp. 111–116). Thousand Oaks, CA: Sage.

Spiro, R. J., Collins, B. P., & Ramchandran, A. R. (2007). Reflections on a post-Gutenberg epistemology for video use in ill-structured domains: Fostering complex learning and cognitive flexibility. In R. Goldman, R. D. Pea, B. Barron, & S. Derry (Eds.), *Video research in the learning sciences* (pp. 93–100). Mahwah, NJ: Lawrence Erlbaum Associates.

Spiro, R. J., Collins, B. P., Thota, J. J., & Feltovich, P. J. (2003). Cognitive flexibility theory: Hypermedia for complex learning, adaptive knowledge application, and experience acceleration. *Educational Technology, 44*(5), 5–10.

Spiro, R. J., Coulson, R. L., Feltovich, P. J., & Anderson, D. (1988). Cognitive flexibility theory: Advanced knowledge acquisition in ill-structured domains. *Tenth Annual Conference of the Cognitive Science Society*. Hillsdale, NJ: Erlbaum.

Spiro, R. J., & DeSchryver, M. (2009). Constructivism: When it's the wrong idea and when it's the *only* idea. In S. Tobias & T. Duffy (Eds.), *Constructivist instruction: Success or failure.* (pp. 106–123). New York, NY: Taylor & Francis.

Spiro, R.J., Feltovich, P.J., & Coulson, R.L. (1996). Two epistemic world-views: Prefigurative schemas and learning in complex domains. *Applied Cognitive Psychology, 10*, 52–61.

Spiro, R. J., Feltovich, P. J., Jacobson, M. J., & Coulson, R. L. (1992). Cognitive flexibility, constructivism, and hypertext: Random access instruction for advanced knowledge acquisition in ill-structured domains. In T. Duffy & D. Jonassen (Eds.), *Constructivism and the technology of instruction* (pp. 57–75). Hillsdale, NJ: Erlbaum.

Spiro, R. J., & Jehng, J. C. (1990). Cognitive flexibility and hypertext: Theory and technology for the nonlinear and multidimensional traversal of complex subject matter. In D. Nix & R. J. Spiro (Eds.), *Cognition, education, and multimedia: Explorations in high technology* (pp. 163–205). Hillsdale, NJ: Lawrence Erlbaum Associates.

Spiro, R. J., Klautke, H., Cheng, C., & Gaunt, A. (2017). Cognitive flexibility theory and the assessment of 21st-century skills. In C. Secolsky & D. B. Denison (Eds.), *Handbook on measurement, assessment, and evaluation in higher education* (2nd ed., pp. 631–637). New York, NY: Routledge.

Spiro, R. J., Klautke, H., & Johnson, A. (2015). All bets are off: How certain kinds of reading to learn on the Web are totally different from what we learned from research on traditional text comprehension and learning from text. In R. J. Spiro, M. DeSchryver, P. Morsink, M. Schira-Hagerman, & P. Thompson (Eds.), *Reading at a crossroads? Disjunctures and continuities in our conceptions and practices of reading in the 21st century* (pp. 45–50). New York, NY: Routledge.

Spiro, R. J., Morsink, P., & Forsyth, B. (2012). Point of view: Principled pluralism, cognitive flexibility, and new contexts for reading. In R. Flippo (Ed.), *Reading researchers in search of common ground: The expert study revisited* (2nd ed., pp. 118–128). New York, NY: Taylor & Francis/Routledge.

Spiro, R. J., & Myers, A. (1984). Individual differences and underlying cognitive processes in reading. In P. D. Pearson (Ed.), *Handbook of research in reading.* (pp. 471–503). New York, NY: Longman.

Spiro, R. J., Vispoel, W. L., Schmitz, J., Samarapungavan, A., & Boerger, A. (1987). Knowledge acquisition for application: Cognitive flexibility and transfer in complex content domains. In B. C. Britton & S. Glynn (Eds.), *Executive control processes* (pp. 177–199). Hillsdale, NJ: Lawrence Erlbaum Associates.

Sykes, G, & Bird, T. (1992). Teacher education and the case idea. *Review of Research in Education, 18,* 457–482.

REACHING OUT TO CAREGIVERS

MODULE 1
Caregivers Who Do Not Respond

SECTION 1: CASE SCENARIO

Context

Ms. Logan is a 40-year-old, White, American woman. She is in her 15th year of teaching in a large suburban district outside of a major city and a university town. She is an English monolingual who teaches 1st grade, and Mitchell is one of her students. Mitchell is a 6-year-old, white, monolingual boy who lives with his father and many siblings. His family qualifies for free and reduced lunch, and some of his siblings receive special education services. Ms. Logan has not met Mitchell's caregiver and does not know a lot about him or his family.

Scenario

Ms. Logan, a 1st-grade teacher, often connects with caregivers at the beginning of the year at open houses, drop-off or pick-up, school events, or conferences; however, Mitchell's caregiver did not attend those school functions. Ms. Logan also writes notes and emails and leaves phone messages; however, Mitchell's caregiver has not responded to these methods of communication. It is October, and Ms. Logan is frustrated that she is missing several documents, homework assignments, permission slips, and take-home books. When she asks Mitchell for the papers and books he says that he gave them to his dad.

Ms. Logan checked with the school office and the kindergarten teacher to see if they had advice for contacting the caregiver. The school office said they are missing many documents as well. The secretary told Ms. Logan that the family lives with extended family in the trailer park outside of town. The kindergarten teacher told Ms. Logan that she never received notes from home last year, and she just gave up. She stopped sending take-home books because she was tired of losing books from her classroom library. The reading teacher told Ms. Logan that the apple hadn't fallen far from the tree, that she had taught the father when he was in elementary school and he wasn't responsible then, either. Ms. Logan does not know what to do.

SECTION 2: EXPLORING CURRENT PERSPECTIVES

 Complete Appendix A, Tasks for Section 2: Exploring Current Perspectives, to consider your initial reactions to the case scenario and the potential underlying needs and emotions of the caregivers, students, and/or teachers.

SECTION 3: GETTING ON THE SAME PAGE

Categorizing caregivers as nonresponsive is a catch-all phrase for families who do not come to conferences, do not greet the teacher at drop-off or pick-up, or who do not send in paperwork or homework. Teachers expect caregivers to do these things, probably because that is what their own caregivers did when they were in school. The belief that all caregivers should respond to school contacts in a highly involved way is an assumption that teachers make about "good" parent involvement. However, labeling caregivers as "nonresponsive" is a deficit way of talking about families and caregivers.

As an elementary classroom teacher and reading specialist for 21 years, I (Ann) worked with caregivers with varying degrees of participation in their child's classroom, and the school as a whole. For example, I learned from one caregiver that work schedules vary for student households. These caregivers had to work during the afternoon and evening and were not available to attend school functions after school. Furthermore, they were on opposite schedules as their children, meaning that they arrived home after work at 1:00 a.m., when the children were sleeping, and the morning time was spent rushing around to get the children out the door. There was little shared time to do homework, look at notes, or sign paperwork. This experience helped reinforce for me that the structures of schooling are not designed to meet the needs of many families. That makes it important for teachers to learn about their students and caregivers to accommodate and understand the needs of all caregivers.

Strategies can be implemented only once teachers shift away from negative stereotypes and assumptions about students and caregivers who do not seem to respond to school initiatives. The main suggestion for what to do or how to get caregivers involved is to take a "never stop trying" stance and slowly build trust with caregivers. Educators can attempt to connect with caregivers who do not respond by intentionally using positive verbal and nonverbal body language when meetings do occur, setting aside assumptions about caregivers, learning about the community that attends the school, and continue trying to connect with caregivers, even when it is difficult.

First of all, educators should reflect on how they use verbal and nonverbal body language with students and their caregivers. According to Jones and Vagle (2013), "Classism in education . . . is often expressed through what we *do* with our body; what we *say* through our language; and simultaneously how we perceive others' bodies and their language" (p. 6). Teachers should think about ways to use positive verbal and nonverbal body language with students and their caregivers and in conversations with other classroom teachers (without the students present) if they notice negative verbal and nonverbal body language. In the scenario above, the teacher and her colleagues used negative language about the family, had negative conversations with other staff members, and stopped supplying resources to the student. In addition, they made assumptions about the student's family status and caregivers' level of education. Remember, it is best to avoid negative talk and negative body language, such as eye-rolling, raised eyebrows, or negative facial expressions.

In addition, teachers should set aside assumptions about caregivers and the communities in which they live. According to Jones and Vagle, "The class-sensitive pedagogue must pay attention to assumptions and perceptions of middle-class normality" (2013, p. 7). As stated earlier, much of the teaching population in the United States is comprised of White, middle-class female teachers with privileged upbringings. First, teachers should think about their own status in society and rethink the assumptions made about caregivers based on race, class, culture, and educational status. Then, educators should learn about the community in which they teach. According to Zeichner and colleagues, "the mission of teacher education is not to try and 'save' students from their communities, but to work with and for communities to help build on their strengths and develop greater community capacity" (2016, p. 12). As stated earlier, many teachers do not live in the communities in which they teach. Teachers can set aside assumptions by embracing and getting to know the community where they teach, instead of trying to fix it. Last, teachers should continue trying to connect with caregivers and students. According to Hampshire and colleagues, there are four dispositions for working with families in education, including partnering with families, valuing and supporting family differences (race, class, culture, and educational status), committing to communication, and "envisioning the teacher as learner" (2015, p. 84). Teachers need to have the dispositions and stance of a learner, and continue to learn about their students and caregivers, how their students learn, their grade-level content, and current best practice and instruction.

As a side note, some education resources suggest home visits, but one of our authors offers advice on home visits based on personal experience. This young family, a teacher and a physician, was expected to participate in home visits for 2 years as part of their son's early intervention. After having this experience, their position about home visits changed. They felt tremendous pressure and unease each time the professional came into their home. They recommend finding a common space at first and waiting until the family invites the teacher to their home. To link this back to our discussion of power, prestige, position, and access, "inviting" ourselves as educational professionals into someone's home is placing much of the power in our hands and lowering that of the caregiver. Caregivers do not have the same power, privilege, or access to "invite" themselves into the teacher's home. Moreover, they probably do not think they have the prestige to even ask, causing one to stop and think about the disparity that home visits create. As a teacher, this mom advocated for home visits. Now, as a parent, her position changed, because she shifted from the role of teacher to that of parent.

SECTION 4: LISTENING TO EXPAND PERSPECTIVES

 Complete Appendix B, Tasks for Section 4: Listening to Expand Perspectives, to reconsider the case scenario and the participants' potential needs and emotions in the context of the background information you read.

SECTION 5: FIXING IT

 This section presents suggestions for working with students who have caregivers who do not seem to respond to school communication Complete Appendix C, Tasks for Section 5: Fixing It, for further reflection and analysis.

Use Positive Verbal and Nonverbal Body Language

- Use positive verbal and nonverbal communication with and about caregivers.
- Do not use negative language about the caregivers.
- Do not have negative conversations with other staff members.

- Do not stop supplying resources to the student.
- Do not make assumptions about the student's family status and caregivers' level of education.
- Avoid negative talk and negative body language, such as eye-rolling, raised eyebrows, or negative facial expressions with colleagues as well as caregivers and students.

Set Aside Assumptions

- Think about your own status as a teacher and how you position caregivers during your attempts to engage with them.
- Rethink the assumptions made about other families based on race, class, culture, and educational status.

Learn about the Community in Which You Teach

- Set aside assumptions by embracing the school community, instead of just trying to fix it.
- Partner with caregivers to build relationships with children and the community.

Keep Trying

- Remember that many caregivers are not able to be as responsive as others in regard to involvement in their child's education, but keep trying to connect.

SECTION 6: REBUILDING THE CASE

Mitchell is a 1st-grader who has regular attendance; however, the teacher has never met his caregivers. Even though Mitchell's teacher, Ms. Logan, has many ways built into her classroom structures to connect with caregivers, Mitchell's caregivers do not attend the events or respond to other methods of communication. In addition, Mitchell does not return materials to school. Ms. Logan refrains from making assumptions and jumping to conclusions about Mitchell and his caregivers, and instead continues to learn more about them in order to help Mitchell learn as much as he can in 1st grade. When Ms. Logan checks with the school office and Mitchell's former kindergarten teacher, she learns that the same pattern occurred the previous year. Instead of falling into negative verbal exchange with other staff members about Mitchell's caregivers' lack of responsiveness, Ms. Logan refrains from negativity and decides to keep trying.

One way that Ms. Logan keeps trying is by figuring out how to meet Mitchell's caregiver.[1] She asks Mitchell how he gets to school each day, and he says his dad drops him off in the morning. Ms. Logan decides to look for the family truck the next morning. She stands outside at drop-off and waves Mitchell's dad down as soon as the children hop out of the car. Mitchell's dad pulls into a space and is able to talk for a minute.[2] Ms. Logan has the paper she needs to be signed on a clipboard and a pen at hand.[3] She explains that she wants Mitchell to receive reading support and needs the form to be signed before the lessons can begin. Mitchell's dad is appreciative that his son will receive support and signs the form.[4] This was the first time that Ms. Logan and Mitchell's dad met. Although it took extra work on Ms. Logan's part, this first meeting was a good start. Back inside the school setting, Ms. Logan refuses to engage in negative talk about where the family lives, about the apple not falling far from the tree, or about how some families are "just broken." She keeps trying and learning instead of falling into negative verbal and nonverbal talk about the family. She asks one of Mitchell's older siblings to help by reminding him to read his take-home books and bring them back the next day.

1. In this scenario, Ms. Logan keeps trying to figure out how to meet Mitchell's caregiver. By asking Mitchell how he gets to school each day, she gathers information about how to meet his caregivers so she can talk about helping Mitchell learn to read. By finding out that Mitchell is dropped off each day, she is able to make a plan to meet Mitchell's father the next morning.

2. By deciding to meet Mitchell's caregiver at drop-off the next morning, Ms. Logan finds nontraditional ways to connect with the caregiver(s). Ms. Logan thought creatively about connecting with other parents of students in her class as well, such as meeting at a local community center or park.

3. If Mitchell's dad couldn't talk right then, Ms. Logan could have asked him if another morning that week would work for a brief chat. Since he was available for only a few minutes, Ms. Logan's readiness with the paper she needed signed on a clipboard and a pen made it efficient to share the reading program with Mitchell's caregiver.

4. By explaining that she wants Mitchell to receive reading support and needs the form to be signed before the lessons could begin, Ms. Logan is respectful of the caregiver's time and is efficient with paperwork for their school's Title I permission requirement. If the drop-off time were too rushed for any discussion, Ms. Logan could mail the paperwork home with a note before meeting Mitchell's father very briefly to get his signature. There are many instances when teachers need to share information with caregivers and collect signatures. Coordinating with caregivers' schedules and life circumstances could help include them in their child's schooling.

REFERENCES

Edwards, P. (2016). *New ways to engage parents: Strategies and tools for teachers and leaders, K–12.* New York, NY: Teachers College Press.

Edwards, P., Pleasants, H., & Franklin, S. (1999). *A path to follow. Learning to listen to parents.* Portsmouth, NH: Heinemann.

Hampshire, P. K., Havercroft, K., Luy, M., & Call, J. (2015). Confronting assumptions: Service learning as a medium for preparing early childhood special education preservice teachers to work with families. *Teacher Education Quarterly, 42*(1), 83–96.

Jones, S., & Vagle, M. D. (2013). Living contradictions and working for change: Toward a theory of social class–sensitive pedagogy. *Educational Researcher, 42*(3), 129–141.

Zeichner, K., Bowman, M., Guillen, L., & Napolitan, K. (2016). Engaging and working in solidarity with local communities in preparing the teachers of their children. *Journal of Teacher Education, 67*(4), 277–290.

ADDITIONAL RESOURCES

Center for Comprehensive School Reform and Improvement (n.d.). Getting parents involved in school. Retrieved from www.readingrockets.org/article /getting-parents-involved-schools

MODULE 2
Caregivers with Low Print-Literacy Levels

SECTION 1: CASE SCENARIO

Context

Mrs. Colvin is a 25-year-old, middle-class, White teacher. She is in her third year of teaching 1st grade in a small rural southern community where she grew up. She knew when she took the job that this school historically had low scores on statewide achievement tests and had been struggling to increase them, and she hoped she could make a difference. She recently graduated from a flagship university and had learned many wonderful strategies for teaching reading and writing.

Scenario

After working as hard as she could at school to improve the reading performance of her students, Mrs. Colvin is now frustrated and feels that her students' caregivers are doing little if anything at home to prepare their children for school. She feels that the caregivers do not read to their children or talk to them. She also feels that the children had very limited opportunities to engage in literacy instruction before they entered kindergarten. She believes that many caregivers do not care whether their children read or not. Every year she tells caregivers what to do, but nothing happens. It seems as if the caregivers don't hear her, or if they do, they just don't plan to do anything. Many of her students are not meeting the grade-level benchmarks. They don't recognize letters of the alphabet or numbers; many can't even recognize the letters in their own name. She has had to retain a large number of 1st-graders each year.

SECTION 2: EXPLORING CURRENT PERSPECTIVES

 Complete Appendix A, Tasks for Section 2: Exploring Current Perspectives.

SECTION 3: GETTING ON THE SAME PAGE

Readers Are Made, Not Born

"No one comes into the world already disposed for or against words in print" (Chambers, 1973, p. 16). Caregivers who read to their children provide their children with those first models of literacy. Reading is an invaluable skill that's important to nearly every aspect of our daily lives, from communications to the way we work to the food we eat. A caregiver is one of the largest influences in a child's life, and with that power comes a great responsibility. Caregiver–child storybook reading exchanges are the focal point for the start of reading, providing the roots of print literacy (Bruner, 1975; Gilberson, Richards, & Topping, 2017; Heath, 1982; Hindman, Skibbe, & Foster, 2014; Mol, Bus, de Jong, & Smeets, 2008; Reese, Sparks, & Leyva, 2010; Sénéchal & LeFevre, 2002;). Caregiver involvement in students' education matters for their achievement, motivation, and well-being at school. Unfortunately, not all students' caregivers can read well, and some cannot read at all.

Approximately 32 million adults in America, 14% of the entire adult population, are considered to be illiterate (Strauss, 2016). This means that many students have caregivers with limited reading and writing skills. Literacy begins at home. Literacy is everywhere and is shaped and reshaped by the spaces we enter and exit (Rowsell, 2006) and by the interactions we have with people in those spaces. For some students whose caregivers are illiterate, teachers need to aid these caregivers in building the desire to read and write in their children by respecting and teaching caregivers ways to support literacy (Edwards, 1989).

In particular, teachers must emphasize to caregivers the importance of oral language development. The importance of early communication skills and their implications for the child's social educational development across the early years and beyond need to be understood by caregivers (Law & Roy, 2015). Some caregivers might need to be given confidence in their ability to partner with the skills and assets that they do have even if they don't read well, or at all. Caregivers can be helped to feel empowered, rather than embarrassed, by being shown the importance of storytelling and oral language.

Misjudging or Misunderstanding Caregivers

Several years ago, I (Patricia) had the opportunity to interview lower–socioeconomic-status kindergarten and 1st-grade caregivers and teachers regarding their thoughts about storybook reading in a school similar to the one at which Mrs. Colvin currently teaches (see Edwards, 1995a). Most of the teachers in that school, like Mrs. Colvin, felt they were doing all they could to help the children during class time. The teachers expected and demanded that these caregivers be involved in their children's education by reading to them at home, which, to the teachers, seemed not an unreasonable request. The teachers were indeed "giving" caregivers the right advice. However, the teachers assumed that the caregivers knew how to read to their children and had a clear understanding of what to do while reading.

Here are the caregivers' responses to the series of questions (Edwards, 1995a, p. 56):

1. What does reading to your child mean?

    "I think it means helping your children sound out words."
    "Reading means opening the book and reading to the end, just try to get the job done. My problem is my children won't sit still."
    "Could it mean selecting fun books for your child?"
    "I really don't know what teachers mean when they say, 'Read to your child.'"
    "I don't read that well myself, so I don't read to my child. I don't know how to get started."

2. Do you understand what the teacher means when he or she asks you to read to your child?

    "No, I don't know what the teacher means."
    "No, I don't know the correct way to begin reading to my child."

"I don't know what to do when I open the book. I mean, I don't know what to do first, second, third, and so on."

"I wish somebody would tell me what to do, because I am fed up with teachers saying 'Read to your child.'"

"I am tired of teachers saying, 'Your child would do so much better in school if you read to them and talked to them.' I do talk to my children. Maybe I don't read to them 'cause I have difficulty reading myself.'"

3.   What difficulties have you encountered when you have attempted to read to your child?

"I guess my answer to this question is if you can't read or don't feel comfortable reading, you ain't gonna want to read to your children."

"I try to read, but I guess I am not doing it right. My child becomes bored, not interested in the book, so I quit trying to read."

"I don't know what books to read to my child."

"Because I don't read well, I don't make time in my schedule. I just pray that they will learn to read in school."

4.   Is storybook reading an important part of your daily interactions with your child?

"No, storybook reading is not an important part of my daily interactions with my child." (This comment was made unanimously by the caregivers.)

These responses confirm that caregivers wanted their children to succeed in school, but the teachers did not provide a plan for helping them to succeed. Perhaps one of the reasons storybook reading was not an important part of the caregivers' daily interactions with their children is that many of them were unable to assume the responsibility of being their child's first tutor in "unraveling the fascinating puzzle of written language" (Anderson, Hiebert, Scott, & Wilkinson, 1985, p. 57). The "global statements teachers made to parents about book reading interactions make it difficult for parents to translate into practice the much-requested teacher directive, 'Read to your child'" (Edwards, 1995b, p. 269).

The Need to Show Versus Tell Caregivers to Read to Their Children

Schools and teachers should develop programs at school to help students from a lower socioeconomic status (SES) make a smooth transition from home to school, but Teale questioned whether the "classroom storybook reading experience [can] substitute for the more intimate one-to-one (or one-to-two or three) interactions typical of the home" (1987, p. 64).

To inform caregivers of the importance of reading to their children is not sufficient. Teachers must go beyond telling lower-SES parents to help their children with reading. Teachers must show parents and caregivers how to participate in parent–child book reading and support their attempts to do so; At the same time, teachers must not assume that lower-SES parents and caregivers cannot acquire the necessary skills to engage in successful book-reading interactions with their children. To make such an assumption only reinforces the self-fulfilling prophecy that lower-SES parents are incapable of helping their children.

Even if caregivers are illiterate, it is important to recognize and emphasize the importance and value of the language skills caregivers do have. Importantly, Heath's (1983) research revealed the importance of the oral language base that parents provide children, the oral stories they tell them, the stories they recite from religious texts that they've memorized, and so on. Heath noted that these are important foundations that teachers can build on and need to recognize in order to have an asset-based view on caregivers.

SECTION 4: LISTENING TO EXPAND PERSPECTIVES

 Complete Appendix B, Tasks for Section 4: Listening to Expand Perspectives.

SECTION 5: FIXING IT

 The following are some suggestions for working with illiterate caregivers to increase their role in their children's learning. Complete Appendix C, Tasks for Section 5: Fixing It, for further reflection and analysis.

Creating a School-Friendly Environment

- When possible, schedule parent–teacher meetings around parents' schedules, and offer child care.
- Hold workshops for parents at the school (as often as there is a need and volunteers) to help parents with their reading skills.
- Recruit other parents who had similar issues and have made progress to be mentors for those parents who are struggling with being illiterate, semiliterate, or functionally illiterate.
- When speaking with parents, always use vocabulary they will understand. When discussing their child's academics, have examples of their work and examples of the academic level their child should be working on or working toward.

- Link parents with resources within the community that could provide
  tutoring for them. Find out if the parent is willing to be tutored by a
  high school or college student (free of charge—check for citizenship
  programs in which students must provide a required number of hours
  of community service).

Showing Caregivers How to Support Literacy Learning

- Encourage parents to listen to audiobooks with their child as they
  follow the literature.
- Make home visits. Since many parents may be uncomfortable even
  coming to the school out of fear, teachers can do home visits, or
  caregivers may be more comfortable meeting at a neutral site that they
  identify, such as a community center or library. During these visits,
  teachers can model reading behaviors that will help caregivers help
  the child, as well as themselves. Teachers can demonstrate matching
  beginning and ending sounds of words with pictures, or matching
  simple pictures with words underneath the picture so that the child and
  caregiver can identify the correct word with the picture. Puppets can be
  used to help the caregiver or child become storytellers.
- Caregivers can be encouraged to use wordless picture books so that the
  caregiver can tell the child a story and vice versa.
- Encourage caregivers to orally share stories about their childhood or
  stories passed down from their relatives with their children. In this
  way, caregivers are helped to understand that storytelling is a literate
  practice that is part of many cultures and helps their children with oral-
  language development.
- Encourage caregivers to read simple children's literature to the
  children (nursery rhymes, preschool books, picture books). This boosts
  caregivers' self-esteem and shows them they can contribute valuable
  lessons even if they are not the best readers.
- Provide visual aids for caregivers instead of a list of literature to take to
  the library. These visual aids require little reading, such as photocopies
  of the covers of picture books, wordless books, and/or predictable books
  to retrieve from the library or a store.

SECTION 6: REBUILDING THE CASE

Concerned and frustrated that most of her students' caregivers were not
reading to them, Mrs. Colvin decided to approach one of the caregivers to
ask about the situation.

Angela, a 32-year-old African American mother with five children ranging in ages from 22 months to 16 years old, explained to Mrs. Colvin[1] that she becomes fearful and sometimes defensive when asked to read to her child. She admits:

> I'm embarrassed, scared, angry, and feel completely helpless because I can't read. I do care 'bout my children and I want them to do well in school. Why don't you believe me when I say I want the best for my children? I know that my children ain't done well in kindergarten and first grade and had to repeat those grades. My older children are in the lowest sections, in Chapter 1, and are struggling in their subjects. My children are frustrated, and I am frustrated, too. I don't know how to help them, especially when the teacher wants me to read to them. Mrs. Colvin, you might think that reading to children is so easy and simple, but it is very difficult if you don't know how to read.

Mrs. Colvin realized that she needed to be sensitive, understanding, and responsive, and not only to the needs of Angela. She understood that Angela's views likely represented[2] those of other caregivers of students in her 1st-grade class. She decided to focus on what caregivers *could* do, not on what they could not do. She organized a series of workshops at convenient times for the caregivers,[3] during which she taught them a variety of strategies: (a) dialogic reading: children lead the conversation around the pictures in the book; (b) the use of strategies to improve the length of children's sentences; (c) the use of complete sentences when speaking to children; (d) the use of books the children can handle; (e) effective play with children and spending more time talking to them; and (f) the use of toys as mediators of spontaneous language use. She also taught caregivers skills they could use to support their children's reading development, such as pointing to words, speaking about illustrations, and labeling.

1. Because of Mrs. Colvin's lack of awareness and false assumptions that caregivers like Angela didn't care about children, she failed to recognize that most of her students' caregivers were illiterate. Her students' caregivers *did* care, but they did not know how to read to their children.

2. In this scenario, Mrs. Colvin realized she shouldn't rush to judgment. Illiterate caregivers might be overly sensitive about not being able to read and write.

3. In order not to single out illiterate caregivers, Mrs. Colvin decided to schedule a series of workshops that focused on ways not only to nurture literacy, but also to promote its value. As she scheduled these workshops, she tried to take into account parents' varied work schedules, their home languages and proficiencies, and convenient locations for all to meet.

REFERENCES

Anderson, R. C., Hiebert, E., Scott, J. A., & Wilkinson, I. A. G. (1985). *Becoming a nation of readers: The report of the commission of reading.* Washington, DC: The National Institute of Education.

Bruner, J. (1975). The ontogenesis of speech acts. *Journal of Child Language, 3,* 1–19.

Chambers, A. (1973). *Introducing books to children.* London, England: Heinemann.

Edwards, P. A. (1989). Supporting lower SES mothers' attempts to provide scaffolding for bookreading. In J. Allen & J. Mason (Eds.), *Risk makers, risk takers, risk breakers: Reducing the risks for young literacy learners* (pp. 222–250). Portsmouth, NH: Heinemann.

Edwards, P. A. (1995a). Combining parents' and teachers' thoughts about storybook reading at home and school. In L. M. Morrow (Ed.), *Family literacy: Multiple perspectives to enhance literacy development* (pp. 54–60). Newark, DE: International Reading Association.

Edwards, P. A. (1995b). Connecting African-American families and youth to the school's reading program: Its meaning for school and community literacy. In V. L. Gadsden & D. Wagner (Eds.), *Literacy among African-American youth: Issues in learning, teaching, and schooling* (pp. 263–281). Cresskill, NJ: Hampton Press.

Gilberson, J., Richards, J. A., & Topping, K. J. (2017). The impact of book reading in the early years on parent–child language interaction. *Journal of Early Childhood Literacy, 17*(1), 92–110.

Heath, S. B. (1983). *Ways with words: Language, life, and work in communities and classrooms.* Cambridge, England: Cambridge University Press.

Heath, S. B. (1982). What no bedtime story means: Narrative skills at home and school. *Language in Society, 11,* 49–76.

Hindman, A. H., Skibbe, L., E., & Foster, T., D. (2014). Exploring the variety of parental talk during shared book reading and its contributions to preschool language and literacy: Evidence from the Early Childhood Longitudinal Study-Birth Cohort. *Reading Writing Interdisciplinary Journal, 27*(2), 287–313.

Law, J., & Roy, P. (2008) Parental report of infant language skills: A review of the development and application of the Communicative Development Inventories, *Child and Adolescent Mental Health, 13*(4), 198–206.

Mol, S. E., Bus, A. G., de Jong, M. T., & Smeets, D. J. H. (2008). Added value of dialogic parent–child book readings: A meta-analysis. *Early Education and Development ,19*(1), 7–26.

Morrow, L. M. (1987). The effect of one-to-one story readings on children's questions and responses. In J. E. Readance & R. S. Baldwin (Eds.), *Research in the literacy: Merging perspectives* (pp. 75–83). Rochester, NY: National Reading Conference.

Morrow, L. M. (1988). Young children's responses to one-to-one story readings in school settings. *Reading Research Quarterly, 23,* 89–107.

NICHD Early Child Care Research Network. (2005). Pathways to reading: The role of oral language in the transition to reading. *Developmental Psychology, 41*(2), 428–442.

Reese, E., Sparks, A., & Leyva, D. (2010). A review of parent interventions for preschool children's language and emergent literacy. *Journal Early Childhood Literacy 10*(1), 97–117.

Rowsell, J. (2006). *Family literacy experiences: Creating reading and writing opportunities for student achievement.* Markham, Ontario: Pembroke Publishers.

Schickedanz, J. (1986). *More than ABCs: The early stages of reading and writing.* Washington, DC: National Association for the Education of Young Children.

Sénéchal, M., & LeFevre, J. A. (2002). Parental involvement in the development of children's reading skill: A five-year longitudinal study. *Child Development, 73*(2), 445–460.

Strauss, V. (2016). *Hiding in plain sight: The adult literacy crisis.* Retrieved from www .washingtonpost.com/news/answer-sheet/wp/2016/11/01/hiding-in-plain -sight-the-adult-literacy-crisis/?utm_term=.356cb49cfc3f

Teale, W. H. (1987). Emergent literacy: Reading and writing development in early childhood. In J. E. Readance & R. S. Baldwin (Eds.), *Research in the literacy: Merging perspectives* (pp. 45–74). Rochester, NY: National Reading Conference.

ADDITIONAL RESOURCES

Edwards, P. A. (2016). *New ways to engage parents: Strategies and tools for teachers and leaders, K–12.* New York, NY: Teachers College Press.

Grahl, A. R. (n.d.). Illiteracy traps adults, and their families, in poverty. Rotary International website. Retrieved from www.rotary.org/en/illiteracy-traps-adults -and-their-families-poverty

Kristof, N. (2012, December 9). Profiting from a child's illiteracy. Retrieved from www .nytimes.com/2012/12/09/opinion/sunday/kristof-profiting-from-a-childs -illiteracy.html

Strauss, V. (2016). Hiding in plain sight: The adult literacy crisis. *Washington Post.* Retrieved from www.washingtonpost.com/news/answer-sheet/wp/2016/11/01 /hiding-in-plain-sight-the-adult-literacy-crisis/

MODULE 3
Caregivers Experiencing Homelessness

SECTION 1: CASE SCENARIO

Context

The setting for this case is an urban kindergarten classroom where residential mobility among the student population is high. Ms. Martin is a 34-year-old, monolingual, middle-class, White, female teacher. The number of families and children experiencing homelessness in this district is steadily increasing.

For example, a White, monolingual, low-income child in her classroom, Kara, and her siblings attended the school the previous year. During the year, school personnel suspected that the family was experiencing homelessness, and an extended family member, the grandmother who lives within district boundaries, confirmed it. The grandmother also shared with the principal that Kara's mother, who was raising four children on her own, had been living with her but that she had asked them to leave her home because Kara's mother refused to quit her use of illegal drugs.

Scenario

In Ms. Martin's classroom, Kara is quiet and well-liked by peers. From the start of the year, she has followed directions the first time they are given, participated in class discussions, and is meeting grade-level expectations. Despite her living arrangements, she arrives at school each morning clean and appropriately dressed. However, Ms. Martin has become increasingly concerned about the dark circles under her eyes, and on numerous occasions Kara has fallen asleep in class. Ms. Martin planned to speak with her mother at fall conferences to share her concerns about Kara's tiredness and dark eyes, but she didn't show up for her scheduled appointment. Ms. Martin has seen Kara's mother a few times from across the parking lot when she picked the children up after school, but they have never exchanged words. Ms. Martin has had no written communication with Kara's mother.

Ms. Martin assumes Kara's mother doesn't care about her children's well-being due to her drug abuse and the fact that the family is homeless. Further, it has been over a month since she missed fall conferences, and she still has not contacted the school to obtain a copy of Kara's report card. Ms. Martin doesn't send it home in Kara's backpack because it is school policy not to send a student's report card home if caregiver(s) do not attend conferences. As such, the report card can be obtained by the caregiver(s) only if they physically come to the school to get it. As Ms. Martin ponders the situation, she begins to question Kara's mother's status as a caregiver. What kind of mother is she? Why doesn't the grandmother take legal action? Should Ms. Martin or someone else in the school contact social services? What if Ms. Martin were to approach Kara's mother in the school parking lot when she picked the children up after school and find her incoherent? Was it even safe to approach her? Last, why should Ms. Martin even bother exerting effort to communicate with Kara's mother when the family would most likely move to another district soon, particularly if social services intervened?

SECTION 2: EXPLORING CURRENT PERSPECTIVES

 Complete Appendix A, Tasks for Section 2: Exploring Current Perspectives.

SECTION 3: GETTING ON THE SAME PAGE

Homelessness in U.S. Schools

Research suggests that the neighborhood in which children and youth live influences their educational attainment (Owens, 2010; Wodtke, Harding, & Elwert, 2011). The issue is complicated by the fact that not all children and youth have a permanent residence. As a result, some children and their families are homeless. The term "homeless," according to the most recent Annual Homeless Assessment Report (AHAR) to Congress, "describes a person who lacks a fixed, regular, and adequate nighttime residence" (U.S. Department of Housing and Urban Development, 2017, p. 2). In 2017, the National Center for Homeless Education (NCHE) reported that the number of homeless students enrolled in public school districts during the 2015–16 school year, as reported by state educational agencies (SEAs), was a staggering 1,304,803.

Whereas experts contend homeless rates are higher in rural areas (Tobin, 2016), others argue that homelessness is a problem in both urban and rural contexts (Cowen, 2017). More African American and Hispanic students are homeless than White students, and not surprisingly, homeless students are "overwhelmingly impoverished" (Cowen, 2017, p. 34). Notwithstanding, homeless children and youth attend schools in multiple contexts, so it is important that educators, researchers, and policymakers have knowledge of this complex phenomenon that increasingly affects far too many children and youth across the United States.

The Effects of Homelessness

As the classroom teacher, it is Ms. Martin's professional and legal responsibility to ensure that students and families experiencing homelessness are supported by the school district. This support is necessary because "studies confirm that homeless children and youth perform worse than housed students on the full array of important measures of academic performance" (Murphy & Tobin, 2011, p. 33). For example, homeless students tend to exhibit more behavioral problems in school (Kurtz, Jarvis, & Kurtz, 1991); have below-average rates of literacy (Herbers et al., 2012); and have lower attendance rates (Rafferty & Shinn, 1991). Understandably, homeless students are also at greater risk for mental illness (Bassuk, Richard, & Tsertsvadze, 2015). The National Center for Homeless Education (2007) notes that less than a quarter of the children experiencing homelessness in the United States complete high school.

Federal Policy for Homeless Children and Youth in School

All children and youth have little to no control over the many factors that affect their daily performance in school, such as falling asleep in class.

Therefore, it is incumbent upon school personnel to offer support rather than unnecessarily punish students or their caregivers for particular behaviors or circumstances. Despite that homeless youngsters are the most vulnerable of the homeless population (Burt, Aron, Lee, & Valenta, 2001), they are more likely to be suspended and expelled from school (Better Homes Fund, 1999).

The McKinney-Vento Act, authorized in 1987 and reauthorized in December 2015 by the Every Student Succeeds Act (ESSA), requires that local educational agencies (LEAs) identify homeless children and youth to ensure that school districts provide additional support and appropriate services to the family, child, and/or youth (NCHE, 2017). Once the determination for eligibility of services is made, the school can enroll students. Next, the school can begin to address basic needs such as food, clothing, and school supplies. They can also provide information to caregivers so they are aware of their rights and can thus advocate for their children in the schooling context.

Understanding Eligibility for Rights and Services

The NCHE (2017) provides recommended practices for determining McKinney-Vento eligibility for children and youth. If Ms. Martin suspects a child, such as Kara, is falling asleep in class because she is homeless, it must be confirmed by the school, as stipulated by law. When she reaches out to Kara's caregiver, she will want to ensure that she first understands the law in order to help her understand her rights as a caregiver. She will want to avoid a threatening situation that may result in absences or Kara's mother placing the children in another school district. Homeless children have an increased rate of absences in comparison to housed peers (Rouse & Fantuzzo, 2009). In other words, a teacher's goal is to establish a partnership between the school and the family

Reaching Out to Homeless Caregivers

According to the NCHE (2017), the McKinney-Vento Act requires that school districts appoint an appropriate staff member as the district's local homeless education liaison who can help locate available resources. Teachers need to contact this person, perhaps by enlisting the help of the principal, a social worker, or a school psychologist.

SECTION 4: LISTENING TO EXPAND PERSPECTIVES

 Complete Appendix B, Tasks for Section 4: Listening to Expand Perspectives.

SECTION 5: FIXING IT

 The following is a framework for better serving students and caregivers who may be experiencing homelessness. Complete Appendix C, Tasks for Section 5: Fixing It, for further reflection and analysis.

Adopting an Educational Framework for Homelessness

Murphy and Tobin (2011) suggest a seven-step framework that schools can implement to care for homeless children:

1. *Develop awareness.* Become familiar with the McKinney-Vento Act and the legal implications for school districts to provide additional support in the form of services and resources to homeless children and families.
2. *Collaborate with other organizations.* Legally, schools are mandated under the McKinney-Vento Act to coordinate with local service agencies to provide services and resources to homeless children and their families.
3. *Attend to basic needs.* Children's basic needs must be met before they can learn. Proactively work to ensure that students have the basics—food, clothing, school supplies, hygiene items, and health services—so that they can learn. These essential items may be donated through community organizations (e.g., businesses, YMCA, local churches). But always remember that charity should be reserved for extras. Under the McKinney-Vento Act, students are entitled to the basics in support of their right to learn. They and their caregivers have a right to know that they have rights under law, and that their school will honor those rights,
4. *Provide effective instruction.* Research suggests that students who are homeless learn best from individualized instruction as well as through cooperative learning models. Murphy and Tobin (2011) note that homeless youngsters do not require a different or separate curriculum. They need access to a high-quality curriculum.
5. *Create a supportive environment.* Help students feel adequate and accepted in the classroom and school environment. Reimagine school more as a stable environment as opposed to an institution.
6. *Provide additional supports.* In addition to meeting basic needs, students may also benefit from tutoring services and the opportunity to participate in nonacademic activities such as after-school clubs and recreational activities.

7. *Promote caregiver involvement.* Educate homeless caregivers about their rights so they can advocate for themselves and their children both in school and the community. For instance, schools can help caregivers find language classes.

SECTION 6: REBUILDING THE CASE

Developing Awareness and Advocating for Homeless Students and their Families

Ms. Martin <u>sends a letter home to Kara's mother requesting a meeting, but she does not respond.</u>[1] <u>Instead of waiting to speak with Kara's mother at fall conferences to share her concerns about the dark circles under Kara's eyes accompanied by falling asleep in class, Ms. Martin contacts the school district's local homeless education liaison, who assists her in developing a plan of action to address and support the family's needs.</u>[2] During recent professional development provided by the district regarding homeless children and their families, Ms. Martin read the McKinney-Vento Act and is therefore aware of the family's rights as well as the school district's accountability to provide support for families experiencing homelessness.[3] She schedules a meeting with Kara's mother. When Kara's mother does not show up for the meeting, Ms. Martin reaches out to Kara's grandmother and establishes a school relationship so the district can support the children and family by providing resources to the family under the McKinney-Vento Act.[4] Ms. Martin also decides to contact a local homeless shelter to inquire about residence and other support services available for the family.[5]

1. If Ms. Martin confirms that Kara's family is homeless, sending home a written letter that contains a bulleted list of supports available to the family as well as their legal rights is one way the district can offer services. This step is important in advocating for students and following the law according to the McKinney-Vento Act.

2. However, Kara's mother does not respond to the letter. Because Ms. Martin understands the impact of homelessness on children's learning, she creates a plan of action with the appropriate school district personnel so that Kara's basic needs are met. Additionally, classroom instruction should include both individualized instruction and small-group projects where Kara can be successful, giving her opportunities to engage with peers and receive academic support as needed.

3. The school district holds itself accountable in addressing needs among its student population by offering personnel professional development to understand the McKinney-Vento Act. In doing so, Mr. Martin had the knowledge, skills, and disposition to help him determine Kara's family's eligibility and rights. Thus, the family has access to the basics (e.g., food, school supplies).

4. In this case, Mr. Martin demonstrates respect, sensitivity, and understanding of the differences in students' residences.

5. Because Ms. Martin is both knowledgeable and persistent in following district protocol for families and children experiencing homelessness, Kara is able to make academic growth while placed in her classroom.

REFERENCES

Bassuk, E. L., Richard, M. K., & Tsertsvadze, A. (2015). The prevalence of mental illness in homeless children: A systematic review and meta-analysis. *Journal of the American Academy of Child & Adolescent Psychiatry, 54*(2), 86–96.

Better Homes Fund. (1999). *Homeless children: America's new outcasts.* Newton, MA: Author.

Burt, M., Aron, L., Lee, E., & Valenta, J. (2001). *Helping America's homeless: Emergency shelter or affordable housing?* Washington, DC: The Urban Institute.

Cowen, J. (2017). Who are the homeless? Student mobility and achievement in Michigan 2010–2011. *Educational Researcher, 46*(1), 33–43.

Herbers, J. E., Cutuli, J. J., Supkoff, L. M., Heistad, D., Chan, C. K., Hinz, E., & Masten, A. S. (2012). Early reading skills and academic achievement trajectories of students facing poverty, homelessness, and high residential mobility. *Educational Researcher, 41*(9), 366–374.

Hubbard, J. (1996). *Homeless children in their own words and photographs: Lives turned upside down.* New York, NY. Simon & Schuster Books for Young Children.

Kurtz, P. D., Jarvis, S. V., & Kurtz, G. L. (1991). Problems of homeless youths: Empirical findings and human services issues. *Social Work, 36*(4), 309–314.

Miller, P. M., Pavlakis, A., Samartino, L., & Bourgeois, A. (2015). Brokering educational opportunity for homeless students and their families. *International Journal of Qualitative Studies in Education, 28*(6), 730–749.

Murphy, J. F., & Tobin, K. J. (2011). Homelessness comes to school. *Phi Delta Kappan, 93*(3), 32–37.

National Association for the Education of Homeless Children and Youth. (2017). *The most frequently asked questions on the educational rights of children & youth in homeless situations.* Retrieved from naehcy.org/wp-content/uploads/2018/02/2017-10-16 _NAEHCY-FAQs.pdf

National Center for Homeless Education (NCHE). (2007). *Best practices in homeless education series: Confirming eligibility for McKinney-Vento services.* Retrieved from files.eric.ed.gov/fulltext/ED522280.pdf

National Center for Homeless Education (NCHE). (2017). *Federal data summary: School years 2013–14 to 2015–16.* Retrieved from nche.ed.gov/downloads/data-comp -1314-1516.pdf

Owens, A. (2010). Neighborhoods and schools as competing and reinforcing contexts for educational attainment. *Sociology of Education, 83*(4), 287–311.

Rafferty, Y., & Shinn, M. (1991). The impact of homelessness on children. *American Psychologist, 46*(11), 1170.

Rouse, H. L., & Fantuzzo, J. W. (2009). Multiple risks and educational well-being: A population-based investigation of threats to early school success. *Early Childhood Research Quarterly, 24*(1), 1–14.

Tobin, K. J. (2016). Homeless students and academic achievement: Evidence from a large urban area. *Urban Education, 51*(2), 197–220.

U.S. Department of Education. (2017). *Education for homeless children and youths program non-regulatory guidelines*. Retrieved from www2.ed.gov/policy/elsec/leg/essa/160240ehcyguidance072716updated0317.pdf

U.S. Department of Housing and Urban Development. (2017). *The 2017 annual homeless assessment report to Congress*. Retrieved from www.hudexchange.info/resources/documents/2017-AHAR-Part-1.pdf

Wodtke, G. T., Harding, D. J., & Elwert, F. (2011). Neighborhood effects in temporal perspective: The impact of long-term exposure to concentrated disadvantage on high school graduation. *American Sociological Review, 76*(5), 713–736.

ADDITIONAL RESOURCES

Briefs on additional homeless educational topics can be accessed at nche.ed.gov/briefs.php

MODULE 4
Caregivers with Complex Job Situations

SECTION 1: CASE SCENARIO

Context

Belding Elementary School is located in a Midwestern metropolitan area. Ferdous is a 4th-grader from a bilingual, working-class family. He is a second-generation American whose caregivers were born in Bangladesh. The family has recently moved to this Midwestern metropolis from the East Coast. Ms. Sanford is an upper-class, White woman in her early 30s who has lived in this metropolis since college graduation. She is monolingual, speaking only English.

Scenario

Ms. Sanford looks at the classroom clock. It is already ten minutes into the school day. Ferdous shuffles into the classroom holding a tardy slip. It's only the eighth week of school, but this is Ferdous's 20th time being tardy. Sometimes Ferdous is late by a few minutes, but other times he can be up to an hour late. Ms. Sanford is becoming increasingly concerned about how much instructional content Ferdous is missing. Also, Ferdous usually comes to class without his homework completed.

After his fifth tardy, Ms. Sanford shared her concerns about Ferdous's lateness and unfinished homework with his caregivers. They told her they would try to get Ferdous to school on time, but didn't offer any explanation for the frequent lateness. The caregivers also agreed to sign Ferdous's nightly reading slip and ensure that all homework was completed. Since the conversation, Ferdous has continued to arrive late without his homework finished.

The previous week, Ms. Sanford requested a meeting with the principal and Ferdous's caregivers to discuss his attendance and homework. Ferdous's caregivers shared that his father works 12-hour shifts (8:00 a.m. to 8:00 p.m.) and that his mother works two jobs, one of them 2 days a week (9:00 p.m. to 7:00 a.m.) and the other 3 days a week (12:00 a.m. to 7:00 a.m.). Ferdous attends after-school care. Ferdous's caregivers expressed that since Ferdous attends after-school care, they expect Ferdous to complete his homework during that time. The meeting concluded with the principal supporting Ms. Sanford's position that Ferdous needed to arrive to school on time with his homework completed.

SECTION 2: EXPLORING CURRENT PERSPECTIVES

Task 1: Initial Reaction

Directions: Consider how you would react to the scenario if you were the student's teacher. The guiding questions below will support your thoughtful reflection. Jot down notes or bullet points that respond to each of the guiding questions.

1. After "experiencing" the scenario, what would your feelings and inner thoughts be?
   » I may be frustrated that Ferdous's parents weren't supporting his education in the ways that I expected.
   » I may be concerned about Ferdous's progress.
   » I may be concerned about my yearly evaluation, since student achievement on the state tests is considered.
2. How would you respond to this situation?
   » I may document instances when Ferdous was late or his homework unfinished.
   » I may inform the principal of any continued concerns so that these could be accounted for on my evaluation.
   » I may schedule a meeting with the principal and caregivers if I have continued concerns about late arrivals or homework.
   » I may speak with the after-school-care staff to learn their preferences for homework completion during after-school care, and would arrange for homework to be done then, if appropriate.

3. What do you know or did you learn about the student as a learner from this experience?
   » Ferdous is a bilingual and second-generation citizen.
   » He is from a working-class family.
   » He is new to the area.
   » He attends after-school care.
   » He is often late to school.
   » He doesn't do his homework independently.
4. What do you know or did you learn about the student's family?
   » They are first-generation citizens.
   » They expect Ferdous's homework to be completed during after-school care.
   » Caregivers work nontraditional hours.
   » They are new to the area.

Task 2: Maslow's Hierarchy

Directions: Consider Maslow's (1943) Hierarchy of Needs (see Figure 2.1). Then complete Table 2.

Table 2. Mapping Individual Needs onto Maslow's Hierarchy

Individual	What are the individual's needs as described in the scenario?	Where do these needs fit on Maslow's Hierarchy of Needs?
The Student	• Possibly communication in English (unclear in scenario) • Possibly relationship-building since new to community • Arrive to school on time • Complete homework	• Belongingness needs • Esteem needs • Self-actualization needs
The Student's Caregivers	• Possibly communication in English (unclear in scenario) • Possibly relationship-building since new to community • Coordinate the schedules and demands of both work and school • Support Ferdous's learning	• Belongingness needs • Esteem needs • Self-actualization needs • Physiological and safety needs, since they need to be employed to provide for family
The Teacher	• Educate all students • Create classroom community of which Ferdous is a member • Meet expectations for student achievement to maintain employment	• Belongingness needs • Esteem needs • Self-actualization needs • Physiological and safety needs, since he/she needs to be employed to provide for self and possibly family

Task 3: Probing Deeper

Directions: Consider issues of power, prestige, positioning, and access as defined in Chapter 2. Complete Table 3, Considerations of Power, Prestige, Positioning, and Access based on the case scenario.

Table 3. Considerations of Power, Prestige, Positioning, and Access

Individual	WHAT ARE THE THREATS (REAL OR PERCEIVED) TO THE INDIVIDUAL'S . . .			
	Power?	Prestige?	Positioning?	Access?
The Student	• Not able to 100% control being on time to school • Unable to sign homework sheet	• Viewed as lower-income student who is struggling • Viewed as not applying himself to learning since he does not do homework	• Lowest positioning of three entities. He must follow the directives of the teachers and caregivers. Status as a second-generation American, possible English language learner, and working class contribute to lower social positioning.	• Possibly limited access if an English language learner. Also, differences in social class and culture might influence access.
The Student's Caregivers	• Limited since school is directing caregivers' actions. Less power since not able to change work schedules to accommodate family's needs.	• First-generation American and working class • Possible English language learner	• Status as a first-generation American, possible English learner, and working class contribute to lower social positioning. Currently positioned lower than the teacher and administrator, since being directed what to do	• Possibly limited access if an English language learner. Also, differences in social class and culture might influence access. Limited access to understanding the educational system since work schedules don't permit engagement with school.
The Teacher	• Most powerful since able to arrange and ask for a meeting • Principal supports her request	• Viewed as the expert who knows what the student needs in order to achieve	• Highest positioned since able to organize the meeting, set the agenda, and determine outcomes	• Understands the school system and how to navigate it

45

Task 4: Summarizing

Directions: For each individual, compare what they need (Table 2) with any threats they are experiencing to their power, prestige, positioning, and access (Table 3). What overlaps exist between Table 2 and Table 3? Write down any overlapping needs and threats in Table 4, Summarizing Overlapping Needs and Threats.

Table 4. Summarizing Overlapping Needs and Threats

Individual	Overlapping Needs and Threats (Real or Perceived)
The Student	• Not completely able to control arriving to school late or finishing homework • May have limited access to instruction due to primary language, culture, and social class • May have limited ability to advocate for supports that he needs or knowledge of available supports
The Student's Caregivers	• Employment obligations may limit parents' ability to get Ferdous to school on time or assist with homework, despite their best intentions • May have limited access to instruction due to primary language, culture, and social class • May have limited ability to advocate for supports that Ferdous needs or knowledge of available supports
The Teacher	• May feel pressure for Ferdous to achieve educational expectations so that her evaluation and employment are not negatively impacted

SECTION 3: GETTING ON THE SAME PAGE

Historical Background

The recession of 2007 to 2009 was a defining moment in U.S. economic history, a moment with far-reaching impacts for teachers, students, and their families. These recent economic fluctuations influenced the American job market, the labor force, and wages. Since World War II, the number of middle-class households has decreased. According to the Pew Research Center (2016), middle-income households are "those with an income that is two-thirds to double that of the U.S. median household incomes, after incomes have been adjusted for household size" (p. 2). As reported in the *Washington Post*, in 1981, 59% of adults could be classified as middle income, but the percentage fell to 51% by 2011 (Tankersley, 2014). This decrease is noted in rural, suburban, and metropolitan areas (Pew Research Center, 2016).

A change related to the shrinking middle class is that students' care-givers might experience the stagnation or reduction of total household income. Nationwide data show that in 2014 the median income of all households was 8% less than in 1999 (Pew Research, 2016). Economic analysts have linked the wage reduction to the outsourcing of middle- and low-skill jobs to either machines or overseas labor markets. Caregivers may have had to enter the workforce, work longer hours, work multiple jobs, or acquire debt in order to increase or maintain their household income (Tankersley, 2014).

Atypical Work Situations

How might the changes in employment influence teachers' abilities to collaborate with caregivers? Caregivers might work atypical hours, such as the evenings or weekends. Atypical work schedules can influence when caregivers are available to meet with school staff as well as the time spent with their children. For example, students might need to spend lon-ger hours in before- and after-school care, at nontraditional day cares that provide overnight supervision, or with friends and family members. Caregivers might also experience financial limitations, since their income might not cover the increased costs of basic living needs (e.g., groceries, housing, transportation) and child care.

My (Marliese's) family falls into the category of having "complex job situations." When I began my doctoral program, my job situation involved working from home 3 or 4 days a week and then commuting 75 minutes to my doctoral program two or three times per week. Agonizingly, there were multiple weeks when I worked 6 days in an attempt to balance my doctoral assistantships along with coursework. When commuting to campus, I left the house by 6:30 a.m. and often did not return until 9:00 p.m., since I had evening courses. On my "at home days," I could shift my schedule to accommodate child care drop-offs and pick-ups. My husband was completing his medical residency and fellowship programs. He worked 6 days a week, approximately 60 to 70 hours. For most weeks, he would be on-call at least 1 or 2 days, meaning he remained at the hospital for the majority of the night to attend to patients' acute medical needs.

Our combined work schedules necessitated that our child care begin at 6:30 a.m. and last into the evening. In our local area, we could not find any day care centers with extended hours. We were financially unable to pay for a nanny, so our extended family offered to visit for 6 to 8 weeks at a time so they could provide child care during the early morning and evening hours. Our children's day care providers and preschool teachers interacted with our extended family. Once our children entered formal schooling, we dedicated time to share information about how our extended family worked collaboratively to support our children's educational progress.

Critical Introspection

When a caregiver seems to be "unavailable" or "difficult to reach," it is easy for teachers to assume a deficit perspective by thinking that the caregiver does not care about their child's education. So how can teachers learn to apply a perspective that views differences as assets? First, it is important to recognize that caregivers haven't changed, but that parenthood or caregiving has. Caregivers continue to love their children and want them to experience academic success. Most caregivers would agree that developing collaborative relationships with their child's teacher is one way to support their child's success (Applebaum, 2009).

While taking steps to develop relationships with caregivers, teachers must also acknowledge the factors contributing to changes in caregiving. Teachers should primarily look to the multiple institutional systems influencing one's role as a caregiver. One such system might be the contemporary job market, with decreasing middle-class job opportunities and wages. A second might be the housing market. Many teachers no longer reside in the neighborhoods and communities in which they teach. Thus, teachers are "outsiders" to the community in which the school is situated. Being outsiders, teachers may have limited knowledge or access to the resources and supports available within the community. To conclude, teachers should acknowledge how complex job situations might influence their mindset and approach for establishing collaborative relationships with caregivers. Only then can teachers brainstorm how to form collaborative relationships from an asset-based rather than a deficit-based perspective.

SECTION 4: LISTENING TO EXPAND PERSPECTIVES

Task 5: Probing Even Deeper

Directions: Let's probe this background information more deeply. What additional potential threats to the individual's power, prestige, positioning, and access were identified in the background information presented? List all potential threats in Table 5, Expanded Considerations of Power, Prestige, Positioning, and Access.

Table 5. Expanded Considerations of Power, Prestige, Positioning, and Access

Individual	BASED ON BACKGROUND INFORMATION, WHAT ARE ADDITIONAL POTENTIAL THREATS TO THE INDIVIDUAL'S . . .			
	Power?	**Prestige?**	**Positioning?**	**Access?**
The Student				
The Student's Caregivers	Employment might be temporary or in jeopardy of being outsourced.			
The Teacher				May be negotiating own complex schedule if need to work multiple jobs

Task 6: Integrating

Directions: After considering this background, revisit the Case Scenario. Review the information in Table 4. Consider how the potential threats listed in Table 5 overlap or extend the needs and threats listed in Table 4.

For each individual, complete Table 6 by revising the needs and threats according to the information contained in Tables 4 and 5.

Table 6. Revised Needs and Threats

Individual	Revised Needs and Threats (Real or Perceived)
The Student	• Not completely able to control arriving to school late or finishing homework • May have limited access to instruction due to primary language, culture, and social class • May have limited ability to advocate for supports that he needs or knowledge of available supports
The Student's Caregivers	• Employment obligations may limit parents' ability to get Ferdous to school on time or assist with homework, despite their best intentions • May have limited access to instruction due to primary language, culture, and social class • May have limited ability to advocate for supports that he needs or knowledge of available supports • Employment might be tenuous so may be overly attentive to work obligations

Table 6. Revised Needs and Threats (continued)

Individual	Revised Needs and Threats (Real or Perceived)
The Teacher	• May feel pressure for Ferdous to achieve educational expectations so that her evaluation and employment are not negatively impacted • May have own complex work schedule if juggling multiple jobs

SECTION 5: FIXING IT

Task 7: Analyzing

Directions: Complete Table 7, ABC Model, below. For each of the listed behaviors, identify the antecedents. These can be either known antecedents identified in the Case Scenario or potential antecedents outlined in Getting on the Same Page. Next, identify consequences (either known or potential).

Table 7. ABC Model

Antecedent	Behavior	Consequence
Parents' work schedules conflict with school start times.	Arriving to school late	Ferdous misses instruction.
Travel times extended due to traffic or weather	Arriving to school late	Ferdous misses instruction.
Attends after-school care so limited time at home with caregivers	Not completing homework	Does not have additional independent practice. Potentially limited academic growth.
Potential status as an English learner could complicate understanding of assignments.	Not completing homework	Does not have additional independent practice. Potentially limited academic growth.

Task 8: Identifying Action Steps

Directions: After completing the ABC chart above, select the desired behavior(s) that you want to encourage. You will complete Table 8 for each identified target behavior. In the table below, phrase the desired behavior in positive terms (i.e., as something you want to happen).

Next, brainstorm ways to alter the antecedents and/or consequences so that the selected behaviors are more likely to occur. By reviewing the expanded perspectives in Getting on the Same Page, you can identify antecedents/consequences that could contribute to increasing the desired behaviors.

While it is important to state target behaviors in a positive manner, there may be instances when this is not possible. For this example, Ferdous and his caregivers are not able to control all potential factors that might impact arriving to school on time. For this reason, it is appropriate to brainstorm altered antecedents and consequences for the instances when Ferdous arrives late. The altered antecedents and consequences should be stated in a positive manner.

Table 8. Target Behaviors

Selected Target Behavior: Arriving to School on Time

Altered Antecedents	Behavior	Altered Consequences
Relatives or friends transport Ferdous to school.	Arriving to school on time	Ferdous does not miss instruction.
Identify additional backup drivers that parents could call if they are running late and relatives/friends are not available.	Arriving to school on time	Ferdous does not miss instruction.
Any academic supports (e.g., English language instruction) are moved to later in the school day.	Arriving late to school	Ferdous does not miss these supports even though he is late to school.
Peer buddy or volunteer catches Ferdous up on items if late.	Arriving late to school	Ferdous has access to the content that he missed.
Parents notify school if they are going to be late so that teacher can audio- or videotape instruction.	Arriving late to school	Ferdous has access to the content that he missed and can view it during after-school care.

Selected Target Behavior: Completing Homework

Altered Antecedents	Behavior	Altered Consequences
Complete during after-school care.	Completing homework	Gets independent practice
Volunteer tutor comes after school to support Ferdous with homework completion.	Completing homework	Gets independent practice
Create checklist or anchor charts to support Ferdous with independent completion of predetermined homework items.	Completing homework	Ferdous increases his positioning and prestige since learning independence and self-monitoring.

Selected Target Behavior: Completing Homework (continued)

Altered Antecedents	Behavior	Altered Consequences
Audiotape reading or quick statements about homework. Send these to caregivers.	Completing homework	Caregivers remain part of the homework process. They have increased access to knowing what Ferdous is learning and can raise concerns based on the recordings.
If receiving academic support, Ferdous can review his homework with his support person to ensure he understands the assignment.	Completing homework	This improves access since language differences would be minimized.

Developing Collaborative Partnerships

- Send home a "Getting to Know Our Family" page at the beginning of the school year. Ask caregivers to complete as much of the page as they wish. Questions might address current employment, best methods and times to communicate, additional languages and literacies used in the home/community environment, potential knowledge/expertise that the family would like to share with the class, and any questions the family has at the present time.
- When addressing multiple concerns, it might be most effective to initially address each concern separately. Identify separate solutions for each concern. Then determine how these separate solutions might be unified to form a cohesive plan.
- Teachers and caregivers can use systematic observations and data recording to track the targeted behavior. These objective data records can be reviewed at a follow-up meeting to determine if the fixes are effective or if alternative solutions should be tried.
- Identify other individuals from the school and community with whom the family has a relationship. Determine if these individuals can help mitigate the challenges experienced by the family's complex job situation (e.g., would a neighbor be able to transport the student to school when needed?).

Communication Approaches

- Do not use language that makes caregivers feel guilty. Instead, use language recognizing the limitations that outside systems might place on each individual, limiting their ability to meet the school's expectations (e.g., getting to school on time, completing nightly homework).

- Establish efficient communication methods between the teacher and caregivers so that everyone can remain abreast of time-sensitive information.

SECTION 6: REBUILDING THE CASE

It is the second week of school, and Ferdous is late for the third time. In addition to the missed instructional time, Ferdous usually doesn't have the caregiver <u>signature for nightly reading completed</u>.[1] Ms. Sanford is increasingly concerned about Ferdous. During lunch, she reviews the <u>"Getting to Know Our Family" page</u>[2] she sent home at the beginning of the school year. The introduction page notes that Ferdous's father works 12-hour shifts (8:00 a.m. to 8:00 p.m.) and that his mother works two jobs. One job is 2 days a week (9:00 p.m. to 7:00 a.m.) and the other 3 days a week (12:00 a.m. to 7:00 a.m.). Ms. Sanford creates a sketch of the family's schedule. Looking at the sketch, <u>Ms. Sanford jots these questions</u>[3] in Ferdous's communication log:

- Where are Ferdous's caregivers' places of employment located in relation to their house and the school?
- Does either caregiver get delayed at work so they can't leave at their usual time?

Ms. Sanford also notices that Ferdous's caregivers indicated emailing was the best communication method. <u>Her first priority is to establish an effective communication plan with the family</u>.[4] She crafts an email sharing positive information about Ferdous and asking, "What is the best way to communicate time-sensitive information with you? For example, if Ferdous gets sick at school, how might I contact you? I ask because I noticed that during school hours Ferdous's father is at work and his mother is preparing to work during the night."

Ferdous's caregivers respond, thanking Ms. Sanford for sharing how Ferdous is doing in school. <u>They explain that their current work schedules keep their family busy, leaving little time for everyone being home together</u>.[5] They ask Ms. Sanford to text Ferdous's dad if there is a need during the school day. Ms. Sanford plans to send a follow-up email, inquiring more about the caregivers' employment since they had shared additional information in their email. She wants to learn more about their employment so she can identify resources, experiences, and out-of-school literacies Ferdous might have access and exposure to. This information will also help her understand what factors might contribute to Ferdous's late arrivals to school and incomplete homework. Ms. Sanford will use asset-based language rather than blaming the caregivers for their complex work schedules.

1. Teachers should consider factors that might contribute to caregivers not signing or participating in homework. For example, caregivers who speak languages other than English might not understand the assignment directions or hold contrasting views of the caregivers' role with homework. Ms. Sanford should learn more about the caregivers' views and understandings of homework to determine why the caregiver signature is not being completed. (For additional ideas, see Modules 5 and 6.)

2. When sending communication home at the beginning of the year, first check the student's file to determine what language is spoken in the home. For students who speak languages other than English, confirm which language parents prefer for home communication. Ms. Sanford could translate her introduction paper into another language using Google Translate or school/community resources. (For additional ideas, see Modules 5 and 6.)

3. Ms. Sanford might have different questions depending on her knowledge and personal experience with complex job situations. For example, some teachers work multiple jobs. Thus, she might have personal experience and knowledge of negotiating complex job situations.

4. If Ferdous and his family already have a relationship with the school, Ms. Sanford might not prioritize establishing a positive, collaborative partnership. It is important to assess what type of partnership the school, other staff, and the family already have. Teachers can build on these previous relationships as they problem-solve the current concerns.

5. Families with complex job situations might seek the support of family, friends, or community resources to help navigate the complexities of their job situations. For example, relatives or friends might provide child care support so children do not have to use after-school care or nontraditional day care settings. As teachers learn more about the caregivers' job dynamics, they should ask about the resources that the caregivers draw on for support.

REFERENCES

Applebaum, M. (2009). *How to handle hard-to-handle parents*. Thousand Oaks, CA: Corwin.

Pew Research Center. (2016, May 11). *America's shrinking middle class: A close look at changes within metropolitan areas*. Retrieved from www.pewsocialtrends.org/2016/05/11/americas-shrinking-middle-class-a-close-look-at-changes-within-metropolitan-areas

Tankersley, J. (2014, December 14). The devalued American worker. *Washington Post*. Retrieved from www.washingtonpost.com/sf/business/2014/12/14/the-devalued-american-worker/?utm_term=.2bd1ef0e1230

ADDITIONAL RESOURCES

Edutopia's Family Engagement Resource Roundup: www.edutopia.org
 /home-school-connections-resources
Family–School Relationship Survey: www.panoramaed.com/family-school
 -relationships-survey
National Association for Family, School, and Community Engagement: www.nafsce
 .org
Panorama Education's guide to reducing barriers to family engagement: go
 .panoramaed.com/whitepaper/reducing-barriers-to-family-engagement

---

MODULE 5
Culturally and Linguistically Diverse Caregivers

SECTION 1: CASE SCENARIO

Context

Ms. Green is a 35-year-old, White, American female. She is in her 10th
year of teaching in a large suburban district outside of a major city and a
university town. She is an English monolingual who teaches 3rd grade,
and Joseph is one of her students. Joseph is a Hispanic, bilingual 8-year-old
who lives with his single mother, Deanna, and he is an only child. Deanna
is a graduate student at the local university, and her son attends the public
school. Joseph qualifies for free and reduced lunch, and he receives English
language (EL) services.

Scenario

Families in this district are diverse and come from a variety of cultures and
socioeconomic backgrounds. The school serves children of university students and faculty, as well as families who have lived in the community for
generations. As a parent, Deanna faces many challenges in working with
the school personnel to understand Joseph's status as an EL student and his
growth in academic areas, particularly in reading and writing. The classroom teacher, Ms. Green, rarely sends home newsletters informing caregivers about goals, content, activities, and expected achievements. Instead,
she wants caregivers to inform her about what they do with their children
at home. This is her way of holding caregivers accountable for their children's education.

The most recent school report card showed that Joseph was below grade level in reading, but Deanna did not understand the schoolwide assessments. Not knowing how else to gain information about her child's progress, Deanna decided to spend a morning at the school during literacy time. During the observation that day, Deanna was faced with resistance from the teacher about her presence in the classroom. That morning, Deanna noticed that the same children were repeatedly called on to answer questions. She also noticed that the same English learners were verbally corrected for being off-task. Before the morning was over, Ms. Brown, the school's principal, insisted that Deanna end the visit and leave the school. Deanna wants Joseph to be successful, but she faces barriers when trying to learn about his progress in school.

SECTION 2: EXPLORING CURRENT PERSPECTIVES

 Complete Appendix A, Tasks for Section 2: Exploring Current Perspectives.

SECTION 3: GETTING ON THE SAME PAGE

Culturally and linguistically diverse students and caregivers are growing in numbers in U.S. schools. The gap between the knowledge required to teach diverse student populations and teacher candidates' preparation is problematic and a nationwide issue for schools hiring teachers (Bunch, 2013; Fillmore & Snow, 2000; Lucas, 2011). Teacher candidates (TCs) report that they do not feel prepared to work with and teach students who are culturally and linguistically diverse (Michigan Department of Education, personal communication, Spring 2016). There are a variety of possible reasons for this problem of preparedness. It could be the lack of content about ELs in methods courses, or the TCs' lack of experience with diversity, or the TCs' own lack of diversity (Bunch, 2013; Fillmore & Snow, 2000; Lucas, 2011). Regardless of the cause, many TCs do not feel prepared to teach all populations of students and caregivers.

Children in U.S. classrooms are more heterogeneous than they were 2 decades ago (Enright, 2011). Children and families for whom English is a second language face many challenges when attending English-speaking schools. One barrier is that the majority of teachers around the country are White, monolingual, middle-class females. As diversity in U.S. classrooms grows, so does the need to prepare teachers in new ways. According to Lucas, "Teachers cannot simply teach ELs the way they teach other students; to teach ELs well, they need special expertise—and this requires special preparation" (2011, p. xiv).

Lucas suggests that critical experiences for TCs in school settings with educators who teach culturally and linguistically diverse students might open dialogue and shift preconceived notions about how to teach students who are culturally and linguistically diverse. Creating experiences to prepare TCs to work with culturally and linguistically diverse students that provide meaningful opportunities and information with and about diverse learners and that are separate from other methods courses might help TCs feel more prepared when they exit teacher preparation programs.

As an elementary classroom teacher and reading specialist for 21 years, I (Ann) worked with culturally and linguistically diverse students and caregivers. I worked with the classroom teachers and data team to analyze the literacy data for all 1st-grade students. The data for one student, Arianna, was puzzling. When we analyzed Arianna's benchmark literacy scores, we were not sure if the emerging scores were a result of limited literacy knowledge or limited knowledge of English. Arianna and her two siblings had come to our school from Mexico that year. Her caregivers worked at the local Mexican restaurant and spoke Spanish at home. The large suburban school district had identified one elementary school as the ESL school, but it was across the district and a long bus ride away. The principal asked the family if they wanted to transfer their children to that school so they could receive EL services, but they wanted to keep the children at our school. As we explored the case, we consulted the district EL teacher for support, and she recommended that we keep Arianna in her 1st-grade classroom to gain as much language experience as possible.

Classroom teachers are called to establish and communicate explicit expectations with families to promote individual student growth academically, socially, and emotionally. Teacher candidates and practitioners must learn to work successfully in any classroom and with any group of students, including linguistically and culturally diverse students (Bunch, 2013; Coady, Harper, & de Jong, 2016; Fillmore & Snow, 2000; Gibbons, 2006; Lucas, 2011).

First of all, educators should make extended efforts to connect with caregivers through the child's native language by finding an interpreter, such as a staff member or community member. They could also try connecting caregivers with bilingual staff members, so they have a contact person. Translating written notes sent home to provide access to information (if the caregivers can read in their native language) and learning some of the child's language themselves are other ways to connect to caregivers through their home language (Calderón & Minaya-Rowe, 2003; Colorín Colorado, 2018). In addition, educators should not assume that all caregivers know how U.S. schools operate. Elements such as school structures, dress codes, rules, and routines vary from school system to school system. For example, caregivers might be expected to send their students in snow pants in the winter, but they might not know what snow pants are—that they are to be worn in the snow only, and that they are worn over regular clothes. It is also critical to know that this might be the child's first time in formal school, even if they are in middle or high school. It is educators' responsibility to teach caregivers how U.S. schools work and that caregivers have rights regarding interpreters, translators, food services, and other support programs. Teachers should learn and share those policies (Calderón & Minaya-Rowe, 2003; Colorín Colorado, 2018).

Further, it is important to visit caregivers' communities, though educators should not assume that all caregivers will welcome them into their homes for a visit. Some caregivers are not comfortable meeting at their child's school or at their homes. Therefore, teachers and caregivers can mutually agree on a location in the community, ask an interpreter to be present, and honor the time caregivers can commit to a meeting (Calderón & Minaya-Rowe, 2003; Colorín Colorado, 2018). Last, educators should invite caregivers into their school, and not assume that they will come on their own. Schools can be intimidating spaces, especially for those who do not speak the dominant language. Often, schools host back-to-school open houses, picnics, and curriculum nights, which are often overwhelming events for all families. Teachers can increase attendance by recruiting volunteers, providing interpreters, arranging transportation, and organizing child care (Calderón & Minaya-Rowe, 2003; Colorín Colorado, 2018).

SECTION 4: LISTENING TO EXPAND PERSPECTIVES

 Complete Appendix B, Tasks for Section 4: Listening to Expand Perspectives.

SECTION 5: FIXING IT

 The following are suggestions for working with students and caregivers who are culturally and linguistically diverse. Complete Appendix C, Tasks for Section 5: Fixing It, for further reflection and analysis. According to Colorín Colorado (2018) and Calderón and Minaya-Rowe (2003), there are many proactive steps for reaching out to caregivers of language learners.

Try Using Caregivers' Language

- Ask caregivers and students about their preferences for communication, specifically if it should be provided in their first language, English, or both languages.
- Ask the child how you might connect through their native language.
- Find an interpreter for school meetings.
- Connect caregivers with a contact person in the school. Ask caregivers if they have already established relationships that you could build on or incorporate into this communication system.
- Translate written notes (if caregivers can read in their first language) before sending them home (Calderón & Minaya-Rowe, 2003; Colorín Colorado, 2018)

Help Caregivers Understand the U.S. School System

- Learn about caregivers' knowledge of how U.S. schools operate; clarify any misunderstandings.
- Find out if the child has formal schooling experiences.
- Review the school calendar, hours, rules, routines, lunch menus, staff member titles, and responsibilities.
- Share the school's curriculum, goals, schedule for special classes (e.g., art, music, physical education), caregiver expectations, and dress code. Learn how these might differ from other formal schooling experiences.
- Explain to caregivers their rights, including interpreters, translated materials, free and reduced lunch, and supplemental programs, including EL, language, and Title I programs (Calderón & Minaya-Rowe, 2003; Colorín Colorado, 2018).

Visit the Caregivers' Communities

- Meet with caregivers to build positive relationships.
- Understand that some caregivers are not comfortable meeting at your school or at their homes.
- Agree to meet at a location in the community and ask an interpreter to be present (Calderón & Minaya-Rowe, 2003; Colorín Colorado, 2018).

Invite Caregivers into Your School

- Understand that schools can be intimidating spaces to caregivers.
- At the beginning of the year, make extra effort to reach out to culturally and linguistically diverse caregivers.

- For meetings, recruit volunteers, provide interpreters, arrange transportation, and organize child care.
- Provide school tours for families (Calderón & Minaya-Rowe, 2003; Colorín Colorado, 2018).

SECTION 6: REBUILDING THE CASE

As an international graduate student, Deanna faces many challenges in working with her son's school. The classroom teacher seems to run the classroom in ways that benefit students and caregivers who know English and know how school works, but Deanna is new to the school and finds it difficult to understand how her son is progressing in the classroom. She does not understand the school report card, the assessment data, or how her son is learning in the classroom. The teacher and principal have not found ways to communicate and build bridges with Deanna. As a result, the school personnel, the caregiver, and the student are frustrated and defensive about the ways each party has reacted to the circumstances. The classroom teacher and school principal realize they need to rethink how they work with caregivers and students who are new to the United States and new to their school. They call Deanna and invite her to talk about how they can support Joseph as a 3rd-grade EL student who is learning English and academic subjects at the same time.

One way that Ms. Green and Ms. Brown (the principal) reach out is by reconnecting with Deanna to find out her concerns and needs as a parent of an EL student.[1] When they call Deanna to set up a meeting, they decide to meet on the university campus because it is a more neutral setting. When they gather, they do not hold onto the incident that happened at school the week before: when Deanna decided on her own to observe Ms. Green's classroom teaching, which led to her getting upset about what she saw, which ended in Principal Brown escorting Deanna out of the building. Deanna, Joseph, Ms. Green, Ms. Brown, and the EL consultant from the district meet after school in the cafe area of a campus building, and they start over.[2] They understand that this 45-minute meeting is the beginning of what needs to be an ongoing dialogue between the caregiver and the school staff. The school team works together to share with Deanna how U.S. schools work in relation to her experiences with her country's educational system. They know this is not Joseph's first formal schooling experience—he did attend school before. They come to this meeting prepared to talk about the school's academic curriculum and share ways the school can collaborate with Deanna and Joseph. The district's EL consultant provides information about the EL program, which helps the teacher, principal, and caregiver understand the WIDA scores and the district's literacy assessments.[3] WIDA (i.e., World-Class Instructional Design and Assessment) "provides language development resources to those who support the academic success of multilingual learners" (WIDA, 2018). Often, classroom teachers and school principals have limited understanding of EL methods of instruction and of WIDA assessments. They all learned something new during this meeting. Ms. Green sets a new time for Deanna to come back to the classroom and observe her 3rd-grade instruction. They also find a day that the EL consultant can co-observe with Deanna so she can help her process the instruction and practices viewed by the caregiver and be open to offering PD to the teacher for improving practice, if appropriate.

1. In this scenario, Ms. Green and Ms. Brown decide to start over and connect with Deanna and her son, Joseph. They try to understand her frustration as a caregiver and invite Deanna to a meeting and include the district's EL consultant as a translator for the nuanced information they want to share, and to allow them to hear Deanna's concerns and requests.

2. By inviting Deanna to a meeting at a neutral site to explain how their school operates, they are meeting their ethical responsibilities as educators in public schools. The school staff goes beyond school hours to find ways to connect with caregivers. Deanna asks her many questions.

3. Hearing the explanation about the district's 3rd-grade curriculum, the district's literacy assessment scores, and the district's EL program, the caregiver begins to understand a little. They work together to continue meeting and building a home–school partnership.

REFERENCES

Bunch, G. C. (2013). Pedagogical language knowledge: Preparing mainstream teachers for English learners in the new standards era. *Review of Research in Education, 37*(1), 298–341.

Calderón, M. E., & Minaya-Rowe, L. (2003). *Designing and implementing two-way bilingual programs. A step-by step guide for administrators, teachers and parents.* Thousand Oaks, CA: Corwin Press.

Coady, M. R., Harper, C., & de Jong, E. J. (2016). Aiming for equity: Preparing mainstream teachers for inclusion or inclusive classrooms. *TESOL Q, 50*, 340–368. doi:10.1002/tesq.223

Colorín Colorado (2018). How to reach parents of ELLs. Retrieved from www.colorincolorado.org/article/how-reach-out-parents-ells

Enright, K. (2011). Language and literacy for a new mainstream. *American Educational Research Journal, 48*(1), 80–118.

Fillmore, L. W., & Snow, C. E. (2000). *What teachers need to know about language.* Washington, DC: Office of Educational Research and Improvement.

Gibbons, P. (2006). *Bridging discourses in the ESL classroom: Students, teachers and researchers.* London, England: A&C Black.

Lucas, T., Villegas, A. M., & Freedson-Gonzalez, M. (2008). Linguistically responsive teacher education: Preparing classroom teachers to teach English language learners. *Journal of Teacher Education, 59*(4), 361–373.

WIDA. (2018). Wisconsin Center for Education Research at the University of Wisconsin-Madison. Board of Regents of the University of Wisconsin System. Retrieved from wida.wisc.edu/grow/research/wcer

ADDITIONAL RESOURCE

Reading Rockets, Reading Topic page on English language learners: www.readingrockets.org/reading-topics/english-language-learners

---

MODULE 6
Caregivers Who Speak Limited or No English

SECTION 1: CASE SCENARIO

Context

Ms. Hanson is a White, English monolingual, upper-middle-class, 43-year-old woman teaching in a district that serves students in both suburban and rural contexts. Her school's boundaries encompass multiple subdivisions in addition to wineries and fruit farms.

Ms. Hanson has taught 2nd grade for 15 years. One of her students, Julia, is quiet and hardworking. Julia and her family are from Mexico, and Julia speaks both Spanish and English, although Ms. Hanson has only heard Julia speak English at school. (Julia goes by the English pronunciation of her name, *Joo-lee-ah*, rather than the Spanish pronunciation, *Hoo-lee-ah*.)

Scenario

Ms. Hanson is concerned because the first field trip of the year is approaching, and Julia still hasn't brought back the signed permission slip. Without the signed slip, Julia cannot go on the trip. Ms. Hanson explains these potential consequences to Julia, who says "okay" and takes another copy. As Ms. Hanson reflects on the situation, she realizes that she hasn't received any signed forms from Julia's parents since the year started. She didn't meet them at Open House, and they had not contributed anything for class parties, even simple things like cups or napkins.

Ms. Hanson asks herself: "Why don't parents look at the papers I send home? Parents today just don't care!" She checks Julia's backpack, but it's empty. Her homework folder and her desk don't have copies of the permission slip either. What is going on?

Ms. Hanson talks to Julia's 1st-grade teacher and discovers that Julia exited the ESL program the previous year. The ESL teacher had shared with Julia's former teacher that Julia's parents are farmworkers who speak little English—their primary languages are a dialect of Mixtec (a group of indigenous languages in Mexico) and some Spanish. Julia's parents don't get home until the evening and leave early in the morning to work in the fields. Julia is the oldest in her family, but a cousin in middle school looks after her and her kindergarten sister after school until her parents get home. This helps explain why Julia's permission slips aren't signed and returned, but Ms. Hanson doesn't speak Mixtec or Spanish (other than a few words such as *hola*, *adiós*, and *baño*), so she wonders how she can communicate with Julia's parents.

SECTION 2: EXPLORING CURRENT PERSPECTIVES

 Complete Appendix A, Tasks for Section 2: Exploring Current Perspectives.

SECTION 3: GETTING ON THE SAME PAGE

First, a quick note about the scenario: Caregivers who are multilingual but who may not speak English or speak limited English come from a variety of countries and socioeconomic backgrounds. The purpose of the scenario is not to pigeonhole Mexicans in a stereotypical role of farmworkers. I (Lisa) wrote the scenario this way because Mexicans are the multilingual population with whom I have worked the most. Presenting the family as farmworkers also introduces contextual factors related to their work lives that complicate the situation. Finally, because the family speaks Mixtec as their primary language, it complicates how the teacher can communicate with them (while challenging the stereotype that all people from Mexico speak Spanish), but it also makes it more likely the family will be in a low-paying job due to the marginalization of First Peoples.

General Lack of Communication

One reason for caregivers' lack of communication with schools could be that they are emergent bilinguals learning to speak English. Caregivers often feel embarrassed and/or frustrated by their inability to communicate with teachers and schools and thus do not reach out, especially if translators are not available (Colombo, 2006; Ji & Koblinsky, 2009). Delgado, Huerta, and Campos (2012) noted, "Limited English proficiency makes many parents feel unqualified and uncomfortable, and often they fear that school personnel will expect them to speak English or that they will encounter negative attitudes about their inability to communicate adequately" (p. 33). Caregivers' perceptions of their language competence and how others perceive them may create a barrier of silence, making caregivers feel powerless. This feeling can extend to their children's needs. For example, teachers may share academic or social concerns about children with their caregivers and not receive much response. This is likely not because caregivers do not care or do not realize what is happening. Instead, while caregivers may have witnessed and/or understand their children's struggles, because everything is in English, a language they may not speak fluently, they may feel powerless to help (Qin & Han, 2014).

Perceived Lack of Help or Participation in School Practices

Another issue is that caregivers who have had a lot of schooling and/ or strong academic skills often struggle to help their children with homework in English because they do not know the technical, academic English vocabulary their children are learning or because they learned different ways of solving math problems or presenting information (Colombo, 2006; Ji & Koblinsky, 2009; Qin & Han, 2014). Providing homework support becomes especially complicated if caregivers' schooling experiences did not provide them with the necessary content knowledge in their home languages. Good, Masewicz, and Vogel, in their 2010 study of Latinx students and caretakers, noted that "parents wanted to work with teachers to help their children with homework and studies, but two factors got in their way: parents' limited English skills and a lack of academic preparation in academic content areas" (2010, p. 329). One or both of these factors can limit caregivers' abilities to provide help with school assignments in the ways teachers traditionally envision homework help.

Often, teachers expect families to participate in school activities in traditional/mainstream ways such as volunteering in the classroom, chaperoning field trips, helping with homework, sending in supplies for classroom needs, and attending school activities. Caregivers cannot do these things if they are not informed in languages they understand. Additionally, families may have different cultural expectations of teachers and schools that influence their communication and involvement—a topic discussed further in Module 7 about immigrant families.

During my (Lisa's) years teaching Spanish–English bilingual students, my ability to speak Spanish continually illustrated the importance of families receiving information in a language they understand. One day, I was calling the mother of one of my students, but my student's aunt answered. When I told her in Spanish that I was a teacher at the school and asked to speak with my student's mother, she excitedly told me that her daughter attended the school. She had received a notice about an upcoming class party, but didn't know what it said, and she wanted to contribute. She asked if I could find out for her. That afternoon, I talked to her daughter's teacher and called her back. She was so grateful. For the first time she could contribute something for her daughter's class because she knew what the note said. Communication in a language she understood empowered her.

Incorporating Caregivers' Strengths

Instead of perceiving a lack of support as a deficit in caregiver involvement, it is important for schools to incorporate caregivers' strengths by recognizing the ways in which caregivers help support their children's educational progress. For example, caregivers may stress the importance of hard work and education (Auerbach, 2007; López, 2001) and provide important life and character advice, called *consejos* in the Spanish-speaking community (Alfaro, O'Reilly-Diaz, & López, 2014).

Schools can also utilize caregivers' multilingual knowledge to help other students and families. Chow and Cummins (2003) described a project in which multilingual students created their own stories in English and their home languages. Caregivers helped children write and translate their stories into their home languages. They also recorded themselves reading other dual-language books aloud. These recordings and their accompanying books were sent home with students for additional reading and language practice. Practices such as these validate students' (and caregivers') identities, help them continue developing linguistic skills and knowledge in multiple languages, and create a more inclusive learning environment. These experiences also provide opportunities for multilingual caregivers to share their expertise in ways that further students' learning.

SECTION 4: LISTENING TO EXPAND PERSPECTIVES

Complete Appendix B, Tasks for Section 4: Listening to Expand Perspectives.

SECTION 5: FIXING IT

 The following are suggestions for working with multilingual caregivers who may not have strong English proficiency, spoken or written. Complete Appendix C, Tasks for Section 5: Fixing It, for further reflection and analysis.

Opening Lines of Communication

- One of the most important things schools can do is to translate important documents sent home. Use multilingual school staff, community resources, other caregivers, or, if necessary, Google Translate to translate key phrases. If caregivers cannot read in their home languages, find ways to provide the translated material in audio format or have it read aloud. Having a multilingual phone line is an option. Google Translate also has some capabilities of reading aloud translated text.
- At conferences or face-to-face meetings, ensure that translators are available. Keep points to share with caregivers short, balance sharing strengths and needs, and do not use jargon. If translators are not available, write down important information and have it translated to give to caregivers.
- To find translators, talk to other teachers in the district as well as other family members or families who may speak the same language. Locate and talk to community resources such as refugee centers, places of worship, and advocacy groups.

Helping Families Support Schoolwork

- If the goal is to have caregivers help children with homework, then provide multilingual glossaries of important academic terms. (Some state departments of education provide these online.) If possible, obtain a translated edition of the curriculum to provide to caregivers. Also, provide explanations and/or examples of how to complete the homework.

Incorporating Caregivers' Strengths

- Get to know caregivers, their linguistic and cultural backgrounds, and the ways they support their children. Build on this information. Value the languages that children speak in the classroom, and use caregivers' multilingual skills to help children learn content and linguistic information, not just in English but in their home languages as well.

SECTION 6: REBUILDING THE CASE

It's almost time for the <u>2nd-grade field trip, and Julia still has not brought back her signed permission slip</u>.[1] <u>Ms. Hanson speaks with Julia's 1st-grade teacher and learns that Julia's parents speak very limited English</u>.[2] <u>They speak mainly Mixtec and a little Spanish</u>.[3] Julia's parents also work long hours on nearby farms. With the field trip only days away, <u>Ms. Hanson decides to use Google Translate to create a simplified Spanish version of the permission slip</u>.[4] The translation isn't perfect, but it communicates the main ideas. Ms. Hanson gives Julia the Spanish translation and <u>asks her to leave the form out so her parents can see it and sign it when they get home from work</u>.[5] The next day, Julia brings the permission slip back signed.

1. As students age and develop language proficiency, they may be able to translate forms and school information for their caregivers themselves, but this depends on the opportunities they have for instruction to build literacy skills in multiple languages. It is important for teachers to ask students and families about their language preferences and abilities to help support communication between caregivers and teachers.

2. Getting to know caregivers' backgrounds and stories is critical for establishing a partnership and learning the reasons behind families' actions. If Julia did not attend kindergarten or 1st grade in Ms. Hanson's school, then Ms. Hanson would need to think of alternative strategies for learning about Julia's family. This might include reviewing Julia's school records or attempting to contact Julia's prior school with administrator and family permission.

3. If caregivers are unable to or struggle reading forms in their home languages, then providing written translations will not help. Instead, teachers may need to turn to multilingual family members or community members to translate forms orally in person or via phone. (See Module 2 for more information.)

4. If Ms. Hanson was bilingual in Spanish and English, she could write the translation herself. If she had the time, she could investigate community and/or school district resources (such as district employees proficient in families' languages or community advocacy groups that provide translation services) to help her translate the permission slip. Or she could encourage the school or district to create a generic field trip form translated in students' and caregivers' home languages. She could then just fill in the specific location and date for each event and reuse the form for years to come.

5. Caregivers' work schedules can also complicate their ability to respond to school requests. Perhaps caregivers do not see the form because they arrive home after the children are in bed and have limited time in the mornings as children get ready for school and caregivers prepare for work. In this version of the scenario, Ms. Hanson tried to consider how to accommodate caregivers' work schedules. (See Module 4 for more ideas.)

It is also important to consider other factors that might affect caregivers' willingness to return school forms. These factors could include not wanting to ask for assistance (e.g., completing free and reduced-price lunch forms), not having the monetary resources to contribute (e.g., contributing snacks, field trip money, etc.), or wishing to first seek advice from a friend or educational advocate (e.g., discussing IEP paperwork or academic or behavior concerns). These additional factors can be more easily identified once paperwork is provided in a manner that parents are able to understand, or a translator is engaged to translate verbally as needed.

REFERENCES

Alfaro, D. D., O'Reilly-Diaz, K., & López, G. R. (2014). Operationalizing consejos in the P-20 educational pipeline: Interrogating the nuances of Latino parent involvement. *Multicultural Education, 21*(3/4), 11–16.

Auerbach, S. (2007). From moral supporters to struggling advocates: Reconceptualizing parent roles in education through the experience of working-class families of color. *Urban Education, 42*(3), 250–283.

Chow, P., & Cummins, J. (2003). Valuing multilingual and multicultural approaches to learning. In S. Schecter & J. Cummins (Eds.), *Multilingual education in practice: Using diversity as a resource* (pp. 32–61). Portsmouth, NH: Heinemann.

Colombo, M. W. (2006). Building school partnerships with culturally and linguistically diverse families. *Phi Delta Kappan, 88*(4), 314–318.

Delgado, R., Huerta, M. E., & Campos, D. (2012). Enhancing relationships with parents of English language learners. *Principal Leadership, 12*(6), 30–34.

Good, M. E., Masewicz, S., & Vogel, L. (2010). Latino English language learners: Bridging achievement and cultural gaps between schools and families. *Journal of Latinos and Education, 9*(4), 321–339.

Ji, C. S., & Koblinsky, S. A. (2009). Parent involvement in children's education: An exploratory study of urban, Chinese immigrant families. *Urban Education, 44*(6), 687–709.

López, G. R. (2001). The value of hard work: Lessons on parent involvement from an (im)migrant household. *Harvard Educational Review, 71*(3), 416–438.

Qin, D. B., & Han, E. J. (2014). Tiger parents or sheep parents?: Struggles of parental involvement in working-class Chinese immigrant families. *Teachers College Record, 116*(8), 1–32.

ADDITIONAL RESOURCES

Multilingual content area glossaries from NYU Steinhardt: steinhardt.nyu.edu /metrocenter/resources/glossaries

Multilingual Reading Tip Sheets for Parents from Colorín Colorado (a website about literacy and language development for educators and families, available in Spanish): www.colorincolorado.org/reading-tip-sheets-parents

NCELA (National Clearinghouse for English Language Acquisition): ncela.ed.gov

MODULE 7

Caregivers Who Are Immigrants or Refugees

SECTION 1: CASE SCENARIO

Context

Ms. Keller is a 24-year-old, middle-class, White teacher. She is in her 2nd year of teaching in a large urban district close to the university where she graduated. She is an English monolingual who teaches 8th-grade science, and Amir is one of her students. Amir speaks English in the classroom, but often seems confused by directions for science labs and experiments. He had a low score on his last science test.

Amir and his family are from Oman and speak Arabic. They were upper-middle-class in Oman, but Amir's father is a graduate student, so his current salary puts him at a working-class or lower socioeconomic status. However, Ms. Keller doesn't know this information about Amir or his family.

Scenario

It's the week after middle school parent–teacher conferences. One of Ms. Keller's students, Amir, seems to speak English fluently, but he is struggling with understanding directions and procedures for science labs and experiments. He also scored low on his last science test. Ms. Keller had hoped to talk with Amir's parents during conferences, but they never came, and she hasn't heard a response from the grade report she sent home.

One day, Ms. Keller vents to other teachers at lunch: "I'm worried about Amir; he's really struggling in science. I've never heard a word from his parents, and they didn't come to conferences. What's up with that? Don't they care?" The ESL teacher mentions that over the summer, Amir's family moved from Oman and that Amir's dad speaks English, but not his mom. This gives Ms. Keller some information to consider.

SECTION 2: EXPLORING CURRENT PERSPECTIVES

 Complete Appendix A, Tasks for Section 2: Exploring Current Perspectives.

SECTION 3: GETTING ON THE SAME PAGE

Diversity Within the Immigrant Experience

Amir and his family are immigrants, and immigrants to the United States come from and face a multitude of challenging situations. Some families are temporarily in the United States to pursue higher education, some are refugees, some are undocumented, and some moved to the United States to join family, pursue work opportunities, or establish citizenship. Students and their caregivers may be fluent in multiple languages (sometimes including English, sometimes not). They may be highly educated, their schooling may have been interrupted, or they may have strong oral language skills but be unable to read and write. There is no single linguistic, literary, educational, or experiential profile that fits all immigrants (e.g., Cho, Chen, & Shin, 2010; Han & Love, 2015). These varied situations lead to a multitude of ways in which caregivers interact with U.S. schools.

Structural Factors Affecting Caregiver Involvement

When caregivers are immigrants, their involvement in schools may be affected by a multitude of structural factors, including the jobs they are able to obtain, legal status, language proficiency, and cultural norms. For some caregivers, the only work they can get in the United States is at low-paying jobs with long hours. This makes it difficult for them to spend time with their children, talk about what is happening at school, attend school events, or communicate with school personnel (Ji & Koblinsky, 2009; Qin & Han, 2014; Rah, Choi, & Nguyễn, 2009). These jobs may also lead to frequent relocation, as is the case with families of migrant farmworkers who move to different areas, states, or countries to follow the harvest. It is important for school staff to recognize the limits and stressors work situations such as these can put on families.

Experiences as refugees or possessing undocumented status can also add great stressors to students' and caregivers' lives. Refugees may have fled violence, natural disasters, or other dangerous conditions, such as famine, and may be dealing with anxiety, depression, and emotional trauma from these experiences that affect how children act at school and how families are able to cope day to day (Tadesse, 2014). In the case of undocumented students and caregivers, they live with daily stressors that they or their loved ones may be deported. According to a brochure published by the American Federation of Teachers (2016), Immigration and Customs Enforcement (ICE) officers are generally not allowed to conduct raids collecting undocumented people at schools, hospitals, or places of worship. Much of this is due to the ruling of *Plyler v. Doe*, a 1982 U.S. Supreme Court case that stated, "undocumented children have a constitutional right to receive a free public K–12 education" (AFT, 2016, p. 1). Therefore, teachers should not ask students or their caregivers about their legal status, since all children have the right to an education.

However, issues related to undocumented status reach farther than one may imagine because "there are 4.1 million U.S.-born children with at least one parent or family member who is undocumented" (AFT, 2016, p. 4), meaning that 4.1 million children are legal citizens who have a parent or family member who may be deported at any time. This weighs heavily on their minds and those of their caregivers. It makes some caregivers especially reticent to visit schools for fear that their undocumented status will be discovered (Levine & Trickett, 2000).

Linguistic and cultural factors also affect how immigrant caregivers interact with schools. As mentioned earlier, caregivers may or may not be fluent in English (see Module 6). Caregivers may also have different cultural expectations for schools (Ariza, 2002). For example, caregivers may not understand students' report cards and what grades mean, as countries have different grading systems (Ji & Koblinsky, 2009). They may also view teachers as experts, people who should not be questioned and whose knowledge should be trusted completely, which makes caregivers reticent to approach teachers with concerns, or they may feel unable to help their child adequately in school or with school expectations (Colombo, 2006; Rah, Choi, & Nguyễn, 2009). Additionally, neither caregivers nor their social networks may have extensive knowledge of the expectations and ways in which U.S. schools work (Gándara & Contreras, 2009; Suárez-Orozco, Suárez-Orozco, & Todorova, 2008). It is important that schools explain in detail not only current classroom expectations, but also how aspects of the school operate, such as Open Houses or Caregiver Nights and the purpose of these events (Guo & Mohan, 2008). In addition, caregivers need specific information on the steps to prepare their children for college and the requirements for application (Auerbach, 2004; Suárez-Orozco et al., 2008). For example, Trevino's study of high-achieving students from migrant families revealed that some school staff did not tell caregivers "about residency and citizenship requirements for college admission and financial aid. As a result, some of the older children despite equally high achievement did not have the same college opportunities as their younger siblings" (2004, p. 158). Ways of navigating the U.S. educational system need to be made explicit for students and caregivers.

One situation I (Lisa) encountered as a teacher helped me realize that U.S. educational practices, which I take for granted having grown up in the United States, are not universal. One of my elementary students had low scores on his weekly spelling tests. When I mentioned my concern to his parents and asked about his study habits, they asked what spelling lists were and what their purpose was. They had not encountered spelling lists and tests in their schooling experiences in their country. When I explained why I assigned a spelling list, what I did in class to support students' learning, and what I expected students to do on their own, the parents seemed to understand and were able to support their son in studying for his weekly spelling tests. This experience helped reinforce that things I assume to be "universal" knowledge are not. That makes it very important for teachers to make school expectations transparent for families.

Changing Educators' Views

In addition to living situations, legal issues, and prior experiences and expectations related to schooling, issues concerning lack of information, misinformation, and/or bias from teachers (or caregivers) have large impacts on the extent to which families, especially immigrant families, interact with schools (e.g., Colombo, 2006; Ramirez, 2003; Tadesse, 2014). Thus it is critical that teachers and school staff get to know families and learn about the ways they already support their children (Alfaro, O'Reilly-Diaz, & López, 2014), even if these ways differ from traditional U.S. educational views. For example, while some families may not be able to provide help with homework assignments, their continual emphasis on the importance of learning and school to their children is a critical educational support.

However, to recognize these supports, school personnel often must change how they view students and their caregivers to avoid making generalizations or engaging in deficit thinking so they can build relationships based on trust and open communication. In the case of migrant families or families who move frequently, it also means viewing families "as long-term 'clients' who happen to be temporarily away from the community" (López, Scribner, & Mahitivanichcha, 2001, p. 267) so that long-term relationships are built, and schools feel invested in their students and caregivers. This is important because families put less emphasis on the school's overall environment and more on how they perceive they are treated (López et al., 2001).

SECTION 4: LISTENING TO EXPAND PERSPECTIVES

Complete Appendix B, Tasks for Section 4: Listening to Expand Perspectives.

SECTION 5: FIXING IT

 The following are suggestions for working with immigrant students and caregivers. Complete Appendix C, Tasks for Section 5: Fixing It, for further reflection and analysis.

Working with Structural Factors Impacting Caregiver Involvement

- Have translators available and translate materials if caregivers do not speak English. (See Module 6 for more ideas and information.)
- Offer flexible meeting times and ways of communicating in respect for caregivers' work schedules and needs.
- Explain what expectations are for the classroom and the school and the purpose for various activities. Make sure caregivers understand what U.S. schools expect for students and provide resources to help them be successful.

Changing Educators' Views

- Get to know caregivers' individual situations. Don't assume anything.
- Honor the ways in which caregivers already support their children, even if it differs from traditional U.S. methods. The emotional support and encouragement to achieve that families may provide is critical.
- Treat caregivers and children with respect; maintain an asset-based perspective.

SECTION 6: REBUILDING THE CASE

Ms. Keller is concerned about her 8th-grade student Amir's struggles in science, but Amir's caregivers did not come to conferences or respond to the grade report she sent home.[1] Ms. Keller has never met or had contact with Amir's caregivers.

Ms. Keller talks to other teachers and anyone else who might have information about Amir and his family situation. The ESL teacher explains that Amir's family moved from Oman and that Amir's father speaks English. The secretary checks Amir's records and learns that Amir's father is attending graduate school at the nearby university. In addition, Ms. Keller asks Amir[2] if his parents see the grade reports or if they check his grades online and what languages his parents speak. She discovers that they have not checked Amir's grades online[3] and that Amir's parents speak Arabic and his dad speaks English. Ms. Keller decides to write the parents a note in English[4] explaining why she would like to meet with them. In her note, Ms. Keller also emphasizes the good things Amir is doing in class.[5] Ms. Keller offers a variety of ways Amir's parents can contact her (email, phone, written note, and so on) so they can set up a meeting or talk on the phone during a time that fits everyone's schedule.[6] Mrs. Keller also considers ways to group students for projects that would promote opportunities for Amir to get to know and interact with other students.

1. Because the grade reports and forms for conferences were in English, perhaps Amir's parents did not understand them. Or perhaps the times at which these events occurred did not fit Amir's family's schedule. Or perhaps caregiver–teacher conferences and/or other school events such as Open House are not part of Amir's family's educational experiences and so they are unsure what is expected of them for these events.

2. In this scenario, Amir is old enough to provide information about his family, but depending on the student's age, they may not be able to offer a lot of information about their caregiver(s). However, it is still good to talk with the student, though when doing so, teachers should not ask about the student's or caregiver's legal status. School secretaries, ESL teachers, and other teachers and support staff are also good sources of information regarding students and their caregivers.

3. School practices such as grade reports, online grade platforms, conferences, and Open Houses may be unfamiliar for Amir's family. These expectations/practices may need to be explained and made more transparent. Also, depending on Amir's parents' work schedule, they may not be able to attend or engage in all of these events/practices.

4. If Ms. Keller knows Arabic, she can write the note in Arabic. She could also use Google Translate to send the note home in both Arabic and English or use other community or school resources for help sending information home in languages families can understand. (See Module 6 for more information.) In addition, it will be important that she ensures that everyone can understand each other at the meeting too—both the language in which the meeting is spoken and the vocabulary that is used. She will need to avoid educational jargon.

5. It is important for Ms. Keller to talk about Amir's strengths and the good things he is doing so that caregivers don't associate teacher contact with problems and negativity. By including positives, it helps caregivers realize that teachers care about the student, and it helps lessen some of their worry. She can ask caregivers about Amir's interests and things that might make him comfortable in the classroom.

6. Work schedules can complicate meeting times. With Amir's father being a graduate student, he may be in classes or working throughout the day and evening. The family may have only one car, and the mother may not have a license to drive in the United States yet, making it harder for her to attend the meeting herself (if translation were provided). It is important to provide multiple options for communication and meeting. (See Module 4 for more information.)

REFERENCES

American Federation of Teachers. (2016.) In collaboration with United We Dream's Dream Educational Empowerment Program, the National Immigration Law Center, and First Focus. *Immigrant and refugee children: A guide for educators and school support staff.* Washington, DC: American Federation of Teachers. Retrieved from www.aft.org/sites/default/files/im_uac-educators-guide_2016.pdf

Alfaro, D. D., O'Reilly-Diaz, K., & López, G. R. (2014). Operationalizing consejos in the P-20 educational pipeline: Interrogating the nuances of Latino parent involvement. *Multicultural Education, 21*(3/4), 11–16.

Ariza, E. N. (2002). Cultural considerations: Immigrant parent involvement. *Kappa Delta Pi Record, 38*(3), 134–137.

Auerbach, S. (2004). Engaging Latino parents in supporting college pathways: Lessons from a college access program. *Journal of Hispanic Higher Education, 3*(2), 125–145.

Cho, E. K., Chen, D. W., & Shin, S. (2010). Supporting transnational families. *YC Young Children, 65*(4), 30–37.

Colombo, M. W. (2006). Building school partnerships with culturally and linguistically diverse families. *Phi Delta Kappan, 88*(4), 314–318.

Gándara, P. C., & Contreras, F. (2009). *The Latino education crisis: The consequences of failed social policies.* Cambridge, MA: Harvard University Press.

Guo, Y., & Mohan, B. (2008). ESL parents and teachers: Towards dialogue? *Language and Education, 22*(1), 17–33.

Han, Y. C., & Love, J. (2015). Stages of immigrant parent involvement—survivors to leaders. *Phi Delta Kappan, 97*(4), 21–25.

Ji, C. S., & Koblinsky, S. A. (2009). Parent involvement in children's education: An exploratory study of urban, Chinese immigrant families. *Urban Education, 44*(6), 687–709.

Levine, E. B., & Trickett, E. J. (2000). Toward a model of Latino parent advocacy for educational change. *Journal of Prevention & Intervention in the Community, 20*(1–2), 121–137.

López, G. R., Scribner, J. D., & Mahitivanichcha, K. (2001). Redefining parental involvement: Lessons from high-performing migrant-impacted schools. *American Educational Research Journal, 38*(2), 253–288.

Qin, D. B., & Han, E. J. (2014). Tiger parents or sheep parents?: Struggles of parental involvement in working-class Chinese immigrant families. *Teachers College Record, 116*(8), 1–32.

Rah, Y., Choi, S., & Nguyễn, T. S. T. (2009). Building bridges between refugee parents and schools. *International Journal of Leadership in Education, 12*(4), 347–365

Ramirez, A. F. (2003). Dismay and disappointment: Parental involvement of Latino immigrant parents. *The Urban Review, 35*(2), 93–110.

Suárez-Orozco, C., Suárez-Orozco, M. M., & Todorova, I. (2008). *Learning a new land: Immigrant students in American society.* Cambridge, MA: Harvard University Press.

Tadesse, S. (2014). Parent involvement: Perceived encouragement and barriers to African refugee parent and teacher relationships. *Childhood Education, 90*(4), 298–305.

Trevino, R. E. (2004). Chapter 11: Against all odds: Lessons from parents of migrant high-achievers. In C. Salinas & M.E. Fránquiz (Eds.), *Scholars in the field: The challenges of migrant education* (pp. 147–161). Charleston, WV: AEL, ERIC Clear-inghouse on Rural Education and Small Schools.

ADDITIONAL RESOURCES

American Federation of Teachers immigration resources page: www.aft.org/our -community/immigration

Colorado Statewide Parent Coalition. (2004). *Engaging Mexican immigrant parents in their children's education: A guide for teachers.* Retrieved from www.cde.state.co.us /migrant/engagingmexicanparentsintheirchildrenseducation

Immigrant and Refugee Children: A Guide for Educators and School Support Staff: www.aft.org/sites/default/files/im_uac-educators-guide_2016.pdf

Information about *Plyler v. Doe* (1982): www.americanimmigrationcouncil.org /research/plyler-v-doe-public-education-immigrant-students

---

MODULE 8

Extended, Reconstituted, or Blended Families

SECTION 1: CASE SCENARIO

Context

Ms. Jansen is a 56-year-old White teacher. She teaches 5th grade at an ele-mentary school located in a suburban middle-class community. In her class, Charles, Breanne, Sharon, Ruth, Chad, and Jennifer are White students from working-class and middle-class homes. Alex and Susan are African American students from middle-class homes.

Scenario

Ms. Jansen has eight students in her classroom who she is concerned about: Alex, Susan, Charles, Breanne, Sharon, Ruth, Chad, and Jennifer. She has noticed that these students are not completing their homework assign-ments on time and have not been attending school events and activities. She can't figure out what's going on, and she's worried because these eight students represent a large part of her class. Sometimes when she asks her students why they didn't complete their homework, they reply, "I was at my dad's" or "I left my backpack at my mom's house." Ms. Jansen looks at the students' files and talks with the school secretary. She learns that these students have varied family situations, living in extended, reconstituted, and/or blended families. She surmises that students may not be attending events because one caregiver may not have appropriate information. However, she fears that students' performance and attendance may suffer and that tension might increase among caregivers, step-parents, and students, leading to greater stress for the students.

SECTION 2: EXPLORING CURRENT PERSPECTIVES

 Complete Appendix A, Tasks for Section 2: Exploring Current Perspectives.

SECTION 3: GETTING ON THE SAME PAGE

"A parent is anyone who provides children with basic care, direction, support, protection, and guidance . . . a parent can be single, married, heterosexual, homosexual, a cousin, aunt, uncle, grandparent, a court-appointed guardian, a brother, a sister, an institution employee, a surrogate, a foster parent, or a group such as a commune" (Morrison, 1988, p. 414). These changing patterns regarding who is considered a parent have important implications for today's teachers.

What constitutes a family and/or a parent has undergone a radical change over the years. The family as a social institution has experienced many transformations that profoundly influence not only the ways in which we understand what constitutes "family," but also the function of the family unit (Tutwiler, 1998). Children are born into many different kinds of families, with a variety of living arrangements. These family structures affect, in obvious and subtle ways, children's development and how teachers relate to them.

One form of family diversity that strays from traditional notions of "family" is the stepfamily—now commonly known as a reconstituted or blended family (Mayntz, 2018). Blended families now make up more than half the families in America (Gonzales, 2009). Living in a blended family has become commonplace, as have significant issues related to family members' adjustment to and day-to-day maintenance of the family unit.

When school's back in session, caregivers everywhere are turning their attention from supplies and clothes shopping to the ongoing challenge of helping their kids succeed academically and socially. For caregivers in divorced and blended families, these challenges are compounded by scheduling logistics, clarifying roles with schoolteachers, trying to provide schoolwork consistency between houses, and handling disagreements among parties that likely already have trouble communicating (Williams,

2014). Add to that the downright confusion and awkwardness that can result from teachers trying to figure out whom to contact on any given day of the week. Lloyd Gallman (cited in Williams, 2014) recommends that caregivers and kids in divorced and blended families who are navigating back-to-school issues should focus on "the three Cs": communication, conflict resolution, and compromise. For teachers, the C of communication is critical. It is crucial that all caregivers receive information about school events and classroom functions, with one important proviso: that there is not a restraining or other court order barring or limiting a caregiver's contact with a student.

SECTION 4: LISTENING TO EXPAND PERSPECTIVES

 Complete Appendix B, Tasks for Section 4: Listening to Expand Perspectives.

SECTION 5: FIXING IT

 The following are some policies and practices that teachers and administrators can implement to establish an accepting climate for blended and reconstituted families. Complete Appendix C, Tasks for Section 5: Fixing It, for further reflection and analysis.

- *Put it in writing.* Adopt an official policy that ensures communication with both of a student's caregivers. Making it official makes it easier to ensure it gets done.
- *Avoid "kidmail" as much as possible.* When students are responsible for passing information to caregivers, the information sometimes doesn't get through. Avoiding kidmail can also reduce a lot of pressure on students who might feel caught in the middle between caregivers who may not have an ideal communication relationship. It is usually best to email or mail information directly to caregivers.
- *Send duplicate copies* of important materials, especially performance reports, notices of fees for field trips and events, and permission forms. All such documents must reach all caregivers at all of the student's households. This can be accomplished through mailings and notices in the school's weekly/monthly newsletters, telephone calls, voicemail, email, texting, Skype, Zoom, Google Hangouts, school websites, or class websites (which should, of course, be shared with all student households, too). Establish pick-up points in the school office so caregivers can drop by for copies of materials.

- *Use more than one means of communication.* Help to ensure that you reach all caregivers by using various modes of communication, including mailings, email, telephone calls, voicemail, texting, Skype, Zoom, Google Hangouts, and school and class websites. The PTA or other parent groups can help here: Try telephone or email round-robins in which one caregiver contacts two others, and then those two contact two others, and so on.
- *Create call-in or online homework hotlines,* event calendars, classroom news bulletins, and a scheduling database that caregivers, students, and staff can access 24 hours a day. These could be maintained by caregiver volunteers, or even by a group of students.

SECTION 6: REBUILDING THE CASE

Ms. Jansen has eight students in her classroom who live in extended, reconstituted, or blended families.[1] She has noticed that these students are not completing their homework assignments on time, and have not been able to attend school events and activities because one caregiver may not have received the necessary information. Ms. Jansen fears that these students' performance and attendance may suffer, and that tension might mount among caregivers, stepfamilies, and students, leading to greater stress for the students. She believes that it is important for her to ease the tensions for children who move between homes.[2] Ms. Jansen assumes that that both a child's caregivers and stepparents want to be as involved as possible in their children's school life.[3] Therefore, she has decided with her principal's support to organize a task force within her school to develop a set of policies and practices for working with extended, reconstituted, or blended families.

1. Ms. Jansen, along with school staff members, should be aware that in the 21st century there are more families that consist of extended, reconstituted, or blended families. Therefore, use of language such as "real mother," "natural father," and "broken home" should not be used at all, and especially not in the classroom. Such terms could create hurt feelings or even cause students to be targeted by bullies.

Teachers and administrators should encourage caregivers to notify them when changes occur. There should be open communication among all involved, including the student.

2. Children want to feel safe and secure, loved, seen and valued, heard and emotionally connected, appreciate and encouraged, and to know their limits and boundaries. Ms. Jansen should integrate discussing all types of families into diversity lessons so that all students will be understanding of their peers who live in blended or reconstituted families. She should try to assist all students in having their needs met during difficult times. She can play an important role in helping

children from blended or reconstituted families make a positive adjustment to their family situation.

3. From talking with caregivers from blended and reconstituted families, Ms. Jansen recognizes that she can play an important role in helping children from blended or reconstituted families make a positive adjustment to their family situation. She has decided to share children's assignment information with all of the caregivers from these blended and reconstituted families. She uses multiple modes of communication and considers caregivers' home languages and proficiencies.

REFERENCES

Allan, G., & Crow, G. (2001). *Families, households and society*. London, England: Palgrave.

Gonzales, J. (2009). Prefamily counseling: Working with blended families. *Journal of Divorce & Remarriage, 50*(2), 148–157.

Mayntz, M. (2018, May 26). Definition of a blended family. Retrieved from family. lovetoknow.com/definition-blended-family

Morrison, G. S. (1988*). Early childhood education today* (4th ed.). Columbus, OH: Merrill Publishing Company.

Tutwiler, S. W. (1998). Diversity among families. In M. L. Fuller & Olsen, G. (Eds.), *Home-school relations: Working successfully with parents and families* (pp. 40–66). Boston, MA: Allyn and Bacon.

Williams, H. (2014, September). Back to school for blended families 101: Parents, stepparents will be tested. Retrieved from www.oregonlive.com/kiddo/index. ssf/2014/09/back_to_school_for_blended_fam.html

ADDITIONAL RESOURCES

Baxter, L. A., Braithwaite, D. O., & Nicholson, J. H. (1999). Turning points in the development of blended families. *Journal of Social and Personal Relationships, 16*(3), 291–314.

Castren, A. M, & Widmer, E. D. (2014). Insiders and outsiders in stepfamilies: Adults' and children's views on family boundaries. *Current Sociology, 63*(1), 35–56.

Labman, S., & Pearlman, M. (2018). Blending, bargaining, and burden-sharing: Canada's resettlement programs. *Journal of International Migration and Integration, 19*(2), 439–449.

Woodbridge, S., & Buys, L. (2018). Grandparents: Meaningful contributors to a changing family landscape. In B. S. Nelson Goff & N. Piland Springer (Eds.). *Intellectual and developmental disabilities: A roadmap for families and professionals* (pp. 117–130). New York, NY: Routledge.

Zurcher, J. D., Webb, S. M., & Robinson, T. (2018). The portrayal of families across generations in Disney animated films. *Social Sciences, 7*(3), 1–16.

BOOKS AND APPS ON SEPARATION AND DIVORCE TO HELP KIDS

The Day the Sea Went Out and Never Came Back (2003) by Margot Sunderland

Divorce is Not the End of the World: Zoe & Evan's Coping Guide for Kids (2008) by Zoe Stern

The Family Book (2009) by Todd Parr (different families)

The Family Forest (2015) by Kim Kane (blended families)

The Invisible String (2014) by Patrice Karst (separation anxiety)

Mom's House, Dad's House: Making Two Homes for Your Child (1997) by Isolina Ricci

Mum and Dad Glue (2010) by Kes Gray

My Family's Changing (1999) by Pat Thomas

Sam's Sunday Dad (1999) by Margaret Wild

Shared Care or Divided Lives: What's Best for Children When Parents Separate (2008) by Phil Watts

Skimming Stones: A Story about Overcoming a Family Breakdown (2007) by Steve Heron

The Truth about Children and Divorce: Dealing with the Emotions So You and Your Children Can Thrive (2006) by Robert Emery

Two Homes (2013) by Claire Masurel

Two of Everything (2000) by Babette Cole

Was It the Chocolate Pudding? A Story for Little Kids About Divorce (2005) by Sandra Levins

What About the Children? Parenting information booklet from Relationships Australia. Available at www.relationships.org.au/relationship-advice/publications /pdfs/what-about-the-children.pdf

Who's in My family: All about Our families (2015) by Robie H. Harris

Kids and Divorce App, An interactive-animation, downloadable app for kids and families going through divorce and different stages of family reorganization: www.kidsanddivorce.co.uk/

Sesame Street Divorce Resource App, available for free download. Designed to help parents and children through this time. Includes tips and art activities to help with emotions: sesamestreetincommunities.org/topics/divorce/

MODULE 9

Families with Incarcerated Caregivers

SECTION 1: CASE SCENARIO

Context

Mr. Murray is a 35-year-old African American teacher who teaches English and History in an inner-city middle school. He knows that many of his male students' caregivers are currently incarcerated or have been in the past.

Mr. Murray has seen the devastating impact the incarceration of caregivers can have on the academic performance of his male students. He graduated from an inner-city school district similar to the one he now teaches in and feels he can serve as a positive role model for his students.

Scenario

Mr. Murray knew it was a common occurrence for many of his male students' fathers to be in and out of prison. He also knew how to relate to his male students because he had an uncle and a cousin who had been to prison. However, he noticed that one of his high-achieving 13-year-old students, Portia, had recently been feeling sad, turning her assignments in late, and falling asleep in class. This was unlike her, so he asked, "What's going on, Portia?" She replied, "I've been living with my grandmother since my mom was put in jail. This makes me angry and embarrassed. My grandmother is raising me and my two younger brothers on Social Security, but it's not enough. My grandmother is trying to get another job, so I've been taking care of my brothers and sisters and everything around the house, and I'm so tired. I barely have any time to do my homework."

SECTION 2: EXPLORING CURRENT PERSPECTIVES

 Complete Appendix A, Tasks for Section 2: Exploring Current Perspectives.

SECTION 3: GETTING ON THE SAME PAGE

What We Have Learned About the Children of Incarcerated Caregivers

The impact of parental incarceration on children and families is one of the most overlooked issues affecting children's education and quality of life. Approximately 1.7 million children under 18 in the United States have a caregiver in state or federal prison (Glaze & Maruschak, 2010). The Children of Incarcerated Parents Library (2017) reported one of every 28 children has a caregiver behind bars. Approximately half of all minor children with caregivers in prison are between the ages of 10 and 17 years, and more than a third will reach age 18 while their caregiver remains incarcerated (Glaze & Maruschak, 2010). Many incarcerated caregivers have little contact with their children because they don't have permission, don't want to, feel ashamed, or are separated by large geographical distances; in fact, many students will go through secondary school without a meaningful connection to their caregivers.

Having a caregiver in prison can have an impact on a child's mental health, social behavior, and educational prospects (La Vigne, Davies, & Brazzell, 2008). The emotional trauma that may occur and the practical difficulties of a disrupted family life can be compounded by the social stigma that children may face as a result of having a caregiver in prison or jail (La Vigne et al., 2008). Children who have an incarcerated caregiver may experience financial hardship that results from the loss of that caregiver's income (General Assembly of the Commonwealth of Pennsylvania, 2011). Furthermore, some incarcerated caregivers face termination of parental/ guardianship rights because their children have been in the foster care system beyond the time allowed by law (General Assembly, 2011). These children require support from local, state, and federal systems to serve their needs.

Children of incarcerated caregivers may also face a number of other challenging circumstances. They may have experienced trauma related to their caregiver's arrest or experiences leading up to it (La Vigne et al., 2008). Children of incarcerated caregivers may also be more likely to have faced other adverse childhood experiences, including witnessing violence in their communities or directly in their household or exposure to drug and alcohol abuse (Centers for Disease Control and Prevention [CDC], 2013; Phillips & Gleeson, 2007).

Teachers, school counselors, and administrators are in unique positions to recognize and ameliorate the difficulties that children of incarcerated caregivers might face. In order to be most effective, teachers and school personnel should be aware, attentive, and knowledgeable (Sullivan, 2018). In the past, practitioners and scholars encouraged schools to make use of all the resources available to children and especially to connect boys and girls whose caregivers were incarcerated with school counselors. This is still considered a good thing to do. However, the latest research encourages schools to train teachers not to make assumptions about how a caregiver's incarceration might affect a child's behavior or academic success and to help lessen the stigma that some of these children may face (University of Wisconsin Institute for Research on Poverty, 2014). Instead of making assumptions, teachers should rely on a continuum of classroom and schoolwide intervention to promote child development and address particular learning needs (Fazel, Hoagwood, Stephan, & Ford, 2014). In other words, teachers might be most effective when they attend to students' diverse learning needs—whether students' caregivers are incarcerated or not—rather than what they assume to be the student's emotional or academic challenges.

Stereotypes and Subconscious Negative Assumptions

People sometimes assume children with an incarcerated caregiver are more likely to engage in criminal or negative activity. Be careful about making such assumptions about behavior, motivation, academic ability, and potential. Research indicates that these assumptions, even when they occur subconsciously, can have detrimental impacts on educational outcomes (Dallaire, Ciccone, & Wilson, 2010). Students who have an incarcerated caregiver, like any other students, have great potential to learn and succeed in school when teachers support them and establish high expectations for them (Hinnant, O'Brien, & Ghazarian, 2009).

Be Sensitive to Certain Trigger Issues

When conversing about current events, crime, criminals, or the police, be mindful of how children with a caregiver who has been arrested or incarcerated might feel. Children usually love their caregivers, even if a caregiver did something illegal. In addition, be careful about making statements about caregiver involvement because Dad might not be there to sign permission slips, or Mom might not be there to help with homework. Across all school settings, pay particular attention to children of incarcerated caregivers being bullied by peers, and help ensure that they are not subjected to biases or stereotypes (Dallaire et al., 2010).

SECTION 4: LISTENING TO EXPAND PERSPECTIVES

Complete Appendix B, Tasks for Section 4: Listening to Expand Perspectives.

SECTION 5: FIXING IT

The following are suggestions for teachers to achieve positive outcomes for students with incarcerated caregivers. Complete Appendix C, Tasks for Section 5: Fixing It, for further reflection and analysis.

Teachers can *collaborate* with the student's other caregiver to create a positive school setting for students of incarcerated caregivers. Collaboration may include

- sharing relevant information with caregivers concerning successes and struggles, as well as emotional and behavioral concerns, and
- becoming aware of community organizations and services available to meet the specialized needs of children with a caregiver in prison, especially mental health resources.

Teachers can *assist* students who have an incarcerated caregiver in reaching their potential and achieving academic and social success by

- implementing behavioral and academic supports that enhance the teaching–learning process,
- engaging in classroom methods and approaches that help students increase their capacities to self-regulate behaviors and develop their academic promise,
- challenging students to do their very best academically by providing support and establishing and promoting high expectations for them, and
- identifying areas of vulnerability, and understanding that negative behaviors and absenteeism may be masking anxiety and depression, which can result from childhood trauma.

Teachers can *advocate* for students with an incarcerated caregiver and educate their colleagues on ways to address the needs of students who have an incarcerated caregiver by

- establishing themselves as trusted and caring adults, serving as role models, and challenging the stigma and shame that can be associated with caregiver incarceration;
- working with other support/ancillary staff (e.g., art teacher, classroom aide, reading specialist, administrators) to provide one-on-one opportunities for students to express feelings openly and freely through art, writing, or other forms of expression, such as writing a letter or poem or drawing a picture to share with their caregiver;
- collaborating with school-based mental health professionals (school psychologists, counselors, social workers) who understand the developmentally sensitive implications of caregiver incarceration and family stress on student well-being; and
- asking librarians to offer books about caregiver incarceration and encourage *all* students to read them, rather than singling out students with an incarcerated caregiver.

SECTION 6: REBUILDING THE CASE

Mr. Murray is concerned about Portia, a 13-year-old student, because she has usually done very well in his class, but lately she has been sad, has not been turning in assignments, and is falling asleep in class. Mr. Murray talks to Portia and discovers that she has lived with her grandmother since her mother was incarcerated. Because her grandmother is raising Portia and her two younger brothers on Social Security payments, which are not enough to cover expenses, her grandmother is trying to get another job, so Portia has been taking care of her siblings and all of the housework.

Mr. Murray reassures Portia that he, the guidance counselor, and other staff are always available to talk, which has the potential to improve her academic, behavioral, and social-emotional outcomes.[1] He sets up a homework plan with Portia to help her complete her assignments and turn them in.[2]

1. Mr. Murray might consider sharing positive news with Portia's grandmother or touching base about upcoming assignments or projects. He needs to be sensitive that Portia might have difficulty concentrating and focusing on learning during days that are reminders of the parent's incarceration, such as birthdays, Father's Day or Mother's Day, the anniversary of the arrest, or trial dates. During these days, knowing her triggers and providing caring reassurances can go a long way.

Mr. Murray may also consider setting up a school fund for students like Portia to provide extra sets of clothing, food, and materials to help meet basic needs or funds for Portia to engage in after-school activities.

2. Although expectations for Portia should remain high, being too rigid can also set a student like Portia up for failure. Use professional judgment in providing flexibility with assignments and extended deadlines.

REFERENCES

Centers for Disease Control and Prevention (CDC). (2013). Adverse childhood experiences study. Retrieved from www.cdc.gov/ace/about.htm

Dallaire, D. H., Ciccone, A., & Wilson, L. C. (2010). Teachers' experiences with and expectations of children with incarcerated parents. *Journal of Applied Developmental Psychology, 31*(4), 281–290.

Fazel, M., Hoagwood, K., Stephan, D., & Ford, T. (2014). Mental health interventions in schools 1: Mental health interventions in schools in high-income countries. *Lancet Psychiatry, 1*(5), 377–387.

General Assembly of the Commonwealth of Pennsylvania. (2011, January 4). *Legislative Journal,* Session of 2011, 195th of the General Assembly, No. 1.

Glaze, O. E., & Maruschak, L. M. (2010). *Parents in prison and their minor children.* Bureau of Justice Statistics Special Report No. NC J222984. Retrieved from bjs.ojp.usdoj.gov/content/pub/pdf/pptmc.pdf

Hinnant, J. B., O'Brien, M., & Ghazarian, S. R. (2009). The longitudinal relations of teacher expectations to achievement in the early school years. *Journal of Educational Psychology, 101*(3), 662–670.

La Vigne, N., Davies, E., & Brazzell, D. (2008). *Broken bonds: Understanding and addressing the needs of children with incarcerated parents.* Washington, DC: The Urban Institute. Retrieved from www.urban.org/UploadedPDF/411616_incarcerated_parents.pdf

Phillips, S. D., & Gleeson, J. P. (2007). *What we know now that we didn't know then about the criminal justice system's involvement in families with whom child welfare agencies have contact.* Retrieved from www.f2f.ca.gov/res/pdf/WhatWeKnowNow.pdf

Sullivan, M. (2018). What to do when a parent is incarcerated. Retrieved from www.amle.org/BrowsebyTopic/WhatsNew/WNDet/TabId/270/ArtMID/888/ArticleID/900/What-to-Do-When-a-Parent-Is-Incarcerated.aspx

University of Wisconsin Institute for Research on Poverty. (2014). *Poverty fact sheet: Life beyond bars: Children with an incarcerated parent.* Retrieved from www.irp.wisc.edu/publications/factsheets/pdfs/Factsheet7-Incarceration.pdf

U.S. Government Accountability Office (GAO). (2011). Child welfare: More information and collaboration could promote ties between foster care children and their incarcerated parents. Retrieved from www.gao.gov/products/GAO-11-863

ADDITIONAL RESOURCES

Annie E. Casey Foundation. (2007). *Focus on the children of incarcerated parents: An overview of the research literature.* Retrieved from www.aecf.org/m/resourcedoc/aecf-FocusonChildrenwith_ncarceratedParentsOverviewofLiterature-2007.pdf

Massachusetts Advocates for Children & Harvard Law School. (2013). *Helping traumatized children learn: Creating and advocating for trauma-sensitive schools* (vols. 1 and 2). traumasensitiveschools.org/tlpi-publications/

National Child Traumatic Stress Network Schools Committee. (2008). *Child trauma toolkit for educators.* Los Angeles, CA & Durham, NC: National Center for Child Traumatic Stress. Retrieved from www.nctsn.org/resources/child-trauma-toolkit-educators. (Also available in Spanish)

Parents behind bars: Children of incarcerated family members: An educator and caregiver's toolkit to Idaho's criminal justice system. (2012). Retrieved from www.idoc.idaho.gov/webfm_send/2303

Promoting social and emotional well-being for children of incarcerated parents: A product of the Federal Interagency Working Group for Children of Incarcerated Parents. (2013, June). Retrieved from csgjusticecenter.org/wp-content/uploads/2013/06/Promoting-Social-and-Emotional-Well-Being-for-Children-of-Incarcerated-Parents.pdf

The San Francisco Children of Incarcerated Parents Partnership. (2005). *The children of incarcerated parents bill of rights.* Retrieved from www.sfcipp.org

Project AVARY's (Alternative Ventures for At Risk Youth) "Top 10 Things Every Teacher Should Know About Children of Incarcerated Parents": www.projectavary.org/resources

What educators and schools need to know when working with children with incarcerated parents. (n.d.). Retrieved from www.spac.k12.pa.us/2010conference/2010%20spac%20conference%20workshop%20handouts/6%20Mona%20Fleeger%20STARS/5%20what%20educators%20and%20schools%20need%20to%20know%20when.pdf

MODULE 10

When School/Neighborhood Demographics Change

SECTION 1: CASE SCENARIO

Context

This case is situated in a 6th-grade classroom in a middle school in a suburban public school district in the U.S. Midwest. This particular district is transitioning from a majority White student population to one that is racially, linguistically, and culturally diverse. The teacher, Ms. Wilson, a 25-year-old, monolingual, White, middle-class American, is finishing up her 3rd year of teaching English language arts in the district. Like Ms. Wilson, colleagues and school-based administrators are also mainly White and middle class.

Scenario

Despite district efforts to address the persistent achievement gaps reflected in district test scores among students living in poverty whose first language is not English, or who are of color, scores are not increasing. Like Ms. Wilson, overall teacher morale is down. In fact, several staff members have recently left the district, seeking employment in other suburban schools with a mainstream population (i.e., White, middle-class, monolingual). Remaining district administrators and teachers face imposed policy mandates at the state level if achievement test scores among students from particular groups do not improve.

Ms. Wilson is stressed in both her personal and professional life. She student-taught in a school with a White, middle-class student population and had few experiences teaching children different from herself. Thus, she only learned to teach children who are monolingual and fluent in dominant American English.

While Ms. Wilson enjoys her grade-level partners and the rest of the staff in her building, these factors aren't enough for her to stay in her current position. Ms. Wilson wonders how different her job would be if she had to focus only on her students instead of stressors such as preparing them for the state achievement test as well as communicating with non-responsive caregivers (see Module 1 for more information on this topic). Further, she feels it is unfair that the quality of her teaching is determined by students' test scores. Although Ms. Wilson cares deeply about the children she teaches, she feels unsupported by some of the new caregivers entering the district and wishes they cared more about their children's academic achievement. Despite her efforts to teach the curriculum, some of her students' test scores are not improving.

SECTION 2: EXPLORING CURRENT PERSPECTIVES

 Complete Appendix A, Tasks for Section 2: Exploring Current Perspectives.

SECTION 3: GETTING ON THE SAME PAGE

Suburban Demographics

While the research community has noted the overwhelming presence in the United States of a mostly White, monolingual, middle-class, female teaching force and their lack of preparedness to teach diverse students in diverse contexts (Gay, 2010; Gilbert, 1995; McIntyre, 1997; Sleeter, 2001), it has paid little attention to the changing demographics among the country's suburban schools (Wepner & Gómez, 2017). This issue is paramount in importance because 85% of teachers are White (Frankenberg, 2013), and most teacher candidates (TCs) learn from White teacher educators who themselves may also have limited teaching experience in diverse contexts (Gay, 2010; Merryfield, 2000). Despite the lack of diversity in many professional teacher preparation programs, a large number of White TCs find their first job in a context where they underprepared for a diverse student population.

The racial, economic, and linguistic diversity in suburban schools is increasing rapidly (Wepner & Gómez, 2017). In fact, the demographic changes in suburban contexts are happening at a greater rate than in any other type of community (Kotok & Frankenberg, 2017). Regardless of their experiences during undergraduate work or where they seek employment, new teachers will deal with various forms of diversity (e.g., race/ethnicity, language, social class, sexuality, religion) during their professional careers. Therefore, this case attends to some of the issues that arise when school/neighborhood demographics change and how they might influence a teacher's ability to establish partnerships with caregivers that ultimately affect students' engagement and academic achievement.

Standardization, Increased Pressure, and Changing Demographics

Ms. Wilson and teachers across the United States are faced with numerous mounting pressures. First, diversity among students is increasing, and many are ill-prepared for such change. Second, teachers are inundated with a proliferation of federal and state policy mandates, high-stakes testing, and standardization. Last, their effectiveness is measured and narrowly defined by the performance of the students they teach on standardized tests. These pressures, particularly early in one's teaching career, are difficult to manage and can lead to burnout. The attrition rate among teachers is highest during their first few years of service (Ingersoll & Smith, 2003). Relatedly, teachers have reported concerns regarding lack of support and poor working conditions (Alliance for Excellent Education, 2005).

In comparison to rural, town, and urban school settings, suburban schools enroll the most students representing the most diverse range of student demographics (Kotok & Frankenberg, 2017). Kotok and Frankenberg (2017) point out that "one-third of suburban students are low-income," and "one in nine suburban students attends a school with between 75 percent and 100 percent of students poor or near-poor" (p. 4). These statistics complicate the notion that all students in suburbia are affluent (Kotok & Frankenberg, 2017). Due to the wide variance in race/ethnicity and social class, it is important to identify the demographic trends in the context of suburban schools.

Depending on the changing demographics, in some locations, suburban school districts across the United States are reconsidering established programs and pedagogical practices to better meet the needs of a changing population that often includes youth of immigrant backgrounds or who speak a language other than English at home (Ghiso, 2017). For instance, many teachers and administrators in schools with large working-class Latinx populations complain that caregivers are not involved in their children's schooling (Poza, Brooks, & Valdés, 2014). Such notions are based on low attendance at school events as well as limited face-to-face communication with school officials (Poza et al., 2014). Despite the deficit perspectives that school personnel tend to hold that immigrant caregivers are incapable or disinterested in playing a role in their child's education, their interviews with Latinx caregivers suggest that they are both interested and involved in their children's schooling (Poza et al., 2014). Their efforts were less visible to school personnel; therefore, they argue that to establish partnerships with caregivers, schools must adopt the mindset of an equal partnership for children's education.

The majority of mainstream classroom teachers have had little to no preparation for providing the type of instruction that English learners (ELs) need in order to successfully learn not only academic content and skills in English, but also develop proficiency in the language (Lucas, Villegas, & Freedson-Gonzalez, 2008). Thus, Ghiso advises that it is important for educators to first examine changing demographics according to the local context. Teachers can then build on and learn from "the cultural and linguistic resources of students and their families" (2017, p. 80). This shifts the focus from what students and their families lack—a deficit perspective—to one that values their cultural and linguistic backgrounds.

SECTION 4: LISTENING TO EXPAND PERSPECTIVES

 Complete Appendix B, Tasks for Section 4: Listening to Expand Perspectives.

SECTION 5: FIXING IT

 The following are considerations that school districts and educators can use to meet the needs of the students they serve, particularly as demographics shift. Complete Appendix C, Tasks for Section 5: Fixing It, for further reflection and analysis.

Before establishing a relationship with caregivers, respect and dignity for the students and families served must be foregrounded. Teachers, administrators, and staff must possess a genuine interest in the personal and community contexts of families (Poza et al., 2014). Doing so might entail, for example, caregiver visits at home or neutral sites, as well as attendance at community events (Ladson-Billings, 2006; Villegas & Lucas, 2002).

Similarly, Edwards (2016) offers *demographic profiles* as a means for schools to describe the caregiver community that exists not only in a particular building, but also individual classrooms. The demographic profile provides school personnel with the tools to gather relevant data that allow them to successfully:

- Develop activities appropriate to the school's population (i.e., ones that caregivers can participate in despite limitations like work schedules, transportation, day care)
- Assist teachers with analyzing trends of caregiver involvement to conceptualize ways that caregivers can be involved in their children's education
- Enhance teachers' success in meeting the needs of individual families
- Help teachers build on family and community strengths
- Offer teachers real data instead of relying on assumptions that are often focused on perceived deficits

SECTION 6: REBUILDING THE CASE

Becoming A Culturally Responsive Educator

The student population in the suburban school district where Ms. Wilson teaches 2nd grade has rapidly been changing since she was first hired and is becoming racially, linguistically, and culturally more diverse.[1] Although it is challenging and, at times, frustrating that her effectiveness as a classroom teacher is based, in part, on her students' performance on standardized tests, Ms. Wilson remains committed to the profession and her students. She believes that *all* children can learn and that those under her care will. On noticing the shift in demographics among her students, Ms. Wilson, for example, took it upon herself to find relevant research that has helped her develop a repertoire of culturally responsive teaching practices.[2] Relatedly, her students' reading achievement scores have begun to steadily increase, albeit slowly. Despite imposed standards and testing, she has developed strategies and tools to adapt standardized curricula and teaching practices such that she is able to build on students' cultural and linguistic backgrounds as resources for the curriculum (Ghiso, 2017).[3] Whereas some teachers in the district are leaving and seeking positions in schools with a less diverse student population, Ms. Wilson has become a known leader and resource for other teachers as well as a highly effective and committed teacher in the district.[4]

1. The U.S. student population is becoming more diverse and will continue to do so. No longer can teachers rely on teaching in a static context (e.g., rural, urban) throughout their career with particular kinds of students (e.g., White, monolingual). Therefore, it is important that teachers have the knowledge, resources, and agency to teach across contexts with diverse student populations.

2. Instead of viewing her students from underserved communities as deficient, Ms. Wilson sees them as capable and believes it is her job to help them reach their learning potential. She demonstrates an inquisitive stance toward learning and thus improving her pedagogy, and toward learning about her students. These are leadership qualities that are not only serving her students well, but also colleagues as they learn alongside her.

3. Educators maintain power in classrooms. They can choose or not choose to make classrooms more inclusive of all students. Ms. Wilson's stance toward inquiry into her profession and her students is not in opposition to preparing them for high-stakes standardized testing. Rather, she mobilizes their racial, cultural, and linguistic resources for learning.

4. Some teachers adhere to the belief that there is a "normal" way in which students develop and should be. Conversely, Ms. Wilson views every child as a unique being with multiple strengths that must be valued in the classroom. Regardless of standardization and high-stakes testing, she advocates for her students and their learning potential.

REFERENCES

Alliance for Excellent Education. (2005). *Teacher attrition: A costly loss to the nation and to the states.* Retrieved from https://all4ed.org/reports-factsheets/teacher-attrition-a-costly-loss-to-the-nation-and-to-the-states/

Edwards, P. (2016). *New ways to engage parents: Strategies and tools for teachers and leaders, K–12.* New York, NY: Teachers College Press.

Frankenberg, E. (2013). Wither the suburban ideal? Understanding contemporary suburban school contexts. In G. L. Sunderman (Ed.), *Changing reform, achieving equity in a diverse nation* (pp. 207–227). Charlotte, NC: Information Age Publishing.

Gay, G. (2010). Acting on beliefs in teacher education for cultural diversity. *Journal of teacher education, 61*(1–2), 143–152.

Ghiso, M. P. (2017). Effective literacy instruction for English learners. In S. B. Wepner & D. W. Gómez (Eds.), *Challenges facing suburban schools: Promising responses to changing student populations* (pp. 79–92). Lanham, MD: Rowan & Littlefield.

Gilbert, S. L. (1995). Perspectives of rural prospective teachers toward teaching in urban schools. *Urban Education, 30*(3), 290–305.

Ingersoll, R. M., & Smith, T. M. (2003). The wrong solution to the teacher shortage. *Educational leadership, 60*(8), 30–33.

Kotok, S., & Frankenberg, E. (2017). Demography and educational politics in the changing suburbs. In S. B. Wepner & D. W. Gómez (Eds.), *Challenges facing suburban schools: Promising responses to changing student populations* (pp. 1–14). Lanham, MD: Rowan & Littlefield.

Ladson-Billings, G. (2006). It's not the culture of poverty, it's the poverty of culture: The problem with teacher education. *Anthropology and Education Quarterly, 37*(2), 104–109.

Lucas, T., Villegas, A. M., & Freedson-Gonzalez, M. (2008). Linguistically responsive teacher education: Preparing classroom teachers to teach English language learners. *Journal of Teacher Education, 59*(4), 361–373.

McIntyre, A. (1997). *Making meaning of whiteness: Exploring racial identity with white teachers.* Albany, NY: State University of New York Press.

Merryfield, M. M. (2000). Why aren't teachers being prepared to teach for diversity, equity, and global interconnectedness? A study of lived experiences in the making of multicultural and global educators. *Teaching and Teacher Education, 16*(4), 429–443._

Milner, R.H. (2015). *Race(ing) to Class: Confronting poverty and race in schools and classrooms.* Cambridge, MA: Harvard Education Press.

Poza, L., Brooks, M.D., & Valdés, G. (2014). *Entre familia*: Immigrant parents' strategies for involvement in children's schooling. *School Community Journal, 24,* 119–148.

Sleeter, C. E. (2001). Preparing teachers for culturally diverse schools: Research and the overwhelming presence of whiteness. *Journal of Teacher Education, 52*(2), 94–106.

Villegas, A. M., & Lucas, T. (2002). Preparing culturally responsive teachers: Rethinking the curriculum. *Journal of Teacher Education, 53*(1), 20–32.

Wepner, S.B., & Gómez, D.W. (2017). *Challenges facing suburban schools: Promising responses to changing student populations.* Lanham, MD: Rowan & Littlefield.

MODULE 11

What to Do When You Have Tried It All

SECTION 1: CASE SCENARIO

Context

Ms. Apple is a 49-year-old, White, American woman. She is in her 25th year of teaching in a large suburban district outside of a major city. She is an English monolingual who teaches 5th grade, and her class is comprised of 30 students with varying backgrounds in regards to race, class, and gender. The school qualifies for schoolwide Title I services, where every student receives free breakfast and lunch each day. Ms. Apple has good rapport with her students and has traditionally connected with most of her students' caregivers.

Scenario

Over her long career as a teacher, Ms. Apple has noticed a gradual change in the ways in which she is able to connect with caregivers and students. This year, she is frustrated that she cannot get Rachel's caregivers to participate in their child's schooling. Rachel is not progressing in literacy this year, and Ms. Apple cannot engage the caregivers to work with her. Rachel is also frustrated because she keeps getting all her spelling words wrong on her weekly tests. Ms. Apple follows all the tried-and-true ways to get caregivers to participate in their children's education. She makes phone calls, writes notes, and sends emails. She sends invitations to school events and parent–teacher conferences. She even asks the older sibling to help transport messages and schoolwork to the caregivers' home. Ms. Apple knows the caregivers were once involved in school volunteer activities, but they rarely attend school events anymore. Ms. Apple would really like more participation from Rachel's caregivers, but she is about to stop trying because she feels she has tried it all.

SECTION 2: EXPLORING CURRENT PERSPECTIVES

 Complete Appendix A, Tasks for Section 2: Exploring Current Perspectives.

Section 3: Getting on the Same Page

Sometimes teachers might think they have tried it all and then decide to give up on connecting with students and families. Learning takes time—often weeks, months, and years, especially when barriers such as language or learning differences slow the process. Teachers must never give up on students and families and must keep looking for ways to unlock learning. According to Clay (2005), "If the child is a struggling reader or writer, the conclusion must be that we have not yet discovered the way to help him learn" (p. 158). This is true for working with caregivers as well. If teachers are unable to connect with caregivers, it is possible they simply have not yet discovered how.

As an elementary classroom teacher and reading specialist for 21 years, I (Ann) worked in situations where I felt that I had tried it all and still could not connect with particular caregivers. As a young, new teacher, I faced a challenging situation where parents of a child were upset with their child's report card and wrote back to me that this was the worst thing that anyone had ever written about their child. As a new teacher, I was horrified. How did my report remarks and comments have such a negative impact on the parents? I contacted the mom as soon as possible and she shared some information about why the dad had a negative reaction to his son's report card. Later in my career, as an experienced teacher, I faced a situation where I could not seem to find the right balance between challenging a student academically and meeting the demands of his caregivers, who told me the work was too difficult. The parents and I could not seem to agree on what the child needed in terms of reading instruction and home reading. This student found learning to read challenging, but I found he was making progress with lots of practice. I think it was hard for the parents to see their child put so much effort into reading, so they put demands on me to lighten up. Like most new teachers, I did not feel prepared to work with caregivers (Edwards, 2016; Edwards et al., 1999; Hampshire et al., 2015), but I continued to find ways of connecting throughout my career, and I used situations like this to continue learning and improving in this area.

Working with caregivers is integral to all the other work educators do as teachers. Some people might view working with parents as separate from or supplemental to the daily work of teaching. But building relationships with children and caregivers should go hand in hand. Therefore, when teachers say, "I don't know how to connect with caregivers because I've tried it all," they might ask themselves, "How am I integrating knowledge of students and caregivers into all areas of my teaching?" It is well known that teaching is complex. Teachers are required to know about their

learners and learning progressions; content knowledge; instructional practices that include assessment, planning, and teaching; and professional responsibilities as educators (Council of Chief State School Officers, 2013).
Working with caregivers can and should be integrated into all of these com-
ponents of teaching.

First, teachers must know about their students and how children learn.
This component of teaching is best filled by an educator who welcomes information from "families, colleagues, and other professionals" (Council of
Chief State School Officers, 2013, p. 16), who "respects learners as individuals with differing personal and family backgrounds" (Council of Chief State
School Officers, 2013, p. 17), and who is "committed to working with learners, colleagues, families, and communities" (Council of Chief State School
Officers, 2013, p. 21). Learning about learners and learning takes time and
effort. Educators cannot expect to learn everything about students from one
beginning-of-the-year survey or questionnaire! Rather, teachers can learn
more and more as they get to know their students, as they teach them each
day, and as they get know their caregivers throughout the school year.

Further, teachers must know about content knowledge and the cycle of
instructional assessment, practice, and teaching. This component requires
a teacher who "takes into consideration the input of learners, colleagues,
families, and the larger community" (Council of Chief State School Officers,
2013, p. 34). Effective teachers learn about their students and caregivers
every chance they get! While planning, teaching, and evaluating student
progress, teachers gather formative information about students as learners and think about ways to connect with them and their caregivers. Last,
teachers must know about their professional responsibilities as educators.
This component welcomes an educator who is willing to expand "understanding of his/her own frames of reference" and "the potential biases in
these frames, and their impact on expectations for and relationships with
learners and their families" (Council of Chief State School Officers, 2013, p.
41) and a teacher who "respects families' beliefs, norms, and expectations"
(Council of Chief State School Officers, 2013, p. 45).

Building relationships with caregivers, and integrating that knowledge
with all other areas of teacher expertise, is not easy. As stated above, teaching is complex, and so is a child's life! According to Bronfenbrenner (1994),
a child's environment can be defined in terms of the bioecological theory.
The five structures in Bronfenbrenner's theory move from the microsystem,
which is the child's immediate environment, such as the home or school, to
the mesosystem, which is the interaction between two environments, such
as the communication between home and school. The exosystem is the
third structure, and it includes contexts in which the family belongs, such
as caregivers' place of employment, family network, or neighborhood. The
macrosystem is the fourth structure, and it includes the family's beliefs and
customs. Last is the chronosystem, which includes "change or consistency

over time" of people or structures in the child's life (p. 40). When teachers think they have tried it all, they must think about integrating knowledge of students across all areas of their teaching, as well as considering all areas of a child's ecological family life when planning to teach them.

SECTION 4: LISTENING TO EXPAND PERSPECTIVES

 Complete Appendix B, Tasks for Section 4: Listening to Expand Perspectives.

SECTION 5: FIXING IT

 The following are suggestions for working with teachers regarding what to do when you feel you have tried everything. Complete Appendix C, Tasks for Section 5: Fixing It, for further reflection and analysis.

Complexities of Teaching

- Consider students as individual learners, and as somebody else's child.
- Consider the age and development of the learners you teach—what did they learn last year? What are they expected to learn this year?
- Consider connecting families with content. Learn about caregivers' backgrounds and interests. How can you connect school to home? What might some of your caregivers have in common with the curriculum or interests of your current class of students?
- Consider learning as much about students as possible while planning, teaching, and assessing student growth. Every teaching opportunity is a learning opportunity for you.
- Consider your ethical responsibilities as a teacher to continue working with students and caregivers, no matter how difficult it is.

Home and School Connections

- Consider the child's immediate environment, such as the home or school (microsystem), and how it affects learning and communication.
- Consider the interaction between two environments, such as the communication between home and school (mesosystem), and how you can contribute as a teacher.
- Consider the contexts in which the family belongs, such as the caregivers' place of employment, family, community, or neighborhood (exosystem), and how that influences the child's schooling.

- Consider the family's beliefs and customs (macrosystem), and how
  you can integrate that in your teaching, and in learning about your
  students.

SECTION 6: REBUILDING THE CASE

Over her long career as a teacher, Ms. Apple notices a change in her ability
to connect with caregivers. This year, she is frustrated that she cannot get
Rachel's caregivers to participate in their child's schooling. Rachel is not
progressing in literacy, and Ms. Apple cannot engage the caregivers to work
with her. Rachel is also frustrated because she keeps getting all her spelling
words wrong on her weekly tests. Ms. Apple knows the caregivers were
once involved in school volunteer activities, but they rarely attend school
events anymore. Instead of giving up on the family, Ms. Apple uses some
of the strategies listed above to problem-solve reasons that the family has
disconnected from school and how she can reconnect with them.

One way that Ms. Apple keeps trying is by inquiring with the school office about what might be going on with Rachel's family. Ms. Apple is careful
not to portray Rachel's family in a deficit way, but is instead genuinely concerned about Rachel's caregivers.[1] Ms. Apple talks with the school principal
and office secretary to find out why there is such a change in Rachel's family
this year. She explains that Rachel is really falling behind in school and that
the caregivers do not respond to communication or help Rachel with her
work. The school principal asks Ms. Apple into the office and shares a little
more about Rachel's family.[2] During their conversation, Ms. Apple learns
that Rachel's father was diagnosed with cancer the month before school
started and that he is no longer able to work. Rachel's mother, who volun-
teered often in previous years, is now trying to balance working full-time,
driving her husband to doctor appointments and treatments out of town,
and taking care of her four children. Ms. Apple is shocked at the news and
feels badly that she jumped to conclusions about the parents.[3] She learns
that the family wants to keep the health diagnosis private because they do
not want other caregivers or school staff talking about Rachel's father in
front of students or their own four kids. Everything seems to make sense
at that moment. Ms. Apple talks with the school principal about the next
steps in working with Rachel to receive the academic support she needs
this school year,[4] while her family is busy with their life-changing events.
In an effort to keep the family's crisis private, the principal and classroom
teacher make a plan to work together to provide Rachel with extra spelling
and literacy support. Ms. Apple understands that a child's circumstances at
home influence performance at school. She knows the mesosystem, or the
interaction between two environments, affects communication between
home and school.

1. In this scenario, Ms. Apple goes to the school office out of concern for Rachel's caregivers. Ms. Apple understands that teaching is complex, and that even when she felt she had tried everything to connect with the caregivers, she could not give up. Instead, she followed her ethical responsibilities as a teacher to continue working with students and caregivers.

2. By deciding to go to the school office, Ms. Apple learned important information about the complexities of school families. Learning about Rachel's family crisis reminds Ms. Apple that each student is an individual learner with unique experiences at home.

3. Ms. Apple is shocked at the news and knows she jumped to conclusions about how the parents did not care about their child's schooling. She also learns how important it is to the family to maintain confidentiality.

4. Ms. Apple talks with the school principal about the next steps to take. She understands that the home and school connect in many important ways. She learns about Rachel's immediate environment, the microsystem, and that home and family health issues can significantly affect school learning.

REFERENCES

Bronfenbrenner, U. (1994). Ecological models of human development. *International Encyclopedia of Education, 3*(2), 37–43.

Clay, M. M. (2005). *Literacy lessons designed for individuals: Why? when? and how?* Portsmouth, NH: Heinemann Educational Books.

Council of Chief State School Officers. (2013, April). *InTASC model core teaching standards and learning progressions for teachers 1.0: A resource for ongoing teacher development.* Washington, DC: Author.

Edwards, P. (2016). *New ways to engage parents: Strategies and tools for teachers and leaders, K–12.* New York, NY: Teachers College Press.

Edwards, P., Pleasants, H., & Franklin, S. (1999). *A path to follow: Learning to listen to parents.* Portsmouth, NH: Heinemann.

Hampshire, P. K., Havercroft, K., Luy, M., & Call, J. (2015). Confronting assumptions: Service learning as a medium for preparing early childhood special education preservice teachers to work with families. *Teacher Education Quarterly, 42*(1), 83–96.

ADDITIONAL RESOURCES

Project Appleseed. (n.d.). Parent involvement checklist. Retrieved from www.readingrockets.org/article/parent-involvement-checklist

HANDLING DIFFICULT CONVERSATIONS

MODULE 12
Honest Caregiver–Teacher Conferences

SECTION 1: CASE SCENARIO

Context

Ms. Carlson is a 31-year-old, English-Spanish bilingual, 5th-grade teacher. She's a White woman from a middle-class background and teaches in a suburban school district. Her student David is a White, English-speaking, middle-class child.

Scenario

Ms. Carlson is worried about David. David is an eager-to-please and kind student who gets along well with others. However, he is struggling academically, especially in math. He cannot remember his math facts, and while he seems to pay attention in class and turns in good homework, he fails the tests.

It is late October, and Ms. Carlson is having her first caregiver–teacher conference with David's family. She opens the conference by saying,

> David is a wonderful child. He is very kind and has many friends in class. He works very hard and turns in good homework. Sometimes he doesn't seem to remember his math facts. Math tests have been hard for him, but I think if he keeps practicing, he'll do well.

David's parents agree, and then Ms. Carlson and David's parents talk about the books David should be reading at home and his enjoyment of art class and recess. Twenty minutes are up, and David's parents feel that he is doing well overall; he just needs to keep working.

SECTION 2: EXPLORING CURRENT PERSPECTIVES

 Complete Appendix A, Tasks for Section 2: Exploring Current Perspectives.

SECTION 3: GETTING ON THE SAME PAGE

Open, Honest Communication

Caregiver–teacher conferences can be intimidating. Teachers have many families to meet in a short time, and there's often much to discuss. Moreover, discussing difficult topics such as students' struggles with academics, behavior, or having basic needs met are never easy. However, glossing over problems does not help them get resolved. When that happens, caregivers are left thinking everything is okay. Then the child does not receive the support they need, and when report cards are later released showing academic struggles, caregivers might feel frustrated and powerless because they did not know a problem existed. As found in Lareau and Horvat's (1999) study of two Midwestern 3rd-grade classrooms, caregivers want to know about issues before they become problems so that they have power to try to remedy them.

Honest communication that is clear and tactful is extremely important. In a study featuring interviews with a variety of caregivers and educators, Blue-Banning, Summers, Frankland, Nelson, and Beegle (2004) found that caregivers want frequent, open, honest communication with the school. They do not want bad news "sugarcoated" or minimized; they do want problems communicated with tact where educators include positive comments and do not blame them or their child. As educators explain issues, they should not use jargon, and both parties should listen to each other without judgment. Also, caregivers want the validity of their viewpoint acknowledged.

Caregivers as Resources

Treating caregivers as experts regarding their children is critical. Often, they know what motivates their children, or they see things happening at home (related to homework, behavior, or emotional or biological issues such as lack of sleep, changes in eating habits, or heightened anxiety) that can affect what is happening at school. Using caregivers' knowledge to inform the ways teachers handle situations and working with caregivers to determine a solution is critical. Rose (1998) recommends this, but also suggests having some possible solutions ready. Caregivers cannot solve the entire problem, and they often look to teachers to be knowledgeable about academics and instruction. However, the combined expertise of teachers and caregivers makes the solution stronger.

In my (Lisa's) teaching career, I found that caregivers expressed frustration if they felt issues or problems were sprung on them. They wanted to be informed in a timely manner so they could do something about issues, but they also wanted to know that I cared about their child and saw their child's strengths, not just the issues or the problems. This meant I had to engage in a delicate balancing act. I found that if I glossed over issues during conferences, in report card comments, or in communications home, then I may have avoided conflict in that moment, but the issue had no chance of being resolved. Also, if I did not document issues in report card comments in an honest (but caring) manner, there would be no record for caregivers or future teachers that a child faced a particular struggle, which could make it difficult to establish a need for extra help in a particular area.

In addition, I found it beneficial and more effective to have ideas for potential solutions ready when I came to meetings with caregivers. However, at these meetings, I talked with caregivers to get their insights and adapted these initial ideas for solutions to fit the information I gleaned and the plans we constructed together. My ideas provided a starting point for the conversation so that we could work together to understand all sides of the issue to find the best potential solution for everyone.

SECTION 4: LISTENING TO EXPAND PERSPECTIVES

Complete Appendix B, Tasks for Section 4: Listening to Expand Perspectives.

SECTION 5: FIXING IT

The following are suggestions for holding caregiver–teacher conferences. Complete Appendix C, Tasks for Section 5: Fixing It, for further reflection and analysis.

Open, Honest Communication

- Try to identify patterns in students' achievement or behavior as early as possible and communicate these promptly with caregivers.

- While beginning with positives is important, glossing over the negatives and assuming things will be fine with more work does not solve the problem. Teachers can talk about observations objectively. For example, a statement such as "I have noticed that . . . ." is helpful because it is objective and can be followed by the concerns.

Caregivers as Resources

- Conversations should not just include the teachers' concerns and observations. Ask for caregivers' ideas or what they have noticed.
- Together, come up with plan of action including ideas both the teacher and caregivers can do to support the student. Maintain communication with caregivers about how the plan is going and formally review any data collected about the plan's effectiveness.

SECTION 6: REBUILDING THE CASE

Ms. Carlson is concerned because David is struggling in math. He cannot remember his math facts, and while he seems to pay attention in class and turns in good homework, he failed the first test. <u>After grading the test, Ms. Carlson asked David to show her how to solve some of the problems on the test, but he still couldn't do them. Therefore, Ms. Carlson doesn't think he was suffering from test anxiety or a bad day, and she cannot figure out what's going on.</u>[1] <u>She decided to talk to his caregivers before the next test and before the scheduled caregiver–teacher conference.</u>[2] She begins the conversation . . .

> *Ms. Carlson:* "<u>David is a wonderful child. He is kind and has many friends in class. He works very hard and turns in good homework, but this first math test did not go well.</u>[3] He scored a 60%. I asked him to show me how to solve some of the problems a couple days later, and he didn't know how to solve them. <u>What do you notice when he's doing his math homework at home?</u>"[4]
> *Caregiver:* "David cannot do his math homework by himself. He doesn't know what to do, so we have to work through every problem with him."

Ms. Carlson nods, now understanding why David does so well on his homework. Then she continues:

> *Ms. Carlson:* "I've also noticed that he does not remember his math facts when we practice them in class. Do you see that too in his homework?"

Caregiver: "Yes. We've tried flashcards, but that hasn't seemed to work."

Ms. Carlson: "There are some fun math games online. Does he enjoy playing on a computer, tablet, or iPad?"

The conversation continues about David's homework and math tests. As Ms. Carlson and David's caregivers talk through potential solutions that might help David and be feasible for Ms. Carlson and David's caregivers, they come up with a plan regarding <u>what Ms. Carlson can do to help David in class and what his caregivers can do at home.</u>[5]

1. Trying to determine the cause of the issues and some potential solutions before contacting caregivers is important. If Ms. Carlson didn't do this, time at the meeting may be spent on discussing whether David has test anxiety without finding potential solutions for David's math struggles. The caregivers may also feel as though Ms. Carlson always contacts them with problems to solve themselves, but that she, as the teacher, should solve problems at school. How caregivers view teachers and their roles varies based on cultural norms, prior schooling experiences, and other factors.

2. If Ms. Carlson waited until conferences or after several tests, David's caregivers may feel frustrated and defeated, like there is nothing they can do because David is already failing. They might also become angry that they were not contacted sooner so they could get David help with math.

When scheduling the meeting, Ms. Carlson will need to take into account David's caregivers' work schedules, preferred communication methods, and their language knowledge/proficiencies.

3. If Ms. Carlson talked only about the problems David is having, David's caregivers may feel that she is picking on their child and does not see his strengths.

4. It is important to get input from caregivers because they know the child in ways that teachers do not, which can provide insights into the issue. It also sets the tone of the meeting as a problem-solving meeting rather than one in which the teacher is the bearer of bad news.

5. Teachers should come to the meeting with an idea or two of how to help the student at school and at home. This helps the meeting be productive. However, caregivers may have specific views about what is the teacher's job and their job. This makes it important to have ideas for how to help the child at school, not just at home. It also creates more of a partnership between teachers and caregivers.

REFERENCES

Blue-Banning, M., Summers, J. A., Frankland, H. C., Nelson, L. L., & Beegle, G. (2004). Dimensions of family and professional partnerships: Constructive guidelines for collaboration. *Exceptional Children, 70*(2), 167–184.

Lareau, A., & Horvat, E. M. (1999). Moments of social inclusion and exclusion race, class, and cultural capital in family–school relationships. *Sociology of Education, 72*(1), 37–53.

Rose, M. C. (1998, October). Handle with care: The difficult parent–teacher conference. *Instructor, 108*(3), 92–93, 101.

ADDITIONAL RESOURCES

Aguilar, E. (2010, November). Tips for parent–teacher conferencing. Retrieved from
www.edutopia.org/blog/parent-teacher-conference-tips-elena-aguilar
Wilson, M.B. (2011). Tips for new teachers: Making the most of parent–teacher
conferences. *ASCD Express, 6*(12). Retrieved from www.ascd.org/ascd-express
/vol6/612-wilson.aspx

MODULE 13
Discussing Academic Concerns

SECTION 1: CASE SCENARIO

Context

Ms. Hernandez is a 46-year-old Latinx, bilingual, middle-class woman
teaching in a suburban school district. The elementary schools in the district all receive Title I funding. Ms. Hernandez is in her 23rd year of teaching, with teaching experience that spans grades K–5. For the last 8 years,
she has taught 1st grade.

Scenario

The student in this particular scenario, Ben, is a White, monolingual, middle-class boy whose reading scores are not at grade level at the end of
the first card marking. At fall conferences while discussing Ben's reading
progress on summative reading assessments (e.g., Developmental Reading
Assessment, Dynamic Indicators of Basic Early Literacy Skills) with his
caregivers, Ms. Hernandez mentioned that he needed to make significant
progress in order to meet end-of-year expectations for 1st grade. His caregivers were shocked to hear this news. They were disappointed that Ms.
Hernandez hadn't contacted them about Ben's struggles with reading.
Further, they had no idea how to help Ben with his reading at home beyond reading to him, which they did most days. Did Ben perhaps have a
reading disability they were unaware of?

Ms. Hernandez, on the other hand, felt it was important to discuss Ben's
lack of reading progress with his caregivers. She didn't understand why

they appeared upset at the end of the conference. It was her duty to share students' assessment scores with caregivers. In doing so, Ms. Hernandez hoped they would help Ben at home so that he could meet grade-level expectations at the end of the next card-marking period.

SECTION 2: EXPLORING CURRENT PERSPECTIVES

 Complete Appendix A, Tasks for Section 2: Exploring Current Perspectives.

SECTION 3: GETTING ON THE SAME PAGE

Established Notions of Children's Development

Whether the issue is academic or social, it is challenging for teachers when they are faced with telling caregivers they are concerned about their child. Equally, it can be difficult for caregivers to learn that a teacher has a concern about their child. Although it is part of teachers' professional responsibility to assess children and use the data to inform instruction, they must do so carefully and critically. In the current era of imposed standardization, high-stakes testing, and accountability, pressure on teachers is increased in ensuring that students under their care achieve at expected levels. Similarly, teachers are expected to teach a particular curriculum that includes administering assessments to not only inform instruction, but also diagnose learning difficulties in, for example, reading. However, these assessments may inaccurately portray what students are capable of because they assess a narrow view of what it means to be literate.

Government-sponsored initiatives such as the No Child Left Behind Act of 2001 (NCLB, 2002) have standardized curriculum and teaching. As a result, a dominant cognitive psychological perspective of how children develop literacy has prevailed. This view emphasizes individual development as occurring inside a child's head. Literacy from this perspective, then, is a distinct set of skills (e.g., rhyming, naming letters) to be learned at particular points in time. Conversely, another perspective views literacy as a social practice (Street, 1984). A traditional notion of literacy perpetuates the idea that there is a "normal" way in which all children develop literacy. Those children who acquire the identified skills, knowledge, and understanding at a different rate from their peers are often identified as inadequate in some way (e.g., "at risk," "struggling reader") (Dyson, 2013; Genishi & Dyson, 2009; Larson & Marsh, 2015). Thus, groups of children who share racial, cultural, and socioeconomic backgrounds are sometimes viewed through a deficit lens (Larson & Marsh, 2015). While Ben is not part of a minority culture, his particular situation is an instance where alternative indicators of academic success and growth should also receive attention.

For instance, on analysis of assessment data, school personnel used labels, referring to some kindergarten children in the classroom as "below average" readers and writers (Yoon, 2015, p. 364). The children labeled as such were racially and economically diverse from their teachers. These assessment practices framed the children's language and literacies as fixed traits. This study foregrounds the complexities of defining and measuring "readiness" by means of literacy assessments that rank, sort, and produce labels that determine children's learning potential. As a result, particular groups of children are pathologized, and educators develop deterministic beliefs about their ability to succeed in school.

Teachers must be cautious when interpreting results so as not to underestimate their students' potential just because they do not fit the traditional notions of literacy development. In the United States, the student population is steadily increasing in terms of race, culture, and language. It is thus important that educators do not perceive diversity as deficit or "at risk."

Because children enter school with various prior learning experiences and acquire school literacy at different rates, teachers must critically examine perceived struggles. Teachers should ask themselves the following question: Is the curriculum creating the perceived academic struggle? In turn, the way in which perceptions of a student's academic struggles are shared with caregivers is important. We do not mean to suggest that some students do not have difficulties in learning—they do. How these concerns are shared affects not only the school–home partnership, but more importantly, the student.

SECTION 4: LISTENING TO EXPAND PERSPECTIVES

 Complete Appendix B, Tasks for Section 4: Listening to Expand Perspectives.

SECTION 5: FIXING IT

 The following are suggestions for discussing academic struggles with caregivers. Complete Appendix C, Tasks for Section 5: Fixing It, for further reflection and analysis.

Challenge the Status Quo

- Critically examine the assessment protocols used to determine whether a student may be struggling academically. A one-size-fits-all standard of development and approach to assessment does not typically account for the racial, linguistic, and cultural diversity among students. Thus, interpret results cautiously to ensure that students' differences are not confused with diversity.

- Remain aware of content standards and hold all students to high expectations, but, at the same time, challenge traditional standards for development that tend to pathologize particular groups of students based on their race, culture, and socioeconomic status.
- While sharing assessment data that suggest a student has a learning difficulty, be sure to explain why the protocol was used, how it was used, and your interpretation of the results.

Use Multiple Assessments

- Teachers do not generally have a choice about what assessments they wish to use with their students because they are mandated at the district, state, and federal levels. Such assessments don't always highlight students' strengths. It is therefore crucial that teachers also use alternative assessments that demonstrate that although a particular concept might not yet be learned according to a standard or benchmark, the student has learning potential.
- For example, a "focused anecdotal records assessment" (Boyd-Batstone, 2004, p. 230) is a helpful tool that teachers can use to observe and capture a close-up snapshot of a student's development across disciplines (literacy, math, science, social studies) in ways that traditional assessments might not. While discussing assessment data that suggest an academic difficulty or concern, teachers can draw on anecdotal records to show caregivers that despite the appearance of an academic struggle, the student is in fact making progress. Anecdotal records indicate what a student *can* do. A teacher can use this information to build on a student's strengths in order to address a learning need. Likewise, if a student is struggling with a concept, the anecdotal records can help pinpoint why and suggest a plan of action.

Plan of Action

- When sharing a student's perceived struggle, it is important to begin with a discussion about observed strengths. This way, when the teacher presents an academic concern, caregivers may be more open to listening. In turn, the teacher is building trust and earning respect that will ultimately benefit the student.
- Next, the teacher will want to present a plan of action. This plan may entail additional help in or outside of the classroom, resources, and school personnel. In order to gain support from caregivers, it's essential that they have ample time to ask questions, share concerns,

and, if possible, meet school personnel who may be administering additional assessments and/or working with their child so that they feel comfortable.

SECTION 6: REBUILDING THE CASE

After Ms. Hernandez has administered the district-mandated 1st-grade literacy assessments, she notices that one particular student, Ben, scored low on two of them. She is filling out report cards and preparing for the first conference of the school year with his caregivers and proceeds carefully and cautiously because, according to the assessment data, Ben is struggling with learning to read. However, she is not worried about him because she is critical of the limitations of the assessments.[1] She regularly uses a focused anecdotal records assessment system (Boyd-Batstone, 2004) to document her students' developing literacy because she is aware that a one-size-fits-all assessment does not account for students' diversity.[2] These notes, along with other informal interview protocols, provide her with evidence that while Ben may not have yet reached expectations for the beginning of 1st grade in the area of reading, he has many strengths that she plans to build on throughout the year in order to help him reach his maximum learning potential. For instance, during a one-on-one interview about his interests, she learned that Ben is motivated to learn to read so that he can explore particular topics (e.g., the solar system, Pokémon).[3]

During the conference with Ben's caregivers, Ms. Hernandez plans to explain why the literacy assessments were used, how she interprets the results, and her plans to help Ben learn to read by making connections between the curriculum and his individual interests. In this way, she will provide him with some additional support but will do so in motivating ways that foreground what he already knows.[4] She begins the conference by sharing anecdotal records that document Ben's willingness and openness to participate in class discussions, his oral language development, and the many relationships he has with his peers. Ben's caregivers leave the first conference pleased with his progress socially. They understand that Ben has plenty of room for growth in learning to read but are assured that he will get there because Ms. Hernandez perceives him as capable and seems to know him well. They're impressed that she knows so much about his personal interest in becoming a Pokémon expert!

1. It is important that teachers understand why they are giving a particular assessment, how to give it, and how to interpret the results to inform instruction, but they must also know how to critically analyze the assessment's limitations. This critical awareness is important because it helps teachers focus on what students can do in order to build on their strengths. A perceived struggle is thus viewed and discussed with caregivers as an opportunity for growth.

2. Rather than assume that some students are more capable of learning than others, Ms. Hernandez believes that all of her students have the potential to learn. Thus, she keeps anecdotal records to inform her instruction on a daily basis. Further, the notes are used when discussing an academic concern to demonstrate to caregivers what their child does well and areas for continued growth.

3. It is important that teachers find and develop alternative means for assessing children beyond the standards. This information is important because it allows teachers to connect the curriculum with students' lives to make learning more equitable. This data can be shared with caregivers when discussing an academic concern to bridge home and school.

4. Ms. Hernandez approaches Ben's need for more practice and access to school literacy from a strengths-based perspective. Instead of discussing his need for support in learning to read with his parents as an academic concern, she presents it as helping him reach his learning potential. In this way, Ben is not perceived as deficient or struggling but as a 1st-grade child learning and acquiring literacy in joyful ways.

REFERENCES

Boyd-Batstone, P. (2004). Focused anecdotal records assessment: A tool for standards-based, authentic assessment. *The Reading Teacher, 58*(3), 230–239.

Dyson, A. H. (2013). *ReWriting the basics: Literacy learning in children's cultures*. New York, NY: Teachers College Press.

Genishi, C, & Dyson, A.H. (2009). *Children, language, and literacy: Diverse learners in diverse times*. New York, NY: Teachers College Press.

Larson, J., & Marsh, J. (2015). *Making literacy real: Theories and practices for learning and teaching* (2nd ed.). Los Angeles, CA: SAGE Publications, Inc.

Street, B. (1984). *Literacy in theory and practice*. New York, NY: Cambridge University Press.

Yoon, H. S. (2015). Assessing children in kindergarten: The narrowing of language, culture and identity in the testing era. *Journal of Early Childhood Literacy, 15*(3), 364–393.

MODULE 14
Discussing Discipline Issues (Positive Discipline)

SECTION 1: CASE SCENARIO

Context

Mr. Jeffrey is a 44-year-old American Black man in his 20th year of teaching in a large urban district in a major city. He is an English monolingual who teaches 6th grade, and his class is comprised of 26 students with varying backgrounds. The school qualifies for schoolwide Title I services, where every student receives free breakfast and lunch each day. Mr. Jeffrey has high expectations for behavior in the classroom and enforces the same classroom management system he has used for 20 years.

Scenario

Mr. Jeffrey has a comprehensive management and organization system in his classroom. He talks loud and uses sarcasm to get students' attention, and expects students to work quietly while they sit with their desks in rows. Mr. Jeffrey hangs a chart with colored cards in the pockets. The pockets are labeled with students' numbers. When students break a school rule, they move their own cards from green, to yellow, to red, and it is no secret which student is associated with which number. At the end of the day, it is always the same students whose cards are red, which means they miss recess, go to the office, get a phone call home, or receive a morning detention. In an effort to recognize positive behavior, Mr. Jeffrey puts a few marbles in a good behavior jar with hopes that the jar will fill up at some point and the class can have a marble party. Unfortunately, on a daily basis, he takes more marbles out of the jar than he puts in, so the class never reaches its goal of a full marble jar. He blames particular students for being loud, and tells them they are the reason the class does not earn marbles for a party. Finally, Mr. Jeffrey passes out tickets, which represent a classroom economy, to children who are well behaved. The students with tickets are able to attend a special celebration at the end of each week, where they can purchase items from the classroom store. The same students get to go to the class store each week, and the same few rarely get to go. Mr. Jeffrey's three management systems—the pocket chart, the marble jar, and the token economy—praise or punish the same students each day. He makes many calls to the same parents, who are resistant to his characterization of their children and feel that he picks on them.

SECTION 2: EXPLORING CURRENT PERSPECTIVES

 Complete Appendix A, Tasks for Section 2: Exploring Current Perspectives.

SECTION 3: GETTING ON THE SAME PAGE

Classroom management and organizing student behavior is part of the complexity of teaching. Both new and experienced teachers must continually consider how to get their students to listen and behave in order to teach them. In the scenario described above, the teacher, Mr. Jeffrey, maintains control in managing student behavior instead of setting up systems of classroom engagement that motivate students to be self-motivated, intrinsic learners. According to Denton (2013), teachers can use positive language that helps students in "gaining academic skills and knowledge, developing self-control, and building their sense of community" (p. 7). In addition, Graham-Clay (2005), recognizes that many teachers are not trained in or know how to implement "proactive communication with parents" (p. 117). Three suggestions for teachers are to balance good news with constructive news when communicating with caregivers, avoid using jargon in conversations, and most importantly, wear a smile when interacting with students and caregivers. The shift from negative language and strict teacher control to positive language and engaged student involvement is possible for all teachers, even for those who have been at it for 20 years.

As an elementary classroom teacher and reading specialist for 21 years, I (Ann) implemented and discussed discipline issues with caregivers. As a new teacher, I began implementation of the three systems discussed above, but I had a difficult time making each system work for me. When I arrived at my school as a new 2nd-grade teacher, I asked my partner teachers for classroom management ideas. Like many new teachers, I did not learn enough about classroom management and organization in my teacher preparation program (Edwards, 2016; Edwards et al., 1999; Hampshire et al., 2015). The two 2nd-grade teachers showed me their colorful pocket charts, their marble jars, and their classroom store. So, I set to work making pocket chart cards, bought marbles for the marble jar, and photocopied tickets for the classroom token economy. I quickly realized that the same students had red cards at the end of each day, the same students prevented our class from having a marble party, and the same students were unable to shop at the classroom store. Those students ended up missing recess and other opportunities because of the structures I had set up in my classroom. I did not like how that made them feel or the way it made me feel as a teacher. I eliminated those systems and began engaging and motivating students in different ways.

Teachers set the tone for classroom climate, management, and organization. Research shows that educators can implement positive discipline systems with students and discuss those systems with parents by following some general guidelines for teacher language, including Denton's (2013) five principles for teacher language: "be direct and genuine, convey faith in children's abilities and interventions, focus on action, keep it brief, and know when to be silent" (p. 31).

First of all, educators should be "direct and genuine" in their communication with students and families (Denton, 2013, p. 13). Teachers are often indirect when talking with students, either by asking questions as a way to get students to follow rules ("Can you join me on the carpet?"), or by praising certain students for following directions with hopes that the rest of the class will follow along ("I like how Sally is already on the carpet"). Denton recommends that teachers "say what we mean, [by] using direct language" (p. 13), by giving clear and direct instructions, and "mean what we say, [by] following through on our words" (p. 17), by only stating demands on which we can follow through. She also suggests that teachers use appropriate voice, avoid sarcasm, and be aware of body language. Denton points out that sarcasm can "wound children and damage trust" (p. 16). Moreover, gestures and facial expressions that do not match a teacher's words can confuse young children.

In addition, teachers should "convey faith in children's abilities and interventions" when communicating with them (Denton, 2013, p. 19). Teachers' comments are often general, such as "great work," when they could be more specific, such as "You are really concentrating on tying your shoes." Denton recommends that teachers "take time to notice the positives" (p. 19), by avoiding general and negative comments; "avoid baby talk" because its use "assumes the listener has limited capabilities" (p. 20), and "be aware of language patterns that treat boys and girls differently" (p. 20) by paying close attention to which students we call on, who receives wait time, and what kinds of feedback we give to boys versus girls.

Further, educators should "focus on action" when communicating with students (Denton, 2013, p. 21). Teachers often use abstract terms, such as asking students to be responsible, respectful, or cooperative, without giving examples of what those terms look like or sound like in the classroom. Denton (2013) recommends that teachers "connect abstract terms with concrete behaviors" (p. 21) by linking the abstract term, such as "be responsible," with examples of what responsibility looks like and sounds like. She also suggests that teachers "describe behavior [of students], not character of [their] attitude" (p. 23), and "keep the wording nonjudgmental" (p. 25) by avoiding using words that attack students' character or that judge them as a person. For example, instead of calling a student careless, teachers should say something straightforward, such as, "You have not followed all the instructions on this assignment."

Teachers should also "keep it brief" when communicating with students, and avoid using warnings and threats (Denton, 2013, p. 26). Teachers can talk for a long time, sometimes repeating themselves over and over. Students may eventually tune out teacher talk. Further, when teachers use warnings and threats, they "undermine both children's self-confidence and their trust in the teacher" (p. 27), which are not useful in building a positive classroom climate. Finally, educators should "know when to be silent" (p. 27). Teachers can use silence in four ways in the classroom: by allowing wait time, by listening to students' comments, by trying not to repeat directions, and by not repeating student answers. Teachers who encourage their own listening, as well as that of their students, build students' responsibility in the classroom. Respecting and listening to caregivers in the same ways can enlist them as partners and elicit new ways to help students.

SECTION 4: LISTENING TO EXPAND PERSPECTIVES

 Complete Appendix B, Tasks for Section 4: Listening to Expand Perspectives.

SECTION 5: FIXING IT

 The following are suggestions regarding positive discipline issues. Complete Appendix C, Tasks for Section 5: Fixing It, for further reflection and analysis.

Proactive Communication with Caregivers

- Smile when talking with caregivers.
- Balance good news with constructive news when talking with parents.
- Avoid using educational jargon with parents.

Create Positive Classroom Environments

- Smile when talking with students.
- Support positive social interactions.
- Support individual and collaborative learning.
- Emphasize what students can do, not what they cannot do.
- Remember that different cultures have different expectations regarding school climate.

Engage and Motivate Students in Learning

- Encourage active engagement in learning.
- Encourage self-motivation

Choose Positive, Powerful Language

- Use language that is direct and genuine.
- Use language that supports children's abilities.
- Use language that focuses on action, not abstract terms.

- Use language that is brief, not long-winded, and without warnings or threats.
- Know when to stop talking and when to be silent (Denton, 2013).

SECTION 6: REBUILDING THE CASE

Mr. Jeffrey has a comprehensive management and organization system in his classroom, including a color-coded pocket chart, a marble jar, and a classroom store. He notices that the same students have red cards each day, the same students prevent the class from earning a marble party, and the same students get to shop at the class store. Further, the same students miss recess, are sent to the office, get phone calls home, and receive detention. Mr. Jeffrey attends a professional development session on implementing positive discipline and decides to make some changes for the upcoming school year.

One way that Mr. Jeffrey makes a change toward positive discipline is by implementing some of the techniques he learned at the summer professional development session.[1] He talks with the other two 6th-grade teachers and the behavior consultant from the district and collaborates with them to implement three new classroom-management practices. The team of four decides to meet every Wednesday at lunch to reflect on how the new strategies are working in the classroom.[2] During their weekly conversations, they choose three practices to implement, including using language that is direct and genuine, using language that supports children's abilities, and using language that is brief, not long-winded, and without warnings or threats. The team reviews how each strategy will look and sound in the classroom.[3] For direct and genuine language, the teachers will eliminate sarcasm and make comments on which they can follow through. For language that supports children's abilities, the teachers will focus on positive behaviors, comment on specific behaviors, and eliminate negative talk about students in front of the class. Last, for using language that is brief, not long-winded, the teachers will eliminate warnings and threats from their vocabulary, and keep teacher talk brief. Mr. Jeffrey and his team of teachers decide to spend a bit of planning time each week observing one another, and giving feedback on their new positive discipline strategies.[4] Mr. Jeffrey is aware that the school principal wants teachers to change their classroom management to a more positive system, but at this point he is more comfortable having his colleagues visit and giving him feedback. The team of teachers notice a positive shift in one another's classrooms. The climate that was once filled with negative consequences, missing recesses, principal visits, and phone calls home is now filled with positive and powerful language. When Mr. Jeffrey does call home, he balances positive and constructive feedback when talking with caregivers.

1. In this scenario, Mr. Jeffrey makes a change toward positive discipline by implementing techniques he learned at a summer professional development session. He collaborates with his grade-level team, works to implement three new classroom-management practices, and shows a willingness to grow professionally.

2. By implementing three new practices—using language that is direct and genuine, using language that supports children's abilities, and using language that is brief rather than long-winded—the team stays focused and takes on just enough to get started.

3. By defining what each strategy will look like and sound like in the classroom, the team has a clear focus. The group works together to be more direct and genuine, while eliminating sarcasm and statements they cannot follow through on. In addition, the group moves away from deficit talk about students and moves toward supporting children's positive behaviors with comments on specific behaviors. Finally, the group stops talking so much, while eliminating warnings and threats from their vocabulary.

4. Mr. Jeffrey is aware that the school principal wants teachers to change their classroom management to a more positive system, which is why she set up professional development opportunities over the summer. At this point in his learning of the new system, Mr. Jeffrey feels most comfortable with his colleagues visiting and giving feedback.

REFERENCES

Denton, P. (2013). *The power of our words: Teacher language that helps children learn.* Turner Falls, MA: Center for Responsive Schools, Inc.

Edwards, P. (2016). *New ways to engage parents: Strategies and tools for teachers and leaders, K–12.* Teachers College Press.

Edwards, P., Pleasants, H., & Franklin, S. (1999). *A path to follow: Learning to listen to parents.* Portsmouth, NH: Heinemann.

Graham-Clay, S. (2005). Communicating with parents: Strategies for teachers. *School Community Journal, 16*(1), 117–129.

Hampshire, P. K., Havercroft, K., Luy, M., & Call, J. (2015). Confronting assumptions: Service learning as a medium for preparing early childhood special education preservice teachers to work with families. *Teacher Education Quarterly, 42*(1), 83–96.

ADDITIONAL RESOURCES

National Institute for Urban School Improvement. (n.d.). Teaching all children. Retrieved from www.readingrockets.org/article/teaching-all-children

MODULE 15

Advocating for a Neurodiversity Paradigm

SECTION 1: CASE SCENARIO

Context

Ms. Shields, the classroom teacher, is a 24-year-old, monolingual, middle-class, American White woman. One of her students, Joel, is a 12-year-old, monolingual, African American, middle-class boy. School personnel speculate that Joel has autism spectrum disorder (ASD). From our perspective, characterizing students as having a "disorder" focuses on perceptions of what they lack rather than on their potential. We advocate instead using the term *neuro-atypical,* which refers to "people who have uncommon makeups in a manner that is less judgmental than mentally ill, mentally disordered, socially deficient, . . . and other deficient-oriented" language (Smagorinsky, 2014, p. 16). Standard terminology in schools has been "learning disabled," but schools are beginning to move away from this deficit labeling to use "differently abled" instead.

Scenario

During the spring of her 1st year of teaching 1st grade, Ms. Shields was looking forward to participating in the end-of-year planning meeting to discuss class lists for the upcoming year alongside colleagues. However, during the planning meeting, she encountered a troubling discussion. A kindergarten teacher made several disparaging comments about a particular student, Joel, who was placed on Ms. Shields's class list. Also, the principal presented letters from caregivers for the upcoming school year requesting that their child not be placed in Joel's classroom because they perceived his behavior as disruptive to their child's learning.

These caregivers felt such disruptions interfered with their child's learning. A few caregivers stated safety as their primary concern.

Ms. Shields left the meeting not only worried about the following year but also concerned about her lack of preparation to work with neurodiverse children and their caregivers. Safety for the other children in the classroom as well as her own was at the forefront of her mounting concerns. To date, the district had not provided employees with professional development (PD) to explore the issue of working with neurodiverse children. In this district, neurodiverse children received special education services outside the classroom.

SECTION 2: EXPLORING CURRENT PERSPECTIVES

Task 1: Initial Reaction

Directions: Consider how you would react to the scenario if you were the student's teacher. The guiding questions below will support your thoughtful reflection. Jot down notes or bullet points that respond to each of the guiding questions.

1. After "experiencing" the scenario, what would your feelings and inner thoughts be?

As a new teacher without a special education background who is learning for the first time about having an autistic child on my future class list, I suspect that I might lack confidence in my own ability to successfully teach Joel while also attending to the myriad needs of the other students in my classroom. I would be fearful of failing students and their families, while at the time worried that I might also disappoint my administrator and colleagues.

2. How would you respond to this situation?

I would look into the resources in my school and district to learn all that I can to be a caring teacher and to create an inclusive learning environment in my classroom where all children feel welcome and valued.

3. What do you know or did you learn about the student as a learner from this experience?

At a young age, Joel's potential has been underestimated. I didn't learn anything helpful about Joel as a learner because his previous teacher only focused on what he could not do yet. Therefore, I don't know much about Joel's learning strengths.

4. What do you know or did you learn about the student's family?

I learned that Joel's caregivers were thankful that I contacted them before the school year began so they could share his interests and strengths with me (e.g., he likes the Pink Panther and Super Mario and enjoys swimming), as well as what accommodations he might need during school (e.g., a quiet place to work when he feels the noise level is too loud).

Task 2: Maslow's Hierarchy

Directions: Consider Maslow's (1943) Hierarchy of Needs (see Figure 2.1). Then complete Table 2.

Table 2. Mapping Individual Needs Onto Maslow's Hierarchy

Individual	What are the individual's needs as described in the scenario?	Where do these needs fit on Maslow's Hierarchy of Needs?
The Student	An inclusive learning environment	Self-Actualization Needs
The Student's Caregivers	A partnership with the school	Love/Affection & Belongingness Needs
The Teacher	Professional support, resources, and belief in her ability to successfully teach all students under her care	Esteem Needs

Task 3: Probing Deeper

Directions: Consider issues of power, prestige, positioning, and access as defined in Chapter 2. Complete Table 3, Considerations of Power, Prestige. Positioning, and Access, based on the case scenario.

Table 3. Considerations of Power, Prestige, Positioning, and Access

Individual	WHAT ARE THE THREATS (REAL OR PERCEIVED) TO THE INDIVIDUAL'S . . .			
	Power?	Prestige?	Positioning?	Access?
The Student	The schooling context requires Joel to act according to "normal" classroom behavior. When he doesn't meet these expectations, he may fear consequences he doesn't fully understand and that may not meet his needs. In turn, he develops anxiety.	Joel's social status as an estranged member of the classroom community threatens his prestige.	Joel is positioned as lacking social skills by some school professionals who have power over him. As a result, he may feel threatened and lash out in ways accessible to him (e.g., throwing game pieces).	Positioning Joel as deficient may affect his access to social and/ or academic status in the classroom.
The Student's Caregivers	Caregivers have less power over Joel in school.	Caregivers may experience compromised prestige if Joel is viewed as deficient.	Caregivers may be positioned as lacking in their ability to discipline their son.	Caregivers may question their son's access to a free and appropriate education.

Table 3. Considerations of Power, Positioning, Prestige, and Access (continued)

| Individual | WHAT ARE THE THREATS (REAL OR PERCEIVED) TO THE INDIVIDUAL'S ... | | | |
	Power?	Prestige?	Positioning?	Access?
The Teacher	The teacher may lose power if her administrator does not perceive her as an effective teacher.	If the teacher's practice is questioned, then she may lose prestige as a capable and knowledgeable educator.	The teacher may be positioned as ineffective.	The teacher could lose access to employment if her administrator does not view her as effective.

Task 4: Summarizing

Directions: For each individual, compare what they need (Table 2) with what threats they are experiencing to their power, prestige, positioning, and access (Table 3). What overlaps exist between Table 2 and Table 3? Write down any overlapping needs and threats in Table 4, Summarizing Overlapping Needs and Threats.

Table 4. Summarizing Overlapping Needs and Threats

Individual	Overlapping Needs & Threats (Real or Perceived)
The Student	Has needs related to belongingness and actualization, but there may be threats to his needs if Joel may not achieve his learning potential if school officials exercise power over him and position him as lacking social skills
The Student's Caregiver (Mother)	Have needs for their child to belong that may leave them powerless if the school does not share concerns about their son with them. include them in making decisions about their son.
The Teacher	Has esteem needs, but her power and prestige might be threatened if she doesn't agree with her colleagues' deficit perceptions of Joel.

SECTION 3: GETTING ON THE SAME PAGE

Recognizing the Pathology Paradigm

In their K–12 classrooms, most teachers have been socialized through an "apprenticeship of observation" (Lortie, 1975) regarding individuals who possess a neuro-atypical mental health makeup (Smagorinsky, 2014).

Through this apprenticeship, both prospective and practicing teachers generally learn to view those with a neuro-atypical mental health makeup as deficient or in need of repair. Some well-meaning educators (e.g., classroom teachers, special education teachers, reading specialists, school psychologists, researchers, teacher educators) participate in, although often unknowingly, and perpetuate the cultural practice of misinterpreting difference—difference from themselves—as deficit (Gorski, 2011). This issue is crucial because educators are in positions to impact whether or not the learning environment is inclusive of neuro-atypical children.

Advocating for a Neurodiversity Paradigm

In this scenario, we advocate that educators adopt a strengths perspective of neurodiverse students and their caregivers in the schooling context. A neurodiversity paradigm, according to Walker (2013), is a conscious shift away from the dominant pathology paradigm, currently prevalent not only in schools but society more broadly, to a *neurodiversity paradigm* inclusive of the entire spectrum of human neurocognitive variation. We thus advocate for a neurodiversity paradigm shift that "defines a child as a unique individual with traits, talents, and resources" that comprise a host of strengths (Saleebey, 1996, p. 298). This shift focuses attention away from what students are not yet able to do to helping them reach their learning potential.

According to the National Institute for Mental Health, autism spectrum disorder (ASD) is defined as persistent developmental deficits in social communication and social interaction across contexts (n.d.). Rather, we argue that the diagnostic and medicalized discourse that pervades schools and society disrespects the whole child. A neurodiversity paradigm, then, is a mindset that rejects the pathology paradigm.

A neurodiversity paradigm is helpful in collaborating with caregivers and, most importantly, for building trust. Establishing a relationship built on trust with caregivers might work to counter other children and caregivers in the school from adopting or transforming a deficit perspective of human difference. Ultimately, it is in children's best interest that the school perceive them as capable of academic achievement as well as able to interact and communicate with others.

A pathology paradigm (Walker, 2013) likely permeates school settings because, as Sheridan and Gutkin (2000) assert, contemporary school psychological services, by their very design and delivery, are built on the premise that referred children require assistance from adults who can "fix" or "cure" them of their ailments. Further, a medical model of diagnosing and treating referred students is the mode for determining if they qualify for professional services. Despite good intentions, practitioners focus on assessing, diagnosing, and treating students' perceived deficiencies. This deficit stance has held sway in school psychology, pathologizing human difference by assuming that some children have disabilities that reside within their corpus. Instead, we propose that it is imperative that we "confront, challenge, and disrupt certain deficit discourses" operationalized by a medical model "while at the same time trying to create an open, honest, and reflective classroom community where teachers can freely discuss their perspectives" (Koestler, 2016, p. 114) without fear of being pathologed themselves.

The medical model for diagnosing incurs an incessant focus on the developmental milestones of the "normally developing child" while ignoring what a child *can* do. Moreover, we argue that a cognitive psychological approach to childhood that assumes there is a static trajectory for all children is false and has led to inequitable learning environments for many children, particularly for those who are misunderstood as inadequate in some way. The medical model and a one-size-fits-all approach to cognitive development reifies the exclusion and pathology of neurodiverse children and can negatively affect the relationship between school personnel and caregivers. Thus, it is critical that educators possess the agency to advocate for a shift to a neurodiversity paradigm that is inclusive of *all* children.

Understanding Federal and State Laws

Similarly, this medical model, in our opinion, has also contributed to an "us versus them" mentality that positions the school against caregivers, and vice versa. Although the IEP is tailored to meet students' individual needs, it does not always translate into instruction and services that best meet their needs. Instead, what often happens is that because a medical model and pathology paradigm undergirds school psychology (Sheridan & Gutkin, 2000), many students are not perceived as capable beings with multiple assets; therefore, they may not benefit from the services offered. Caregivers must then navigate an institution that perceives their child's difference as deficit and that does not always operate in the child's best interest. Understandably, caregivers may feel that they are not only battling the school for the services and instruction they feel best meets their children's individual needs, but also demanding the dignity and respect that their children deserve to help them reach their learning potential, along with discourse that respects the whole child.

Effective Communication with Caregivers

Despite that educators may advocate for a neurodiversity paradigm, it is likely more difficult for neuro-atypical children to reach their learning potential without first establishing a positive relationship with caregivers. Thus, neuro-atypical children are best served when teachers and other school personnel who work with them develop a family–school partnership. Having a conversation with caregivers about a child can be unnerving for many reasons, and particularly for a child who appears neuro-atypical. For legal reasons, when meeting with caregivers, educators must choose their words carefully, which should be discussed with the special education teacher, principal, and perhaps the district superintendent. Also, educators should understand that caregivers may be wounded from past experiences in which their child was not viewed from a strengths-based perspective; thus, if a conversation does not begin well, it may be because caregivers are reluctant to trust school personnel.

Suggestions for effectively communicating with caregivers include meeting them before the school year begins and listening with an open mind and heart. While it may sound simplistic, educators often don't have the time or space to meet caregivers prior to the start of the school year—partly because demands on teachers are always increasing. This issue is challenging, particularly if caregivers aren't able to attend events such as Open House.

We therefore recommend that teachers initiate a meeting with caregivers and students before the first day of school. Perhaps caregivers can be reached by phone or email. In either case, the conversation should provide the teacher with knowledge about what the student *can* do, incorporating prompts such as, "Tell me about your child's strengths and interests."

SECTION 4: LISTENING TO EXPAND PERSPECTIVES

Task 5: Probing Even Deeper

Directions: Let's probe this background information more deeply. What additional potential threats to the individual's power, prestige, positioning, and access were identified in the background information presented? List all potential threats in Table 5, Expanded Considerations of Power, Prestige, Positioning, and Access.

Table 5. Expanded Considerations of Power, Prestige, Positioning, and Access

| Individual | BASED ON BACKGROUND INFORMATION, WHAT ARE ADDITIONAL POTENTIAL THREATS TO THE INDIVIDUAL'S . . . | | | |
	Power?	Prestige?	Positioning?	Access?
The Student	(no additional threats)	(no additional threats)	Joel's positioning in the classroom could affect how he is perceived by society more broadly.	(no additional threats)

Table 5. Expanded Considerations of Power, Prestige, Positioning, and Access (continued)

| Individual | BASED ON BACKGROUND INFORMATION, WHAT ARE ADDITIONAL POTENTIAL THREATS TO THE INDIVIDUAL'S . . . | | | |
	Power?	Prestige?	Positioning?	Access?
The Student's Caregivers	May feel powerless if the school doesn't communicate their concerns.	(no additional threats)	(no additional threats)	(no additional threats)
The Teacher	(no additional threats)	(no additional threats)	(no additional threats)	(no additional threats)

Task 6: Integrating

Directions: After considering this background, revisit the Case Scenario. Review information in Table 4. Consider how the potential threats listed in Table 5 overlap or extend the needs and threats listed in Table 4.

For each individual, complete Table 6 by revising the needs and threats according to the information contained in Tables 4 and 5.

Table 6. Revised Needs and Threats

Individual	Revised Needs & Threats (Real or Perceived)
The Student	Has belongingness and actualization needs; however, how school personnel perceive Joel's potential will affect his ability to achieve his full potential.
The Student's Caregivers	Belongingness, but if the school does not establish a partnership with Joel's caregivers to understand his strengths and needs, then they may feel their son is positioned as deficient.
The Teacher	Has esteem needs, but her power and prestige may be threatened if she does not agree with her colleagues' deficit perceptions of Joel.

SECTION 5: FIXING IT

Task 7: Analyzing

Directions: Complete Table 7, ABC Model, below. For each of the listed behaviors, identify the antecedents. These can be either known antecedents identified in the Case Scenario or potential antecedents outlined in Getting on the Same Page. Next, identify consequences (either known or potential).

Table 7. ABC Model

Antecedent	Behavior	Consequence
Joel's kindergarten teacher views his social behavior in the classroom as "abnormal."	School professionals label Joel as autistic.	Joel is viewed as lacking. School personnel only use deficit language and do not focus on his strengths.

Task 8: Identifying Action Steps

Directions: After completing the ABC chart above, select the desired behavior(s) that you want to encourage. You will complete Table 8 for each identified target behavior. In the table below, phrase the desired behavior in positive terms (i.e., as something you want to happen).

Next, brainstorm ways to alter the antecedents and/or consequences so that the selected behaviors are more likely to occur. By reviewing the expanded perspectives in Getting on the Same Page, you can identify antecedents/consequences that could contribute to increasing the desired behaviors.

Table 8. Target Behaviors

Selected Target Behavior: School Professionals Adopt a Strengths-Based Perspective of Students.

Altered Antecedents	Behavior	Altered Consequences
Ms. Shields is worried that she does not have the background or experience to a child on her class list who school personnel speculate is autistic. She finds resources in the district and enrolls in professional development. and outside to prepare her.	Ms. Shields to learns how to accommodate neurodiverse students so that the learning environment is inclusive, allowing her to meet all students' needs.	Ms. Shields has more confidence in her ability to work with autistic students. She reaches out to Joel's caregivers before school begins and establishes a relationship with them.

Working Together

In this scenario, the first and foremost concern is creating an environment that builds on Joel's strengths. Adopting this stance does not suggest that he may not have some needs that must be addressed, but it does advocate that those needs are met in collaboration with him and his caregivers using a strengths-based perspective. There is not one best solution for meeting Joel's needs, nor will a specific set of strategies work for every neurodiverse student. For example, some students are less disruptive if they are allowed to signal the teacher and receive permission to walk around the classroom, and other students are helped to understand that this is a legitimate accommodation. Sometimes the neurodiverse student can provide ideas for how they can be less disruptive. We recommend that with a strengths perspective some of the ideas offered below may help in creating a more inclusive classroom and school for neurodiverse students and their caregivers. Armstrong (2012) developed the concept of "positive niche construction," which means establishing an environment that enables all children to flourish (p. 4).

Identifying Students' Strengths

- Communicate with students identified as neurodiverse. What do they enjoy? What do they care about? What are they good at? Look for ways that their interests can be incorporated into the curriculum (Armstrong, 2012).

Establishing a Relationship/Partnership with Caregivers

- Initiate a conversation with caregivers to find out more about neurodiverse students and their family. Develop a list of 5 to 10 questions that will allow caregivers an opportunity to educate you about their child from their perspective.
- Provide caregivers time to ask you questions. Also, if you don't have an answer to a question, it's okay to say that you don't know or to ask for suggestions.
- Listen carefully to caregivers' responses and leave behind assumptions about neurodiverse students that you might hold that have been influenced by the deficit language used by other school personnel. Alternatively, caregivers may hold deficit assumptions themselves.
- Consider the context and timing for an interview with Joel's caregivers. Perhaps visiting them in their own home would be more comfortable and convenient for them and offer you the opportunity to see Joel in a different context in which he is more comfortable. If the parents/caregivers decline your offer, let them choose the location. This gesture demonstrates respect.

Model Advocacy for Inclusive Learning Environments

- Resist deficit talk about students when participating in conversations with other educators. According to Armstrong (2012), the following are examples of specific words that are regularly used to describe students: *disability, disorder, deficit,* and *dysfunction* (Armstrong, 2012, p. 3; emphasis in original). When the focus is on what students *cannot* do, change the conversation by asking what they *can* do. A statement as simple as "tell me about Joel's strengths" can quickly turn a negative conversation around, and lets those around you know that your disposition toward students is professional and that you promote your students.

- Model to other students and caregivers within the classroom and school communities that you are an advocate for all students by mentioning Joel's strengths in authentic situations.
- Understand that the discourse used in federal, state, and local policy may or may not reflect an asset-based perspective of neurodiverse students; however, using the language in documents (e.g., IEP) might be necessary to advocate for services.

Foregrounding an inclusive learning environment for all students also entails safety. Develop a plan to grow a learning community that is reinforced through positive language and, if necessary, appropriate accommodations for individual students. For example, if students respond to their own frustration in ways that might harm others in the classroom, then work with school personnel (e.g., school psychologist, learning consultant), caregivers, and individual students to develop a plan so they can seek refuge when needed in the classroom or, if necessary, another space in the school where the student feels safe.

SECTION 6: REBUILDING THE CASE

Although Ms. Shields is nearing the end of a successful 1st year of teaching 1st grade, she is concerned about a particular child, Joel, who has been placed in her classroom for the following year. While developing class lists for the upcoming year at a planning meeting attended by the school principal, the school psychologist, the learning specialist, and the other kindergarten and 1st-grade teachers, Ms. Shields hears Joel's kindergarten teacher make disparaging comments about Joel and his caregivers. Further, some caregivers have written letters to the principal requesting their child not be placed in a classroom with Joel the following year for issues related to safety.[1] The teacher states that she believes Joel has autism spectrum disorder (ASD) and that she has strategically placed him in Ms. Shields's classroom to ensure that he receive special education testing for a proper diagnosis.[2] This comment worries Ms. Shields because she doesn't feel prepared to teach an autistic child.[3] Although she deeply respects her colleagues, their behavior surprises her and she feels alone and unsupported.[4] Ms. Shields wonders who will help her work with Joel and his caregivers the following year. How will she manage a classroom with an autistic student? She also wonders what strengths Joel will have.[5]

1. While the kindergarten teacher's comments are unacceptable, she is enmeshed in a society where the pathology paradigm is normalized. If she has not had previous experience in working with neurodiverse students, she may lack both the confidence and resources to teach neurodiverse children. The principal should address concerns expressed by caregivers by listening and responding honestly and thoughtfully. School personnel should work together using human resources to develop an environment that supports Joel's needs as well as those of his classmates. In other words, the environment should accommodate all children. Caregivers can therefore be reassured that the school understands all children are different and that they are working to ensure that each child's needs are fairly and appropriately met, with safety as the primary concern.

2. Rather than assume that something is biologically deficient with Joel and that he needs to be "fixed" or "repaired," school personnel should reflect on the environment. Has the teacher developed an inclusive classroom? Is every child respected? Is the school, as a whole, inclusive of all students? A neurodiversity paradigm assumes there is no "normal" way for human brains to function (Walker, 2012).

3. Rather than agreeing with the teacher, Ms. Shields can change the conversation by inquiring about Joel's strengths and interests. This information provides her with ideas on how she should begin to build a curriculum that builds on his interests.

4. Although Ms. Shields does not support pathologizing language (e.g., "disorder"), she understands that federal, state, and district policy requires that she and colleagues use deficit discourse to advocate for services for Joel. He may, for example, benefit from particular services such as speech and language. School personnel can and should advocate and model a neurodiversity paradigm shift by using different terminology (e.g., neurodiverse, neuro-atypical) when discussing such students in the school context and in conversation with caregivers. It may be helpful to explain the purpose in using these terms to others in order to advocate for this paradigm shift.

5. Ms. Shields might consider contacting Joel's caregivers before the start of the new school year to meet with them and establish a relationship. These actions demonstrate that she not only cares about Joel, but also that she respects his caregivers and values their opinion and input. Establishing a family–school partnership is an effective way to find out about Joel's strengths and areas for growth to help him reach his potential.

REFERENCES

Armstrong, T. (2012). *Neurodiversity in the classroom: Strength-based strategies to help students with special needs succeed in school and life.* Alexandria, VA: ASCD.

Autism Spectrum Disorder. (n.d.). Retrieved from www.nimh.nih.gov/health/topics/autism-spectrum-disorders-asd/index.shtml?

Durgunoglu, A. Y., & Hughes, T. (2010). How prepared are the US preservice teachers to teach English language learners? *International Journal of Teaching and Learning in Higher Education, 22*(1), 32–41.

Edwards, P. A. (2016). *New ways to engage parents: Strategies and tools for teachers and leaders, K–12.* New York: NY. Teachers College Press.

Epstein, J. L. (2011). *School, family, and community partnerships: Preparing educators and improving schools* (2nd ed.). Boulder, CO: Westview Press.

Ferlazzo, L. (2011). Involvement or engagement? *Educational Leadership, 68*(8), 10–14.

Gorski, P. C. (2011). Unlearning deficit ideology and the scornful gaze: Thoughts on authenticating the class discourse in education. *Counterpoints, 402,* 152–173.

Koestler, C. (2016). Challenging and disrupting deficit notions in our work with early childhood and elementary teachers. In D. Y. White, S. Crespo, & M. Civil (Eds.), *Cases for mathematics teacher educators: Facilitating conversations about inequities in mathematics classrooms* (pp. 113–120). Charlotte, NC: Information Age Publishing, Inc.

Lortie, D. C. (1975). *Schoolteacher: A sociological study.* Chicago, IL: University of Chicago Press.

McDermott, R., & Varenne, H. (1995). Culture as disability. *Anthropology & Education Quarterly, 26*(3), 324–348.

Milner, H. R. (2012). But what is urban education? *Urban Education, 47*(3), 556–561.

Rozema, R. (2015). Manga and the autistic mind. *English Journal, 105*(1), 60–68.

Saleebey, D. (1996). The strengths perspective in social work practice: Extensions and cautions. *Social Work, 41*(3), 296–305.

Sheridan, S. M., & Gutkin, T. B. (2000). The ecology of school psychology: Examining and changing our paradigm for the 21st century. *School Psychology Review, 29*(4), 485.

Smagorinsky, P. (2014). Who's normal here? An atypical's perspective on mental health and educational inclusion. *English Journal,* 15–23.

Walker, N. (2013, August). Throw away the master's tools: Liberating ourselves from the pathology paradigm. Retrieved from neurocosmopolitanism.com/throw-away-the-masters-tools-liberating-ourselves-from-the-pathology-paradigm

---

MODULE 16

Families with Students Experiencing Life-Altering Developmental Disabilities

SECTION 1: CASE SCENARIO

Context

Autumn is a 7th-grade African American student at Parkway Middle School in a rural town in southwestern United States. Her family is considered upper middle class and speaks English in the home. Ms. Callahan is a White, middle-class woman in her late 40s. She has taught 7th grade at Parkway for 15 years and speaks only English.

Scenario

Ms. Callahan's class is hosting a Poetry Slam to celebrate the end of the first quarter. During the event, the students' caregivers seem to enjoy listening to the students perform their poetry. When Ms. Callahan calls Autumn to read her poem, she isn't in the classroom. After 20 minutes of searching, Autumn is found in one of the school bathrooms. Autumn says, "I am tired of my family not coming to school events because of my brother's disabilities." While Ms. Callahan thinks Autumn's behavior is inappropriate, she understands her feelings. Autumn's parents often say that Autumn's brother has doctor appointments or that he will disrupt the event, so they don't attend school events.

SECTION 2: EXPLORING CURRENT PERSPECTIVES

 Complete Appendix A, Tasks for Section 2: Exploring Current Perspectives.

SECTION 3: GETTING ON THE SAME PAGE

Defining Life-Altering Developmental Variations

Commonly, life-altering developmental variations are referred to as developmental disabilities or developmental delays. The U.S. Department of Health and Human Services (2017) defines *developmental disabilities* as "a group of conditions due to an impairment in physical, learning, language, or behavior areas. These conditions begin during the developmental period, may impact day-to-day functioning, and usually last throughout a person's lifetime" (para. 1). Recent data shows that in the United States approximately one in six children (about 15%) between the ages of 3 and 17 have at least one developmental disability (U.S. Department of Health and Human Services, 2017). We advocate for the use of *developmental variations* to explain the developmental profiles of these children. This terminology shifts viewing differences as deficient forms of development to a nondeterministic developmental trajectory. The phrase "life altering" does not mean that the developmental variation has a negative impact on the child and/or caregivers' daily lives, but rather connotes only that daily life changes in some manner. For example, a child with hearing loss might use a personal FM system in public spaces—a life-altering change that is minimally invasive and provides access to hearing.

Shifting to an Asset-Based Approach

As in the previous module, we propose shifting to an asset-based approach, which involves mindful action to (1) acknowledge the pervasive influence of the deficit-based approach on the medical and educational fields, and (2) change how society talks about and positions individuals with developmental variations.

Within the educational field, the Individuals with Disabilities Act (IDEA) (2009) formalized the language regarding differences in learning and ability. Each of the 14 designated disability categories situates the cause for a child's difference within the child. Further, eligibility for special education services requires that there is an *adverse effect* on the child's educational performance due to the disability. This foregrounds a deficit perspective that defines differences as internalized deficiencies requiring remediation via specialized instruction.

Impacts of Life-Altering Developmental Variations

The identification of a life-altering developmental variation may usher in a complex life that caregivers weren't expecting to live. For many families, the prognosis and path of this change are unknown. A second impact is experiencing chronic sorrow (Roos, 2002), a normal grief response for those living with daily loss. Caregivers grieve as they repeatedly experience a chasm between their family and child's current realities, the previous expectations for the future, and memories of the past. Societal and institutional barriers can exacerbate this grief experience. Third, families' weekly schedules may be affected due to the multiple therapy and doctor appointments. Caregivers typically encounter deficit approaches and terminology during these appointments, reflecting the prevalence of the deficit mindset within the medical and educational fields. As one caregiver reflected: "In my life, this has meant learning therapies that dictate the details of virtually every interaction I have with my daughter. . . . I have had to be trained in how to be with my kid" (Savoie, 2017, n.p.). In addition, caregivers might feel that doctors and therapists judge their abilities to support their child's development (Zero to Three, 2016).

Enacting an Asset-Based Approach

Teachers who work directly with students who have developmental variations, as well as teachers who teach the siblings/relatives of a student who has developmental variations, might try the following suggestions. First, use asset-based terminology by referring to a child's difference in a way that connotes a positive image of the child. Some asset-based terms include the terms "difference" or "variation." This positive image of variation can be incorporated into how we teach children to talk about development and plans for the future. For example, we can teach children to say that a child is "not yet" able to perform a skill rather than saying he/she can't or won't ever learn the skill.

Second, promote family/caregiver resilience as family members/ caregivers confront the effects of deficit-based perspectives and issues of inaccessibility. As teachers, we can frame "challenges" the family experiences as "barriers" caused by societal expectations or limitations to accessibility. For example, families might not be able to attend a school event since it is not a sensory-friendly environment, an environmental accessibility barrier.

Third, foster proactive caregiver engagement rather than involvement (Ishimaru et al., 2016). Often, caregivers of students with developmental variations are simply invited to be involved in the student's education. For example, caregivers may participate in the student's annual individualized education plan (IEP) meeting by sharing about their child's strengths and areas of need. Then other team members determine how to "fit" the student into the current educational system. To avoid positioning parents as informants, establish trusting and collaborative relationships that are sustained beyond the IEP process.

SECTION 4: LISTENING TO EXPAND PERSPECTIVES

 Complete Appendix B, Tasks for Section 4: Listening to Expand Perspectives.

SECTION 5: FIXING IT

 The following are suggestions for working with families who have a child with a life-altering developmental variation. These considerations are applicable for both children with life-altering developmental variations and their siblings. Complete Appendix C, Tasks for Section 5: Fixing It, for further reflection and analysis.

Enacting an Asset-Based Approach

- Establish respectful and trusting relationships with caregivers.
- Use asset-based language when speaking about the child who has life-altering developmental variations. Examples include "variation," "different," and "not yet being able to do a skill."

- For all students, develop goals linked to students' development and learning. Caregivers should help create these goals so they are connected to their family's knowledge and skills.
- Remember that you are the teacher for *all* the children in your classroom. Even if some students receive support from special education teachers or other specialists because of a life-altering developmental variation, the classroom teacher is each child's teacher and must collaborate with caregivers to find each child's strengths to propel them forward.

Acknowledging the Impacts of Life-Altering Developmental Variations

- Use asset-based approaches, recognizing that all students are different and that these differences can be used in ways that promote development and learning rather than limit them.
- Consider all forms of difference and the integrated impact that these differences have on the lived experiences for the student and family/caregivers.
- Build your capacity to view caregivers as capable and competent partners who contribute to their child's development. This can be done by participating in professional development opportunities, attending professional conferences, and reading publications addressing implementation of research-based family engagement practices.
- Develop strong and collaborative relationships with community partners who support the family.

SECTION 6: REBUILDING THE CASE

Ms. Callahan notes that Autumn's caregivers haven't attended any school events, so she calls them for input about the poetry cafe. The next day, Ms. Callahan calls Autumn's mom and shares, "I want to make the Poetry Slam accessible and enjoyable for everyone, so I am reaching out to a few families to see if they have ideas about ways to accomplish this."

Autumn's mom pauses. Then she says, "Well, one thing that comes to mind is to hold the event in the evening so that parents don't have to take time off work.[1] We can't miss work since we have to reserve our days for Autumn's brother's doctor appointments." Autumn's mom then takes a deep breath and says, "We don't want to make it hard for anyone, but it is a challenge for our family to attend school events because they aren't accessible for Autumn's brother. Autumn's brother is nonverbal and has intellectual disabilities. He makes loud sounds as a way to communicate, and people usually don't like this. Also, if the event is loud, he gets overstimulated."[2]

Ms. Callahan asks, "When you attend other social or public events, are there things you have found to be helpful?" Autumn's mom responds that having seats near an exit so the family can leave without too much commotion is helpful. Also, having a microphone so that the audience can hear the speaker over any additional sounds seems to reduce other people's irritation with their son. Ms. Callahan thinks these strategies[3] will be easy to incorporate and again thanks Autumn's mom for sharing.

1. For families with complex work situations, holding school events during the evening hours might still limit their engagement. Ms. Callahan could schedule her school events during various times (e.g., before school, during the lunch hour, on the weekends) throughout the year so that parents with complex work situations could potentially attend. She could also use video recordings to share these events with parents who cannot attend.

2. Accessibility needs for materials, social interactions, education, and physical spaces likely vary among individuals with developmental variations. Teachers should thus address accessibility at an individual level. Ms. Callahan can learn about accessibility by asking what types of things make experiences positive and which hinder participation.

3. If Ms. Callahan and Autumn live in an urban or suburban context, their school district and community might have additional accessibility resources, such as community organizations that provide respite care or child supervision during school events. When considering any accessibility resource, always remember to coordinate these efforts with caregivers.

REFERENCES

Individuals with Disabilities Education Improvement Act. (2009), 20 U.S.C. § 1400.

Ishimaru, A. M., Torres, K. E., Salvador, J. E., Lott, J., Cameron Williams, D. M, & Tran, C. (2016). Reinforcing deficit, journey toward equity: Cultural brokering in family engagement initiatives. *American Educational Research Journal, 53*(4), 850–882.

Roos, S. (2002). *Chronic sorrow: A living loss.* New York, NY: Brunner-Routledge.

Savoie, H. (2017). Don't know any young moms with special needs kids? They probably unfriended you. *Romper.* Retrieved from www.romper.com/p/dont-know-any-young-moms-with-special-needs-kids-they-probably-unfriended-you-73270

U.S. Department of Health and Human Services, Centers for Disease Control and Prevention. (2017). Developmental disabilities. Retrieved from www.cdc.gov/ncbddd/developmentaldisabilities/about.html

Zero to Three. (2016). *Tuning in: Parents of young children speak up about what they think, know, and need.* Washington, DC: Zero to Three.

ADDITIONAL RESOURCES

Council for Exceptional Children: www.cec.sped.org

Special Needs Project at the Ackerman Institute for the Family: www.ackerman.org
    /special-projects/resilient-families-children-with-special-needs-project

U.S. Departments of Education and Health and Human Services Joint Policy State-
    ment on Family Engagement: www2.ed.gov/about/inits/ed/earlylearning/files
    /policy-statement-on-family-engagement.pdf

MODULE 17
Caregivers Who Challenge Teaching

SECTION 1: CASE SCENARIO

Context

Ms. Danielson is a 26-year-old, White, English-speaking 1st-grade teacher from a middle-class background. She teaches at a suburban school.
Rebecca is a White, English monolingual, upper-middle-class student in
her classroom.

Scenario

Ms. Danielson's class has recently begun learning addition and subtraction
using math triangles and base-10 drawings to help students visualize parts,
totals, tens, and ones. She does not want students only to memorize facts
but also to understand what happens when they add and subtract.

However, after sending home the first homework assignment, Ms.
Danielson gets an email from Rebecca's father requesting a meeting. At
the meeting, Rebecca's father is upset because he does not know what
Rebecca is supposed to do on the homework: What are math triangles?
How is she supposed to draw the numbers? He just wants her to know
that 8 + 7 = 15; he doesn't want to teach her something that will confuse
what she is learning in school. He asks, "Why do schools keep changing
the methods? I memorized my addition and subtraction facts just fine.
As I read this homework, I can't understand what Rebecca needs to do. I

have two college degrees and can't even help my 1st-grade daughter with her work!"

SECTION 2: EXPLORING CURRENT PERSPECTIVES

 Complete Appendix A, Tasks for Section 2: Exploring Current Perspectives.

SECTION 3: GETTING ON THE SAME PAGE

Questioning Content

Caregivers might challenge pedagogy in multiple ways. They might object to books read in the classroom, question the content of lessons taught, or voice frustrations related to homework and teaching methods. When caregivers object to books and/or lesson content, this often involves conflicts with caregivers' values and the ways in which they see their children and wish to have them raised. For example, Brkich and Newkirk (2015) describe simulations they conducted with prospective social studies teachers to practice encounters with caregivers challenging their lessons. In their simulations, the authors found prospective teachers to be more successful when they justified their lessons and corresponding book selections using the standards they were teaching.

Muzevich (2008) reinforced this idea in her discussion of book challenges. She told teachers to "always preview and read a book first before sharing it with students. Know your purpose and how using the book with your students will help you achieve state standards for literacy instruction" (p. 24). She also suggested knowing the larger community and its general viewpoints on controversial issues. If book choices are challenged, Muzevich's first recommendation is to "listen calmly and respectfully to the parent's concern" (p. 24). Listening to caregivers is one of the first and most important things a teacher can do. Applebaum (2009) also recommends listening to caregivers, even when they sound like they are telling teachers how or what to teach. In addition, she recommends acknowledging caregivers' knowledge/expertise and being prepared for the conversation (such as being able to explain why teachers are teaching in this way and how it connects to the standards).

Questioning Methods

Caregivers might not only question content; they may also question homework or the methods used to teach a concept. Often these concerns stem from their seeing their child struggle and their feelings of being unable to help. For example, in a case scenario similar to this module published by the Harvard Family Research Project (2004), a child's father feels frustrated that he cannot help his daughter with math, that not only does he (and his child) not fully understand what is required for the homework assignment, but there is also no textbook to use for reference. The Harvard Family Research Project recommends that homework should be used for practicing familiar strategies, not new material. They also suggest taking video of children learning math or being taught math strategies so that caregivers can learn along with their students and see the lesson in action.

In my (Lisa's) experience, when I taught new methods for mathematics, I sometimes received push-back from caregivers. This stemmed from their feelings of frustration that they didn't know what was expected of their children or how to help them because they were unfamiliar with the methods we were using, and they didn't want to confuse their children. I found success when I sent caregivers the "take-home letters" for each unit explaining aspects of the curriculum and why I taught particular methods. In addition, I emailed caregivers copies of the math problems we completed in class with all of the work shown (and sometimes keys to the math homework if I knew it might be challenging and would not be graded for accuracy). In these ways, I tried to lessen the stressors for caregivers, work with them to help their children understand the content, and provide them with resources so they felt knowledgeable and empowered.

SECTION 4: LISTENING TO EXPAND PERSPECTIVES

 Complete Appendix B, Tasks for Section 4: Listening to Expand Perspectives.

SECTION 5: FIXING IT

 The following are suggestions for working with caregivers who may question or challenge teachers' pedagogy. Complete Appendix C, Tasks for Section 5: Fixing It, for further reflection and analysis.

Questioning Content

- Be prepared by having reviewed and read materials before teaching them and by knowing how lessons and pedagogy address standards.

Questioning Methods

- Find ways of helping caregivers learn about and understand what is expected and done in class, such as through videos, letters, example assignments/problems, and so on.

Developing Dispositions

- Listen to caregivers' concerns. Acknowledge their feelings and expertise. (This might mean allowing caregivers to teach their children other methods of learning the information while letting caregivers know that the ultimate goal is understanding rather than following specific steps or procedures.)
- Work hard to ensure that all assignments students must complete at home are within their independent ability level. If they are difficult and still must be assigned, consider how to provide help and scaffolding for both students and caregivers.

SECTION 6: REBUILDING THE CASE

Ms. Danielson is teaching mathematics in ways that are different from traditional methods of memorizing addition and subtraction facts. Because she knew this would be different for families, she sent home example problems that show what students are expected to do on their homework.[1]

However, Ms. Danielson receives a meeting request from Rebecca's father because he is frustrated that even with two college degrees he doesn't understand Rebecca's homework and cannot help her. Ms. Danielson listens to Rebecca's father's concerns and hears that he wants to support his daughter and her homework, but that he needs more support in knowing what Ms. Danielson expects. Ms. Danielson responds: "I understand you are trying to help Rebecca with her homework, which I really appreciate. The reason we are learning these methods is so that children understand what it means to add and subtract before they memorize the facts. I will try to send home more example problems and information showing how we use math triangles and base-10 drawings to solve these types of problems. Is there anything else I can do to help make the homework process easier?[2] Also, if Rebecca struggles with particular problems, if you circle them and write a quick note on her homework, I'll make sure to review those problems with her at school."[3]

1. It is very important that communication sent to caregivers is written so they can understand. This means limiting jargon and explaining any specialized terms used, as well as considering if caregivers speak languages other than English. If caregivers cannot read, consider whether audio or visual methods would help communicate the ideas.

If students live in multiple households, consider ways for all caregivers to access this information. Sending one copy of a paper in take-home folders likely will not be enough. Perhaps you can email caregivers or send home multiple copies.

2. It is important that the teacher gain input from the caregiver. The caregiver knows the student's interests, strengths, needs, and home situation—all of which is important information to facilitate collaboration to support the student's learning and growth.

3. Depending on work schedules and/or schooling and background knowledge, caregivers might not always be able to help with homework. By having caregivers note children's struggles with homework and by supporting them at school, teachers learn more about and continue to support students' learning. They also increase communication with caregivers while being flexible to their needs.

REFERENCES

Applebaum, M. (2009). *How to handle hard-to-handle parents*. Thousand Oaks, CA: Corwin.

Brkich, C. A., & Newkirk, A. C. (2015). Interacting with upset parents/guardians: Defending justice-oriented social studies lessons in parent–teacher conference simulations. *Theory & Research in Social Education, 43*(4), 528–559.

Harvard Family Research Project. (2004). Family engagement teaching cases: "Daddy says this new math is crazy." Retrieved from www.hfrp.org/publications -resources/publications-series/family-engagement-teaching-cases/daddy-says -this-new-math-is-crazy

Muzevich, K. (2008, October/November). Defending intellectual freedom. *Reading Today, 26*(2), 24.

ADDITIONAL RESOURCES

Cerra, C., & Jacoby, R. (n.d.). How to solve six tough parent problems. Retrieved from www.scholastic.com/teachers/articles/teaching-content/how-solve-six-tough -parent-problems

MODULE 18

Caregivers with Frequent Concerns

SECTION 1: CASE SCENARIO

Context

Ms. Wyler is a White, 46-year-old, English-speaking, upper-middle-class, 3rd-grade teacher in a suburban school. One of her students, Marilyn, is a White, English-speaking child from an upper-middle-class family.

Scenario

Each morning, Marilyn's mother walks her to her locker, holds her books as she takes them out of her backpack, and makes sure Marilyn has everything she needs before saying goodbye when the bell rings. If Marilyn forgets something—lunch money, a snack, homework, money for the Book Fair—her mother immediately brings it to her. It is a similar routine at the end of the day, with her mother waiting outside the classroom to help Marilyn pack up before she takes her home.

At Open House before the school year started, Marilyn's mother expressed concerns that her daughter does not have many friends. She asked to have a meeting with Ms. Wyler the first week of school to discuss ways to help Marilyn make friends.

Even after the meeting, Marilyn's mother frequently emails to check on her daughter's friendships or talks to Ms. Wyler after school. This usually happens on the days she volunteers in Marilyn's younger brother's kindergarten class. She finishes volunteering around lunchtime, walks by the cafeteria, and sees Marilyn sitting next to peers—but not interacting with them. Sometimes Ms. Wyler passes Marilyn's mother in the hall on the way to the staff lounge to eat her own lunch, and Marilyn's mother again brings up her concerns.

SECTION 2: EXPLORING CURRENT PERSPECTIVES

Task 1: Initial reaction

Directions: Consider how you would react to the scenario if you were the student's teacher. The guiding questions below will support your thoughtful reflection. Jot down notes or bullet points that respond to each of the guiding questions.

1. After "experiencing" the scenario, what would your feelings and inner thoughts be?

   As a teacher, I may feel frustrated and overwhelmed that Marilyn's mother is constantly contacting me. I have a full class of students to get to know, support, and help learn as well as a lot of lesson planning to do and other responsibilities. While I definitely care about Marilyn, I need to attend to all of my students.

2. How would you respond to this situation?

   I would hope to be understanding and respectful and try to get to the heart of Marilyn's mother's concerns, but I may jump to conclusions about her actions and/or be reluctant to respond to her emails and requests to talk since they are so frequent.

3. What do you know or did you learn about the student as a learner from this experience?

   This scenario was more focused on Marilyn's mother. I would need to observe Marilyn more and get to know her better to try to determine what might be affecting her ability to form friendships in the classroom.

4. What do you know or did you learn about the student's family?

   Marilyn's mother seems to want to be involved and worries about Marilyn making friends.

Task 2: Maslow's Hierarchy

Directions: Consider Maslow's (1943) Hierarchy of Needs (see Figure 2.1). Then complete Table 2.

Table 2. Mapping Individual Needs onto Maslow's Hierarchy

Individual	What are the individual's needs as described in the scenario?	Where do these needs fit on Maslow's Hierarchy of Needs?
The Student	Friendship and perhaps more opportunities for independence	Belongingness and perhaps esteem
The Student's Caregiver (Mother)	Be involved and take care of her daughter	Belongingness and supporting her daughter's self-actualization needs
The Teacher	To be able to run her classroom and support all of her students' academic and social needs	Esteem

Task 3: Probing Deeper

Directions: Consider issues of power, positioning, prestige, and access as defined in Chapter 2. Complete Table 3, Considerations of Power, Positioning, Prestige, and Access, based on the case scenario.

Table 3. Considerations of Power, Positioning, Prestige, and Access

Individual	WHAT ARE THE THREATS (REAL OR PERCEIVED) TO THE INDIVIDUAL'S . . .			
	Power?	**Prestige?**	**Positioning?**	**Access?**
The Student	Mother's frequent presence and help at school with tasks may affect opportunities for independence	—	Potentially positioned as dependent on her mother	Mother's frequent presence could affect access to opportunities for socialization
The Student's Caregiver (Mother)	Doesn't have as much power/control over school environment as she does at home	May feel a loss of prestige as school takes a larger role in her daughter's life	May feel positioned as taking a less central/less important role in her daughter's life	May feel worried about access to her daughter and school
The Teacher	May feel power to run the classroom is being affected by frequent communication from and worries of Marilyn's mother	May feel some of her authority or knowledge of teaching is questioned, which would lead to a loss of prestige	May feel positioned as inadequate in her role as teacher because of frequent concerns	Her own access is not threatened, but may feel caregiver has too much access

Task 4: Summarizing

Directions: For each individual, compare what they need (Table 2) with what threats they are experiencing to their power, prestige, positioning, and access (Table 3). What overlaps exist between Table 2 and Table 3? Write down any overlapping needs and threats in Table 4, Summarizing Overlapping Needs and Threats.

Table 4. Summarizing Overlapping Needs and Threats

Individual	Overlapping Needs & Threats (Real or Perceived)
The Student	Has needs related to belonging and self-esteem, but there may be threats to this based on how she is positioned.
The Student's Caregiver (Mother)	Has needs related to belonging, but likely feels a loss of power and prestige by how she is positioned.
The Teacher	Has esteem-related needs, but likely feels potential threats to her power and prestige by how she is positioned.

SECTION 3: GETTING ON THE SAME PAGE

Caregivers' Concerns

Caregivers might have many concerns about their children at any given time. They want their children to be happy and successful. They might worry and want to be kept abreast of their child's grades because their child struggles in a subject or might not work to their potential without someone monitoring their progress. Caregivers' concerns might also involve ongoing behavior issues. However, some caregivers are in frequent, almost constant, contact with teachers and/or the school about their worries.

Sometimes caregivers' concerns manifest themselves in actions they take to make their children's lives easier by shielding them from potential problems or stumbling blocks, such as retrieving forgotten homework, asking teachers to lessen or remove consequences for misbehaviors, doing school projects for their children, asking for special classmate or teacher pairings for their children, and so on. If their children are upset to miss recess to complete a missing assignment or as a behavior consequence, they step in and try to request a change to alleviate the children's anxiety. When caregivers are hovering nearby, ready to land and fix any problems their children may have, caregivers may be termed "helicopter" parents/caregivers (Cline & Fay, 2006; Hiltz, 2015). However, as Hiltz (2015) reiterates, not all "helicopter" caregivers are alike, and this negative stereotype can be detrimental. In fact, negatively stereotyping caregivers in this way is no less harmful or counterproductive than doing the same with students. Some parents might be overprotective, others want to be involved, and others want to be heard because in the past their needs and concerns have not been met. As Hiltz (2015), a teacher and parent, reminds us: "A parent's perception is their reality" (p. 28); "by encouraging open communication, teachers can begin to understand the motivations of these parents and find creative ways to connect them with opportunities to promote their students' academic success and the school's overall effectiveness" (p. 29). Engaging in open dialogue with caregivers and trying to understand their underlying motivations and needs is critical.

Considering Underlying Needs or Motivations

Once teachers have some ideas about caregivers' needs and motivations, they can try to determine how to meet these needs (and even ward off future worries/concerns) in ways that are feasible for the teacher and satisfactory for the caregiver. Perhaps caregivers who want to keep track of their children's grades know their children have a history of not bringing home papers, and they want to make sure that if their children are not understanding something, they can help before their children get too far behind. In this case, maybe an electronic weekly grade report without the comments section would suffice. Then caregivers dependably receive information and can act on it as necessary.

If caregivers are worried about their children's behavior, they might be trying to align their home expectations with those at school. If students already bring home a daily folder or planner, maybe teachers can draw a quick behavior symbol (such as a smiley face) or write a short note—something that would support communication with caregivers but require little time and effort.

If caregivers are always at the school wanting to check in with their children or are worried about their children's interactions or achievement, perhaps teachers can involve them with a meaningful classroom volunteer opportunity. This could give the caregiver peace of mind as to the classroom environment and how teachers interact with their class while offering help through extra skill reinforcement for students who need it. When scheduling these volunteer opportunities, ensure that the main focus is on helping students, as too many caregivers volunteering at once can be overwhelming for everyone, and caregivers want to be useful, not just an extra body. This leads to Cleaver's (2008) recommendation about setting boundaries—that teachers should acknowledge the caregiver's needs, but the volunteer situations must be feasible for teachers. However, most importantly, the volunteer opportunities should also meet the children's needs.

Learning about and being responsive to children's and caregivers' needs in these situations is critical. To do so, teachers might need to observe the student in question more closely to learn more about the caregivers' concerns or perhaps intervene to take care of an issue. It might also mean that teachers hold fast to their convictions and enforce the set consequences for students' behavior/action/lack of action in a consistent-but-caring manner while helping the caregiver and student see the imposed consequence as a learning opportunity and a short-term event that will help them in the future.

There have been instances when I (Lisa) had caregivers who frequently contacted me with concerns or to check in or who wanted to change or avoid consequences their child encountered. It became important for me not to focus exclusively on what parents said or did, but instead to focus on what their underlying, often unsaid, needs were. If caregivers were trying to lessen negative consequences for their child, I tried to make sure there were opportunities for children to make mistakes without negative consequences, such as having a free forgotten assignment each marking period. However, I also explained my reasoning for my class policies and explained the ways in which I was trying to support their child in developing responsibility because learning it at a young age would set them up for later success.

For caregivers who wanted to frequently be involved in the classroom, I tried to design volunteer opportunities that supported everyone's needs. Having weekly math groups during which caregivers facilitated small-group math games or activities allowed me to provide targeted reteaching or extension based on students' needs. In this way, caregivers made substantive contributions to the classroom.

SECTION 4: LISTENING TO EXPAND PERSPECTIVES

Task 5: Probing Even Deeper

Directions: Let's probe this background information more deeply. What additional potential threats to the individual's power, prestige, positioning, and access were identified in the background information presented? List all potential threats in Table 5, Expanded Considerations of Power, Prestige, Positioning, and Access.

Table 5. Expanded Considerations of Power, Prestige, Positioning, and Access

| Individual | BASED ON BACKGROUND INFORMATION, WHAT ARE ADDITIONAL POTENTIAL THREATS TO THE INDIVIDUAL'S . . . | | | |
	Power?	**Prestige?**	**Positioning?**	**Access?**
The Student	No additional threats	No additional threats	The ways in which Marilyn is positioned in the classroom or in school could also be affecting her socially.	Underlying Marilyn's mother's actions seems to be a genuine concern about threats to Marilyn's access to opportunities, success in school, and friendships.
The Student's Caregiver (Mother)	Might feel her ability or opportunity to advocate for her daughter is diminished	No additional threats	No additional threats	No additional threats
The Teacher	No additional threats	No additional threats	No additional threats	No additional threats

Task 6: Integrating

Directions: After considering this background, revisit the Case Scenario. Review the information in Table 4. Consider how the potential threats listed in Table 5 overlap or extend the needs and threats listed in Table 4.

For each individual, complete Table 6 by revising the needs and threats according to the information contained in Tables 4 and 5.

Table 6. Revised Needs and Threats

Individual	Revised Needs & Threats (Real or Perceived)
The Student	Has needs related to belonging and self-esteem, but there may be threats to this based on how she is positioned as well as lack of access.
The Student's Caregivers	Has needs related to belonging and supporting her daughter's self-actualization needs, but likely feels a loss of power and prestige by how she is positioned.
The Teacher	Has esteem-related needs, but likely feels potential threats to her power and prestige by how she is positioned.

SECTION 5: FIXING IT

Task 7: Analyzing

Directions: Complete Table 7, ABC Model, below. For each of the listed behaviors, identify the antecedents. These can be either known antecedents identified in the Case Scenario or potential antecedents outlined in Getting on the Same Page. Next, identify consequences (either known or potential).

Table 7. ABC Model

Antecedent	Behavior	Consequence
Marilyn's mother is worried that Marilyn does not have friends.	Marilyn's mother frequently contacts Ms. Wyler with concerns via email and in person.	Ms. Wyler may feel frustrated or overwhelmed and be reluctant to talk to Marilyn's mother.
Marilyn's mother is worried about her daughter being successful and may also feel she has a diminished role in her life compared to school.	Marilyn's mother brings anything Marilyn forgets and stays at school longer than typical drop-off and pick-up times.	Marilyn may struggle with independence. It's possible that she misses time to socialize with peers because her mother stays longer at drop-off and pick-up.

Task 8: Identifying Action Steps

Directions: After completing the ABC chart above, select the desired behavior(s) that you want to encourage. You will complete Table 8 for each identified target behavior. In the table below, phrase the desired behavior in positive terms (i.e., as something you want to happen).

Next, brainstorm ways to alter the antecedents and/or consequences so that the selected behaviors are more likely to occur. By reviewing the expanded perspectives in Getting on the Same Page, you can identify antecedents/consequences that could contribute to increasing the desired behaviors.

Table 8. Target Behaviors

Selected Target Behavior: Marilyn's mother contacts Ms. Wyler less frequently.

Altered Antecedents	Behavior	Altered Consequences
Ms. Wyler tries different grouping strategies and ways of partnering students to help Marilyn get to know her classmates. She creates a plan with Marilyn's mother for when she will contact Marilyn's mother with updates. Marilyn's mother schedules some playdates for Marilyn with her classmates.	Marilyn's mother contacts Ms. Wyler less frequently.	Marilyn's mother feels her concerns are being addressed, and she is receiving updates, so she contacts Ms. Wyler less frequently.

Selected Target Behavior: Marilyn's mother provides Marilyn with more opportunities for independence.

Altered Antecedents	Behavior	Altered Consequences
Ms. Wyler lets Marilyn and her mother know that if Marilyn forgets her money for the Book Fair, there are other days she can shop; that if she forgets lunch money, there is always an alternate lunch available; that if she forgets homework, she has a free missing homework pass each marking period. Therefore, Marilyn has opportunities to develop independence in an environment where the potential consequences are light and Marilyn's needs will still be met. Ms. Wyler and Marilyn's mother also discuss how some days it might help Marilyn to spend time before school alone on the playground before the bell rings to provide more opportunities to socialize with classmates.	Marilyn's mother provides Marilyn with more opportunities for independence.	Marilyn has more opportunities to develop independence and to socialize with her classmates.

Selected Target Behavior: Marilyn interacts with her classmates more.

Altered Antecedents	Behavior	Altered Consequences
Ms. Wyler looks for ways to support Marilyn's socialization at school by putting Marilyn in work groups that require conversation and interaction.	Marilyn interacts with her classmates more.	Marilyn has more opportunities to socialize with her classmates.

Considering Underlying Needs or Motivations

- Find ways to recognize students' talents and positive attributes (in class and sharing this information with caregivers). This helps students feel they are competent and contributing members of the larger classroom community, making them feel safe and cared for, which can alleviate caregiver concerns.
- Engaging caregivers in classroom volunteering for those with frequent concerns may help them feel more a part of the classroom community and gives them opportunities to see their child's interactions in class as well as the instruction they receive.
- Sometimes boundaries need to be set regarding pick-up, drop-off, and classroom space. School staff might ask all caregivers to wait outside the building to pick up their children because students are learning right up until the bell rings and are often distracted when seeing caregivers waiting outside their doors.
- Expectations regarding forgotten items (and other classroom procedures and expectations) need to be established and communicated from the beginning of the year. Then they need to be consistently enforced in a caring manner. Let caregivers and children know there will be times in life that they won't have someone who can get forgotten things for them (or that caregivers may have other commitments with their time), but let children and caregivers know how their important needs will still be met—for example, there will be an alternative lunch, there will be other opportunities to order from the Book Fair, and so on.

SECTION 6: REBUILDING THE CASE

Marilyn's mother is at school every day and brings anything Marilyn forgets. She expresses concerns to Marilyn's 3rd-grade teacher, Ms. Wyler, that Marilyn does not seem to have close friendships. Marilyn's mother schedules a meeting with Ms. Wyler during the first week of school to discuss ways to help Marilyn make friends and how Ms. Wyler groups students in the classroom. At this meeting, Ms. Wyler explains how she provides many opportunities for students to interact and work together in various ways and that she will be observing Marilyn interact with peers over the next few weeks of school.[1] Ms. Wyler promises to email Marilyn's mother in approximately 2 weeks to share her observations.[2]

During these 2 weeks, Ms. Wyler observes Marilyn working in activities alongside her peers, but not engaging directly with them. Therefore, Ms. Wyler structures her activities in ways that require students to talk and interact. She also groups students in multiple ways to practice the content so that Marilyn works with many different peers throughout the week, but she also strategically partners students for some long-term activities so they can get to know each other more deeply.[3] After 2 weeks, Ms. Wyler emails Marilyn's mother to share her observations, steps she has taken to help Marilyn, and positive things she has noticed Marilyn doing.[4] Ms. Wyler agrees to talk with Marilyn's mother briefly the next day when she comes to pick up Marilyn to discuss next steps at school and at home.[5]

1. Instead of focusing on how Marilyn's mother is always at school or her frequent communication and worry, Ms. Wyler focuses on Marilyn's mother's underlying concerns and works to address them.

2. Creating a communication plan helps reassure Marilyn's mother while also lessening her need to check in and communicate. However, Ms. Wyler needs to follow through on her promise and make sure she communicates using a method that works best for her and Marilyn's mother. If Marilyn's mother is illiterate, speaks a language other than English, works multiple jobs or evening hours, or is a noncustodial parent, Ms. Wyler may need to find other communication methods.

3. It is important that Ms. Wyler try some solutions at school based on what she has control over. This helps caregivers see that Ms. Wyler is both validating and trying to address their concerns.

4. Making sure to mention positives is important in building relationships with caregivers and students.

5. Similar to the comments about the email communication plan above, Ms. Wyler needs to find a meeting time, place, and method that works for everyone, taking into consideration caregivers' work schedules, languages, past experiences with school that affect their comfort levels meeting at school, and so on.

It is also important that Ms. Wyler create a plan for both parties—herself at school and the caregivers—so that everyone is working together to support Marilyn. (In this case, Ms. Wyler may recommend that Marilyn and her family try to schedule playdates with specific students.)

REFERENCES

Cleaver, S. (2008). Meet the micro-managers. *Instructor, 118*(3), 30–36.
Cline, F., & Fay, J. (2006). *Parenting with love and logic: Teaching children responsibility.* Colorado Springs, CO: NavPress.

Hiltz, J. (2015). Helicopter parents can be a good thing. *Phi Delta Kappan, 96*(7), 26–29. Retrieved from www.kappanonline.org/helicopter-parents-can-good-thing

ADDITIONAL RESOURCES

Cox, J. (n.d.). Classroom management tips to tame helicopter parents. Retrieved from www.teachhub.com/classroom-management-tips-tame-helicopter-parents
Gatens, B. (2015, July 13). Helicopter parents: How teachers can bring them back to Earth. *Room 241.* Retrieved from education.cu-portland.edu/blog/curriculum -teaching-strategies/helicopter-parents-teachers

MODULE 19
Adversarial/Confrontational Caregivers

SECTION 1: CASE SCENARIO

Context

Alex is an African American student in Ms. Petty's 3rd-grade class at Brentwood Elementary in the southeastern United States. Alex's mother, a single parent, works as a security guard. Their family is considered lower working class.

Ms. Petty is a White, middle-class woman in her late 20s. She is in her 6th year of teaching at Brentwood, an urban school funded by Title I.

Scenario

Thanksgiving is quickly approaching, and Ms. Petty has recently finished conducting parent–teacher conferences, for those caregivers who attended. Student report cards were distributed after parent–teacher conferences. Alex is a child in Ms. Petty's 3rd-grade class who is often disruptive to learning in class at times. Alex's mother did not sign up for a conference. Ms. Petty's few interactions with Alex's mother include a couple of phone calls about Alex's behavior. Each time they speak, Alex's mother asks Ms. Petty for her "side of the story," which leaves Ms. Petty feeling that Alex's mother thinks she is wrongly accusing Alex. Ms. Petty is concerned that Alex's behavior negatively affects classroom learning. Since Alex's mother did not attend a conference, Ms. Petty has yet to discuss the academic implications of his behavior.

Most recently, Alex's mother came to Ms. Petty's classroom during the students' arrival and confronted Ms. Petty in front of her students. She walked into the classroom, pointed her finger, and accused Ms. Petty of targeting her child. Although Alex had admitted to Ms. Petty that he had caused disruptions for students at his table by shaking a water bottle in their faces, his mother was upset because Ms. Petty asked him to throw away the disposable bottle. She claimed that Ms. Petty deprived her child of water and that Ms. Petty had been "picking on her child." As Ms. Petty calmly tried to explain that Alex's mom should make an appointment for a meeting, Alex's mother continued to yell. Finally, after a few minutes, she stormed out. Ms. Petty was left wondering how she could move forward with this parent and create a positive learning environment for Alex.

SECTION 2: EXPLORING CURRENT PERSPECTIVES

 Complete Appendix A, Tasks for Section 2: Exploring Current Perspectives.

SECTION 3: GETTING ON THE SAME PAGE

Establishing positive relationships can sometimes be difficult. Some caregivers may not know how to begin talking with a teacher to help their child. Caregivers' own challenging school experiences in the past might tarnish their perspective on their child's schooling. As a result, a caregiver might come across as difficult or confrontational. There are often steps teachers can take to preempt any confrontational situations by building trust and helping caregivers set the stage for their child's success. Other times, however, teachers should be prepared with strategies for how to best react and handle potentially hostile situations.

Building Trust

Adams and Christenson (2000) emphasize the importance of collaboration and cooperation between caregivers and teachers. The authors report how trust between caregivers and teachers is a critical component of fostering collaboration. When a caregiver–teacher relationship is founded on mutual trust from the beginning, hostility and confrontations are less likely. Teachers can build trust with caregivers by demonstrating an openness to learn about the differences between the teacher and the student's caregivers. One way is by inviting caregivers to share their "stories," as recommended by Edwards, Pleasants, and Franklin (1999). Having caregivers share their stories of their family and perhaps their own schooling provides an opportunity for caregivers to feel understood, or heard, as well as begins to foster an open line of communication, in turn beginning to build trust.

Adams and Christenson (1999) assert that if a "crisis" occurs in a classroom situation, having a relationship with a child's caregiver that is founded on mutual trust will help all parties navigate the situation better.

Setting the Stage

Robinson and Harris use the metaphor of "setting the stage" to refer to family support of their children's academic success (2014, p. 199). There are two steps that caregivers can take to set the stage for their child's academic success. First, caregivers conveying the importance of education is critical. Second, caregivers can take measures to help children maximize their opportunities for learning (Robinson & Harris, 2014). At times, some caregivers may have difficulty in conveying positive messages about schooling and education. By providing space for caregivers to reflect on their own schooling experiences, teachers can help caregivers envision how they would like to see their child's education proceed.

Teachers can set the stage for students' academic success in ways that might preempt any potential miscommunications or confrontations with caregivers. One way teachers might do this is by consciously making an effort to start the year off with positive communications with caregivers. Such communication might take different forms. For example, teachers might make a point to send a positive note home at the beginning of the year in which they have noted something positive or interesting about a particular student. The note might say, "Alex enjoyed reading about spiders in our reading group today. Ask him to share what he learned." This communication is a quick way for caregivers to see that teachers are taking time to get to know each student as an individual and hoping to work alongside caregivers to help their children. Another way to set the stage for positive communication is to make a point to briefly connect with the caregiver in passing. If a teacher sees a parent at carpool or drop-off, the teacher might take the opportunity to say, "Alex worked really hard in math today. He shared his thinking and taught his classmates a new way to solve addition problems." This quick connection also shares with families a teacher's acknowledgment of a child as an individual and demonstrates a caring attitude. Setting the stage through ideas like these will help parents see that teachers are hoping to work with them and build partnerships, thus preventing future confrontations. For communication to be genuine, teachers must be always on the lookout for positive progress and behaviors to support.

Strategies for Reacting to Confrontation

Teachers work with children from many walks of life. Occasionally, teachers encounter situations with difficult caregivers, ranging from a caregiver who sends an excessive amount of emails to a confrontation at school. When entering the teaching profession, many teachers are underprepared for how to react to confrontational family members. Boutte and colleagues (1992) urge teachers, when faced with a confrontational caregiver, to remain calm and not to argue. It is human nature to defend oneself, but becoming defensive may only heighten the situation. Instead, Boutte and colleagues recommend that teachers seek the assistance of a colleague, preferably an administrator. It is within a teacher's rights to ask a caregiver to make an appointment to meet and to invite an administrator to be present at the meeting. Also, documenting any meeting or contact, by keeping notes or a journal, is helpful for when situations like these occur. These days, for everyone's safety, most schools have procedures in place for notifying the office that support is needed if a parent is confrontational.

SECTION 4: LISTENING TO EXPAND PERSPECTIVES

Complete Appendix B, Tasks for Section 4: Listening to Expand Perspectives.

SECTION 5: FIXING IT

Teachers can potentially preempt any potentially hostile or confrontational situations by taking some of the following steps. Complete Appendix C, Tasks for Section 5: Fixing It, for further reflection and analysis.

Building Trust

- Consider asking caregivers to fill out a brief survey when they come to the first open house. Ask questions like, "What concerns might you have about your child's schooling this coming year?" or "How does your child learn best at home?"
- Consider reaching out to caregivers, via email, conference, or phone call, about a positive experience you have had with their child. Hearing positive sentiments about their child may help them warm up to you and see that you are working to help their child. Sometimes caregivers who previously have heard only negative things about their child may enter new teacher–family relationships with hard feelings. Sometimes inviting caregivers to talk about negative experiences and assuring them that you hope to work with them in positive ways can forge a productive partnership.

Setting the Stage

- Ask caregivers to share stories from their own education experiences. Ask them to reflect on how their experiences might affect their interaction with their children. Ask them to think about their goals for their child's education. You might consider doing this during parent–teacher conferences.
- Consider sharing with families that school involvement involves more than helping out with special school events. Caregivers can be involved by talking with their children and encouraging them to do their best in school. This type of involvement is more important than showing up at schools. Because of hectic work schedules, many caregivers cannot make it to school events. It would be helpful for them to know that being involved can be as simple as talking with their children.

Strategies for Reacting to Confrontation

Sometimes, building trust and setting the stage might not deter a caregiver from being confrontational. In such cases, it is helpful for teachers to know appropriate ways to react. Below are some tips for teachers to consider when facing confrontational situations involving caregivers.

- Remain calm. Despite a caregiver's behavior toward you, make sure you take a deep breath and stay calm.
- Do not argue with the caregiver. Getting into a heated exchange might only make things worse. You will have an opportunity to share your thoughts in a calm way at some point, but during a confrontation is probably not the best time.
- If a confrontation occurs during a caregiver–teacher meeting, remind the caregiver of the purpose of the meeting. You might remind them of your partnership and how you both are working for the best for their child.
- It's okay to end the meeting early and reschedule it (even with an administrator).

SECTION 6: REBUILDING THE CASE

Thanksgiving is quickly approaching, and teachers are finishing conducting fall parent–teacher conferences, for those caregivers who attended. Student report cards were distributed after conferences. Alex is a child in Ms. Petty's 3rd-grade class who has proven to be disruptive to learning in class at times and is performing below grade-level academic expectations. Ms. Petty was disappointed that Alex's mother did not sign up for a conference. Their initial interactions were centered on Alex's mom asking Ms. Petty for her "side of the story" when Ms. Petty called to notify Alex's mom about his disruptive behavior. Ms. Petty feels strongly that conducting a conference will help build a partnership with Alex's mom. She decides to make the effort to reach out to her to connect about Alex's work in a positive way. She sends home a note letting Alex's mom know how hard Alex has worked on a project. She also saw Alex's mom at dismissal one day and informed her of Alex's demonstration of kindness to his classmates.[1] Although Alex's mother didn't seem very warm in the moment, she has stopped asking Ms. Petty for her side of the story. Instead, she asks, "What happened?" and says she will speak with Alex about it.

Ms. Petty also called Alex's mom to personally invite her to come in for a conference. Prior to parent–teacher conferences, Ms. Petty had surveyed caregivers on their child's strengths and what the caregiver's goals were for their children. Alex's mom came to the conference, and Ms. Petty began by asking her to tell her more about her survey answers.[2] Alex's mom shared some anecdotes about Alex's at-home behavior and strategies she used at home. Although she questioned Ms. Petty about a few incidents in which Alex was disruptive, Alex's mom listened to the concerns about how his learning was being affected. She also said she would like to know what Alex needed to be able to be promoted to the next grade level. Ms. Petty feels encouraged that she is open to a positive relationship and has hopes of continuing to work with Alex's mother.

1. Teachers can build trust with caregivers by sending positive stories about children home. Often, caregivers are contacted by teachers only when something negative has occurred. Teachers can work to build trusting partnerships with caregivers by showing them they are looking for strengths their child exhibits.

2. Asking caregivers to share their goals and information about goals they have for their child helps set the stage for children to learn how their caregivers and teachers value building partnerships to work toward supporting the child's education.

REFERENCES

Adams, K. S., & Christenson, S. L. (1998). Differences in parent and teacher trust levels. *Special Services in the Schools*, 14(1–2), 1–22. doi:10.1300/j008v14n01_01

Adams, K. S., & Christenson, S. L. (2000). Trust and the family–school relationship: Examination of parent–teacher differences in elementary and secondary grades. *Journal of School Psychology*, 38(5), 477–497. doi:10.1016/s0022-4405(00)00048-0

Boutte, G., Keepler, D., Tyler, V., & Terry, B. (1992). Effective techniques for involving "difficult" parents. *Young Children*, 47(3), 19–22.

Edwards, P. A., Pleasants, H. M., & Franklin, S. H. (1999). *A path to follow: Learning to listen to parents*. Portsmouth, NH: Heinemann.

Robinson, K., & Harris, A. L. (2014). *The broken compass: Parental involvement with children's education*. Cambridge, MA: Harvard University Press.

ADDITIONAL RESOURCES

American Federation of Teachers. (n.d.). Building caregiver–teacher relationships. Retrieved from www.readingrockets.org/article/building-parent-teacher-relationships

Colorín Colorado. (n.d.). The parent-teacher conference. Retrieved from www.colorincolorado.org/article/parent-teacher-conference

Teaching Channel's tips for caregiver–teacher conferences: www.teachingchannel.org/video/parent-teacher-conference-tips

MODULE 20
Caregivers of Students Who Have Suffered Trauma

SECTION 1: CASE SCENARIO

Context

Luciana is an 8th-grade Latina student at Park Lake Middle school, which is located in a middle-class suburb. Luciana speaks Spanish and English. Ms. Rider is a middle-class African American woman in her late 30s. She speaks mainly English but has learned a few conversational Spanish phrases from her students during her 15 years of teaching.

Scenario

Ms. Rider has received an email from Luciana's caregiver, Raúl Sanchez, who shared that Luciana's cousin had been playing with a handgun he had found. The cousin had died after the gun accidentally went off. Mr. Sanchez asked Ms. Rider to help determine how to share this information with Luciana. When Ms. Rider started teaching, she never expected that she would have to address students experiencing such traumatic events. She feels it is beyond her training to know how to respond to the many forms of trauma, including gun violence, sexual assault, and bullying. She wondered how to respond to this caregiver's email. What was the best way for caregivers to tell a young teenager that her beloved cousin had passed? And, as her teacher, how could she best support Luciana over the coming weeks and months?

SECTION 2: EXPLORING CURRENT PERSPECTIVES

 Complete Appendix A, Tasks for Section 2: Exploring Current Perspectives.

SECTION 3: GETTING ON THE SAME PAGE

Research indicates that nearly one in four children experiences a traumatic event prior to turning 3 years old (Briggs-Gowan, Ford, Fraleigh, McCarthy, & Carter, 2010; Mongillo, Briggs-Gowan, Ford, & Carter, 2009). Teachers should be knowledgeable about how trauma affects the nation's youth so they can assist students with making sense of traumatic events when they do occur.

Defining Trauma

According to the National Child Traumatic Stress Network (2003), trauma is defined as an experience that significantly threatens or negatively impacts an individual's physical, physiological, or emotional well-being. Figure 20.1 depicts common types of trauma that children experience. It is important to remember that experiencing a traumatic event does not always result in traumatization. Traumatization occurs when there is prolonged activation of a stress response without the presence of protective supports and relationships (Grant, 2017).

Indicators of Trauma and Traumatization

Experiencing a traumatic event can interfere with how students engage in daily tasks and responsibilities as well as their interactions with others. According to the Centers for Disease and Prevention (n.d.), common indicators of trauma can be emotional (e.g., fear, grief, depression) and/or behavioral (e.g., nausea, dizziness, changes in appetite or sleep, withdrawal from activities). Children typically experience these types of responses for a few weeks to months. However, if the response persists or worsens, the child might be experiencing traumatization. Within classroom spaces, students who experience traumatization may display defiance, aggression, manipulation, inattention, or withdrawal (Grant, 2017). As Terrasi and de Galarce (2017) have suggested, "teachers who are unaware of the dynamics of complex trauma can easily mistake its manifestations as willful disobedience, defiance, or inattention, leading them to respond to it as though it were mere 'misbehavior'" (p. 36). Teachers should thus be aware of the indicators of trauma so they do not incorrectly assume a student is misbehaving.

Figure 20.1. Types of Trauma Commonly Experienced by Children.

*Adverse childhood experiences are divided into three categories: (1) abuse, which can be physical, mental, or emotional; (2) neglect, which can include emotional or physical forms; and (3) household challenges, including exposure to domestic violence, low levels of caregiver supporting, hostile caregiving styles, substance abuse, mental illness, caregiver divorce or separation, and exposure to crime within the household, larger family network, or neighborhood (Barr, 2018).

Preparing for and Responding to Traumatic Experiences

When students experience traumatic events, teachers should support their resilience. The National Child Traumatic Stress Network (n.d.) has outlined a three-step process to guide educators' actions: Step 1: Readiness, Step 2: Response, and Step 3: Recovery.

During the readiness phase, schools and teachers establish relationships with local entities, such as law enforcement, community organizations, religious institutions, students' families, and mental health resources. Teachers foster secure relationships with students so they feel safe within classroom spaces. These secure relationships can extend beyond the classroom by identifying family members, friends, or community members with whom each student already has or could establish a supportive relationship. In addition to relationship-building, teachers can create a safe, stable, and caring classroom environment by thoughtfully considering how students perceive different classroom interactions and activities (Perry, 2009).

During the response phase, the goal is to reestablish the sense of security and safety. Students and staff should view the school environment as being conducive to learning rather than causing fear and anxiety. Remember that there are limits to one's capacity to address trauma. Many teachers have limited training on how to address traumatic experiences. It is essential to recognize personal limitations so outside supports and experts can assist when needed.

For example, trained professionals (e.g., school counselors, school mental health professionals, social workers) should determine the degree of exposure for all staff and students involved in the traumatic experience. Then the experts can identify appropriate intervention efforts, determining what is needed and with whom efforts should begin. In addition, this group of trained professionals can assist students and staff with understanding reactions to the trauma, verbalizing their feelings, and learning to recognize triggers that might renew feelings of fear and anxiety. It is important to inform caregivers about response efforts and any important changes (e.g., new security measures or a review of the school safety plan).

During the recovery phase, remember that experiencing trauma and traumatization affect brain functioning. Therefore, teachers' actions must focus on changing how the brain functions and perceives experiences rather than changing students' behaviors. This process of recovery will vary among individuals, so those who are supporting the process need to remain steadfast in their efforts. To create long-term recovery, teachers should initially focus on ensuring that students' basic needs are consistently and positively met. Within school spaces, teachers should maintain routines and activities so that there is a sense of comfort and a natural opportunity for students to collectively process their experiences. Following initial efforts, teachers, alongside caregivers and community members, can establish partnerships and support networks addressing the complexities of traumas and restoring a positive, caring, and safe school environment that promotes individual and collective well-being.

SECTION 4: LISTENING TO EXPAND PERSPECTIVES

 Complete Appendix B, Tasks for Section 4: Listening to Expand Perspectives.

SECTION 5: FIXING IT

 The following are suggestions for working with families whose child is experiencing trauma. Complete Appendix C, Tasks for Section 5: Fixing It, for further reflection and analysis. While many of these strategies are appropriate for multiple phases, they are listed under the ideal phase when teachers might engage in the suggested action step.

Preparation Phase

- Refer to the student's educational records, conversations with caregivers, and previous teachers to resolve knowledge gaps about the student's history.
- Attend professional development opportunities addressing trauma.
- Establish a positive, safe, and caring classroom and school environment that promotes social, emotional, and mental health competence.
- Validate students' input by using communication strategies such as a calm voice and neutral body language.
- Organize the classroom with neural colors, natural lighting, and decluttered walls.
- Educate caregivers, students, and staff about symptoms of and supports for mental health concerns.

Response Stage

- Recognize when trained help to support recovery is needed.
- Follow directives from trained professionals who are leading response efforts.
- Identify pathways to refer students to recovery efforts.
- Inform caregivers about changes to procedures, processes for gaining information, and indicators that their child might need professional assistance with recovering from the trauma.

Recovery Stage

- Critically evaluate classroom projects for potential triggers. If a project could be a trigger, consider if there is an alternative project that would be better. Speak with caregivers about potential triggers and how best to design alternative projects.
- Consider how to adapt the daily classroom schedule to include appropriate supports such as predictable transitions, check-ins with caregivers, visual cues, or sensory breaks.
- Provide sensory items (e.g., stress balls, chewing gum, limited visual distractions, calming music) that help students to regulate. Never penalize students by withholding these as a consequence for misbehavior.
- Resume daily routines as soon as possible. Daily routines should be kept unchanged when possible so that a sense of familiarity is fostered.
- Resolve day-to-day conflicts so stress levels don't increase.
- Seek support for the student from his or her current relationships so the student can talk freely about feelings and experiences.

SECTION 6: REBUILDING THE CASE

When Ms. Rider started teaching she never thought she would have to address students experiencing traumatic events. Now she needs to know how to respond to the many forms of trauma such as gun violence, sexual assault, and bullying. Thankfully, each year, trained mental health and social workers provide staff in Ms. Rider's district with professional development about preparing for, responding to, and recovering from trauma.[1]

Ms. Rider is distressed by the email she received from Mr. Sanchez earlier in the evening[2] about the sudden death of her student's beloved cousin.[3] Ms. Rider is thankful that Mr. Sanchez shared the unfortunate news, as this alerts her that Luciana might need support during the upcoming days, weeks, and months. It also creates the space for future conversations about how Luciana is processing this event. Ms. Rider responded to Mr. Sanchez by offering her deepest sympathies. She asked for permission to reach out to their district's social worker and grief-counseling team[4] since they would have ideas on how to share the news with Luciana and support her initial processing of the information. She let Mr. Sanchez know that she would report back within 24 hours. Ms. Rider plans to watch for indications of extreme grief or distress so she can alert Luciana's caregivers. She knows that supportive relationships[5] will help Luciana feel secure and safe to talk about how she is feeling as she grieves the loss of her cousin.

1. Alternatively, school districts may not have access to funding or trained trauma experts. The increased national focus on trauma has led to increased accessibility of resources, of which many are free. For starters, see the additional resources and readings listed below.

2. Caregivers might not readily share details about out-of-school traumatic experiences with the school, so it is important to note any changes in students' behaviors and dispositions so that you can inquire about what might cause these changes.

3. If the scenario had been different, such as the death of a different relative or a different outcome (e.g., severe injury but not death), this might alter Ms. Rider's immediate and future responses. For example, if a caregiver had passed, Ms. Rider might take different steps initially to support Luciana since losing a caregiver is likely even more traumatic than losing a close cousin.

4. Districts might not have personnel whose responsibilities are to support students experiencing trauma. If there are no trained professionals within the school district, it might be necessary to seek the support and assistance from outside professionals. Remember to identify times when there is a need for trained help.

5. The student might be new to the district, or the trauma could occur near the beginning of the school year. In these circumstances, the relationships among the student, caregiver, and teacher are still developing. Relationship-building can occur while you provide supportive response efforts. Try to establish a sense of security and support with the student.

REFERENCES

Barr, D. A. (2018). When trauma hinders learning. *Phi Delta Kappan, 99*(6), 39–44.

Briggs-Gowan, M. J., Ford, J. D., Fraleigh, L., McCarthy, K., & Carter, A. S. (2010). Prevalence of exposure to potentially traumatic events in a healthy birth cohort of very young children in the northeastern United States. *Journal of Traumatic Stress, 23*, 725–733.

Grant, S. (2017, August). Creating a trauma-informed school. Presentation to public schools in Holland, Michigan.

Mongillo, E. A., Briggs-Gowan, M. J., Ford, J. D., & Carter, A. S. (2009). Impact of traumatic life events in a community sample of toddlers. *Journal of Abnormal Child Psychology, 37*, 455–468.

National Child Traumatic Stress Network. (n.d.). Families and trauma. Retrieved from www.nctsn.org/resources/topics/families-and-trauma

National Child Traumatic Stress Network. (2003, Fall). What is child traumatic stress? Retrieved from www.samhsa.gov/sites/default/files/programs_campaigns /childrens_mental_health/what-is-child-traumatic-stress.pdf

Perry, B. D. (2009). Examining child maltreatment through a neurodevelopmental lens: Clinical applications of the neurosequential model of therapeutics. *Journal of Loss and Trauma, 14*, 240–255.

Terrasi, S., & de Galarce, P. C. (2017). Trauma and learning in America's classrooms. *Phi Delta Kappan, 98*(6), 35–41.

ADDITIONAL RESOURCES

Center for Mental Health Services resources for educators: www.mentalhealth.org /talk/educators

Child Welfare Information Gateway. (2013). *What is child abuse and neglect? Recognizing the signs and symptoms.* Retrieved from www.childwelfare.gov/pubPDFs /whatiscan.pdf

Child Welfare Information Gateway. (2015). Mandatory reporters of child abuse and neglect. Retrieved from www.childwelfare.gov/pubPDFs/manda.pdf

Collaborative for Academic, Social, and Emotional Learning (CASEL): casel.org

National Center for School Crisis and Bereavement: www.schoolcrisiscenter.org

National Child Traumatic Stress Network's resources for school personnel: www .nctsn.org/resources/audiences/school-personnel

Substance Abuse and Mental Health Services Administration's National Child Traumatic Stress Initiative: www.samhsa.gov/child-trauma

INVOLVING AND EMPOWERING CARETAKERS

MODULE 21
Curriculum-Based Versus Event-Based Caretaker Involvement

SECTION 1: CASE SCENARIO

Context

Ms. Evans is 27-year-old White teacher who teaches 5th grade in a rural setting. Her principal is constantly encouraging her to find ways to involve her caregivers. She has held events such as school carnivals, bake sales, ice cream socials, Donuts for Dads, and Muffins for Moms, but she feels frustrated because she believes these events are not adequately reaching all of the families and caregivers in the community.

Scenario

Ms. Evans is frustrated because she feels that caregivers are not involved in their children's education. Many caregivers never return notes, answer phone calls, attend meetings, or check their child's homework. However, the improvement plan for her school states that teachers must work on caregiver engagement, so she organizes events such as ice cream socials, Donuts for Dads, and Muffins for Moms. While turnout for the school carnival is large, only a few caregivers attend the Donuts for Dads and Muffins for Moms, and those who do attend are the same ones who serve in the PTA. While her planned events draw a few caregivers into the building, Ms. Evans doesn't see any improvement in her students' learning.

Ms. Evans entered teaching because she wanted to make a difference in the lives of young students, but she feels the students' caregivers just aren't helping her in the ways she envisioned. It is now November, and she's concerned about her students' academic achievement as well as caregiver involvement initiatives. Similar to what has happened over the past years, she feels she's losing control.

SECTION 2: EXPLORING CURRENT PERSPECTIVES

 Complete Appendix A, Tasks for Section 2: Exploring Current Perspectives.

SECTION 3: GETTING ON THE SAME PAGE

Caregiver involvement in children's education matters for their achievement, motivation, and well-being at schools. Overwhelmed with curriculum, assessment, and meetings, among many other expectations, teachers continuously express a desire for caregiver support and involvement (Croft, 1979; Edwards, 2016; Lareau, 2000). Epstein (1982) expressed a similar view: "School cannot always provide individual attention to children who need extra help on skills, nor can schools always offer a range of activities to enrich the basic education program" (p. 1).

As a society, we have focused our energy on trying to change schools and have ignored the home experience. It is possible that in placing so much of the responsibility of developing successful adults into the hands of the schools, we have not been clear on what we want from caregivers. We have not been able to clearly express to caregivers what we would like them to do for their children beyond suggesting general activities such as "help with homework," "read, talk, and listen to your child," "tell them stories, play games, share hobbies," and so on. While schools cannot assume sole responsibility for developing family–school partnerships, they should be the ones to make the first step in initiating the partnership process. In many cases, caregivers do not know the discourse of school well enough or have the confidence in their own educational abilities to take the lead in fostering academically supportive relationships with their children and their children's teachers.

Caregivers are the acknowledged first teachers of their children and need to maintain their role in their children's academic life. Unfortunately, most caregivers do not know where to start. When caregivers are not sure how to support their children's literacy learning or how to integrate themselves into the business of the school, many feel paralyzed, inadequate, and powerless (Clark, 1988). And what, exactly, should caregivers be doing to help their child become academically successful?

Caregiver involvement means more than getting parents to attend school carnivals, bake sales, and ice cream socials. This type of limited involvement is often accessible mainly for parents who are not employed full time, which involves only a small percentage of students' caregivers. Seefeldt (1985) noted that schools should capitalize on the curriculum as an ongoing means of communicating with parents about their child's day and the school's goals and objectives.

While schools might feel overburdened by all the roles they are already expected to assume, I (Pat) would like to suggest that by taking seriously the role of caregivers in the educational process and becoming specific about the actual help from caregivers we need, burdens actually become lifted as responsibilities are shared. Before collaborating with parents, Edwards and Danridge (2001) suggest that teachers should "think about the specific goals and expectations. It would be helpful for teachers to connect these goals and expectations to curricular and instructional practices" (p. 254). Although teachers may do all they can to provide successful literacy for their students, continued success is "dependent upon people and factors outside the classroom and beyond their control" (Hannon, 1998, p. 123). Classroom teachers, therefore, need to ensure that the literacy curriculum is open to home–school partnerships.

This requires that teachers and caregivers establish collaborative relationships around specific goals. Edwards (2016) suggests that curriculum-based caregiver involvement provides a rich context for children's learning, but it is also an opportunity for further enriching children's learning through new forms of caregivers' participation in the curriculum. However, general ideas such as "helping the child to succeed this year" or "providing a good education" can be frustrating and confusing to caregivers because expectations and goals are not explicit enough to provide direction to caregivers who themselves may have a history of school failure. When vague pronouncements dominate, important differences between teachers and caregivers remain unexplored. Little negotiation about meaning and action occurs, and the collaborative effort suffers (Corbett, Wilson, & Webb, 1996). Many caregivers have begged for teachers to instruct them on what to do, but they are often not given clear directions at each grade level on how they might best contribute, especially in relation to the literacy curriculum. The failure of schools to successfully address such issues is yet another reason why family–school partnerships have been difficult to create.

I (Pat) suggest a scope and sequence as a new form of caregiver participation in the curriculum. I define scope and sequence as grade-level caregiver involvement activities that are based on shared decisionmaking and built around the elementary school literacy curriculum (Edwards, 2004, p. 283). I believe that very few schools schedule activities in August that they want caregivers to participate in throughout the year. As a result, caregiver involvement does not become a set of structured activities that caregivers can expect to participate in throughout the year. Here is a sample of scope and sequence of caregiver involvement within the literacy curriculum:

Kindergarten—Sharing Time
1st Grade—Emergent Literacy
2nd Grade—Reading and Writing Connections
3rd Grade—Writing Process
4th Grade—Content Area Reading
5th Grade—Content Area Reading

This scope and sequence can become the foundation for meetings in which teachers and parents collaborate on a grade-level project (see Edwards, 2004). The meetings establish a predictable structure for parents to communicate information about how their child is responding to instruction in school. Caregivers become more knowledgeable about the school curriculum, but they also contribute information about their children's struggles, concerns, and progress. Many caregivers offer each other ideas about how they have worked successfully with their children.

By schools taking seriously the role of caregivers in the educational process and becoming specific about the help needed from caregivers, burdens are lightened as responsibilities are shared. This requires that teachers and caregivers establish collaborative relationships around specific goals.

SECTION 4: LISTENING TO EXPAND PERSPECTIVES

 Complete Appendix B, Tasks for Section 4: Listening to Expand Perspectives.

SECTION 5: FIXING IT

 The following are suggestions for involving caregivers in curriculum-based activities. Complete Appendix C, Tasks for Section 5: Fixing It, for further reflection and analysis.

- Provide information and ideas on how best to assist with homework and other curriculum-related activities. Encourage reading at home by creating a custom reading list based on each student's personality, interests, and skill level.

- Keep a notebook of classroom facts, the curriculum, study resources, contact information, key terminology, and tips detailing how caregivers can support their child's progress. Establish a homework hotline that families can call to retrieve forgotten or missed assignments.
- Start a blog. A blog can be a fantastic tool to share classroom updates and involve caregivers throughout the year. Public or private, your blog can become the place where you discuss study activities, your personal philosophy on teaching, field trips, and more.
- Record videos. Seeing your face is a good way to humanize communications and help parents connect with you. This can be a friendly way for you to share major updates and methodologies with parents if you can't do it in person.

SECTION 6: REBUILDING THE CASE

Ms. Evans is frustrated because she feels that caregivers are not involved in their children's education. Many caregivers never return notes, answer phone calls, attend meetings, or check their child's homework. However, the improvement plan for her school states that teachers must work on caregiver engagement. Instead of holding another bake sale,[1] Ms. Evans decides to organize caregiver informant meetings[2] to provide an opportunity for teachers and caregivers to participate in conversations that will promote caregivers' understanding of how their children are developing as readers and writers. These meetings will establish a predictable structure for caregivers to communicate information on how their children respond to instruction in school and for teachers and caregivers to collaborate on grade-by-grade activities around curricular issues.

1. Perhaps such events are not held at times that align with caregivers' work schedules, or communication is not sent home in languages that caregivers understand. But more importantly, these events are not supporting children's academic achievement.

2. When scheduling these meetings. Ms. Evans considers caregivers' varied work schedules and availability. She also ensures that communication about the meetings is sent home in multiple modes and in languages caregivers understand and to all of the caregivers in blended or reconstituted families.

REFERENCES

Clark, R. M. (1988). Parents as providers of linguistic and social capital. *Educational Horizons, 66*(2), 93–95.

Corbett, H. D., Wilson, B., & Webb, J. (1996). Visible differences and unseen commonalities: Viewing students as the connections between schools and communities. In J. G. Cibulka & W. J. Kritek (Eds.), *Coordination among schools, families, and communities: Prospects for educational reform* (pp. 27–48). Albany, NY: State University of New York Press.

Croft, D. J. (1979). *Parents and teachers: A resource book for home, school, and community relations.* Belmont, CA: Wadsworth Publishing Company.

Edwards, P. A. (2004). *Children's literacy development: Making it happen through school, family, and community involvement.* Boston, MA: Allyn & Bacon.

Edwards, P. A. (2009). *Tapping the potential of parents: A strategic guide to boosting student achievement through family involvement.* New York, NY: Scholastic.

Edwards, P. A. (2016). *New ways to engage parents: Strategies and tools for teachers and leaders, K–12.* New York City, NY: Teachers College Press.

Edwards, P. A., & Danridge, J. C. (2001). Developing collaborative relationship with parents: Some examples. In V. Risko & K. Bromley (Eds.), *Collaboration for diverse learners: Viewpoints and practices* (pp. 251–272). Newark, DE: International Reading Association.

Epstein, J. L. (1982). Student reactions to teacher practices of parent involvement. Paper presented at the annual meeting of the American Educational Research Association, New York City.

Hannon, P. (1998, May). Family literacy in a balanced early childhood program. Paper presented at the 43rd annual meeting of the International Reading Association, Orlando, Florida.

Lareau, A. (2000). *Home advantage: Social class and parental intervention in elementary education* (2nd ed.). Lanham, MD: Rowman, & Littlefield Publishers, Inc.

Seefeldt, C. (1985). Communicate with curriculum. *Day Care and Early Education, 13*(2), 22–25.

ADDITIONAL RESOURCES

Dye, J. S. (1989). Parental involvement in curriculum matters: Parents, teachers and children working together. *Educational Research, 31*(1), 20–35.

Reading Rockets: Launching Young Readers website: www.readingrockets.org/launching

Get Ready to Read, a website with tips and activities for parents with young children: www.getreadytoread.org

MODULE 22
Connecting Caregivers with Community Resources

SECTION 1: CASE SCENARIO

Context

Michael is a White, male 2nd-grader at Armstrong Elementary, situated in a suburban city in the Midwest. He, his siblings, and his single mother have moved around a lot, due to their low-income financial situation. His mother currently is on disability and unable to work due to a health condition.

Mr. Ward, a White male in his mid-30s, chose teaching as a second career and has 7 years of teaching experience. He previously worked in customer service.

Scenario

It is about the middle of the school year in Mr. Ward's 7th year of teaching. Michael is a student in Mr. Ward's 2nd-grade class. He is 7 years old and has a brother in 4th grade and a baby sister at home. Michael is an energetic child who is friendly with most of his classmates.

Having administered the district's reading assessments, Mr. Ward noticed that while Michael is a strong math student, he is currently performing below the district's grade-level reading expectations. Mr. Ward plans to differentiate instruction and provide reading intervention in order to meet Michael's learning needs. Also, Mr. Ward would like to help make sure Michael has a consistent routine for reading at home to reinforce what he is learning in school.

Mr. Ward believes a home–school connection is critical for students and hopes caregivers will encourage their children to read at home. During open house, Mr. Ward passed out a list of book recommendations for caregivers and told them about a weekly reading log he would be sending home. Over the first 3 months of school, Michael has turned in only one reading log, partially completed. When Mr. Ward asked him to describe his at-home reading, Michael shrugged it off and said he wasn't sure why he doesn't turn in completed reading logs.

Mr. Ward sees Michael's mom at dismissal one day and decides to ask her about Michael's at-home reading routine. She tells Mr. Ward their family owns very few books. She says that they have moved a few times and have not been able to maintain a good collection of books. Michael's mom also says that when she asks Michael to read, he sometimes refuses and says he doesn't like the books at his house and that they have "nothing to read." Michael's mom also says she isn't sure what types of books Michael should read.

Michael's mom asks Mr. Ward if he has any books he could let them borrow. He is tempted to loan Michael's mother some books, but in the past some students have lost books when they borrowed them. Mr. Ward has paid for most of the books with his own money and cannot afford to replace more books. The principal has also stated that teachers are not permitted to send home books that are owned by the school. Mr. Ward wants to increase Michael's access to at-home reading materials but isn't sure how to do so.

SECTION 2: EXPLORING CURRENT PERSPECTIVES

 Complete Appendix A, Tasks for Section 2: Exploring Current Perspectives.

SECTION 3: GETTING ON THE SAME PAGE

A child's experiences with reading largely depend on their family/caregiver upbringing as well as the community in which they live (Neuman & Celano, 2001). Providing children with access to books can increase their motivation for reading, improve their reading performance, and help them learn the basics of reading. Teachers often tell caregivers and students that they should be reading at home, yet may not consider children's individual level of access to texts. They may also make assumptions that children have home libraries or easy access to purchasing or borrowing books that might be needed. Many factors influence children's access to print, including the type of community in which they live and their socioeconomic status. It is critical for teachers to understand what resources students have access to and to help caregivers learn how to obtain additional print resources if necessary. It is also important for teachers to understand that sometimes, out of fear or pride, caregivers are reluctant to ask for help in accessing resources (Edwards, Pleasants, & Franklin, 1999), so teachers might need to take the reins and send out information to the class as a whole.

Location Is Important

The type of community a school is located in can affect the availability of resources for students. Whether a school is located in a rural, suburban, or urban setting might factor into the types of resources available. Caregivers in urban areas are likely to be close to a public library, whereas rural families might live very far from their community library.

Teachers should consider the district in which their school is located. If it is a rural district, how might teachers help caregivers locate literacy resources? They might try local organizations, such as churches, that could offer transportation for families who are unable to get to the library easily. Additionally, a library in a rural community might offer online resources that families could access inside their homes, making literacy accessible without travel. If a school is located in an urban community, the resources available to students might extend beyond churches and libraries to include YMCA/YWCA programs and local shelters. Educators should learn which resources are available in a school's community or district and how they might be accessible to students and caregivers.

Edwards, Pleasants, and Franklin (1999) provide teachers with practical ways to provide resources for students' caregivers. They discuss how teachers can create a resource file tailored to their students' situation. Through getting to know students' families, teachers can collect and distribute information about community resources that will best meet the individual needs of all caregivers. Additionally, Edwards (2016) recommends that schools and teachers determine local "voluntary and legal organizations" that can provide resources for caregivers. Some examples include the following:

- Sports clubs/activities for children and adults
- Religious and cultural groups and organizations
- Voluntary and community organizations
- Key services such as doctors, clinics, libraries, dentists
- Community and adult learning providers
- People who represent the official or formal community such as city council members, police, firefighters

Money Matters

A caregiver's ability to build a home library depends on many factors, including their financial status and their ability to purchase books. There are, however, organizations that donate books to children. Dolly Parton's Imagination Library is one example of a way for children to receive free books. Some community agencies sponsor their community through Imagination Library, and when children sign up they receive a free book in the mail every month from birth to age 5. This is just one example of an organization working toward getting books inside all children's homes. Many book-donation organizations are specific to a community, so teachers can search what is available in their school's area.

In addition, public libraries regularly hold sales or giveaways of their discarded books, most of them in fine condition. Teachers can gather information about local libraries and find out if and when they might hold sales. Caregivers might be able to purchase books at minimal cost.

Finally, caregivers can seek free reading resources by searching for Little Free Libraries in their community. The Little Free Library organization's motto is "Take a book. Share a book." The program is set up by community members who build small shelters to house books. Community members then donate books for others to take as they please. The idea is that people are consistently rotating and sharing books. Teachers might help caregivers locate a Little Free Library close by, or encourage volunteers to build one in the school neighborhood.

Free Technology Resources

- *Apps.* Many families have access to smartphones or tablets at home. Thousands of apps have been designed to enhance children's education. Many literacy resources are available to caregivers at no charge. Teachers can preview some of the apps, especially ones they use in class, and share a list with caregivers. Free apps are ideal for many students. Teachers should consider which apps are most appropriate for the students they teach.
- *Online books.* Many books are available online for children and adults alike. Both nonprofit and commercial organizations provide a variety of texts online. Teachers can preview the texts prior to recommending to ensure the recommended texts are representative of diverse racial, ethnic, and socioeconomic groups. Such organizations include the following:
  » The Library of Congress Center for the Book. This organization promotes books and libraries, providing many classic titles online: read.gov/cfb/about.html
  » Storyline Online. This resource provides videos of celebrities reading popular children's titles aloud: www.storylineonline.net
  » Public libraries, many of which have recently added free electronic books to their collections. A library card can provide caregivers access to a wide variety of electronic books.

SECTION 4: LISTENING TO EXPAND PERSPECTIVES

 Complete Appendix B, Tasks for Section 4: Listening to Expand Perspectives.

SECTION 5: FIXING IT

 The following are some items to consider for teachers looking to connect students and caregivers to literacy resources available in their community. Complete Appendix C, Tasks for Section 5: Fixing It, for further reflection and analysis.

- Available resources might vary widely across communities. For example, rural communities might lack resources that urban communities make accessible.
- Educators might try reaching out to community organizations, such as churches, to learn if they offer educational outreach for individuals or families. They would then share this information with students and their caregivers.
- Before sharing resource ideas with caregivers, teachers should consider the expense involved. Many caregivers are unable to afford "extra" educational resources, in which case teachers would want to help them locate resources that are available for free.
- While printed books are critical to a child's reading development, sharing technological resources that caregivers could use on smartphones, tablets, or computers might be a good idea for some households.
- Before recommending books or other reading materials to students and their caregivers, always consider what types of book recommendations are appropriate to make. Do the books cover a variety of genres? Are the books representative of diverse racial, ethnic, and socioeconomic backgrounds?

SECTION 6: REBUILDING THE CASE

Knowing that a home–school connection is critical to a child's literacy development, Mr. Ward took steps to help direct caregivers to literacy resources available within the school's community. Over the summer, he had contacted various local legal and volunteer organizations and created a folder of potential literacy resources that Michael's mom and other students' caregivers could use.[1] Mr. Ward also found a local church that would provide transportation to and from the library for families that would like to access books.[2] When meeting with Michael's mom, Mr. Ward shared with her some examples of resources she could get from the library. He also shared some caregiver–child classes that the library was offering. Michael's mom feels encouraged by Mr. Ward's help, and plans to reach out to the church and library.

Within a few short weeks, Mr. Ward has noticed that Michael has turned in a completed reading log three times. Michael is excited to be able to choose new books, and has even brought in his own library copy of a book Mr. Ward reads aloud to the class each day. Mr. Ward decides to write a quick note to Michael's mom to inform her of Michael's excitement and to thank her for getting involved in helping Michael access more literacy resources.

1. Location is critical when teachers consider community literacy resources. In urban settings, public transportation may be much more available than in rural settings.

2. Local, nonprofit organizations are often motivated to help students and caregivers in need. Churches, for example, will provide transportation to caregivers in need.

3. Libraries are also wonderful resources for students and their caregivers. Teachers should consider barriers that some families might experience when planning a visit to a library (e.g., transportation, time constraints, etc.).

REFERENCES

Edwards, P. A. (2016). *New ways to engage parents: Strategies and tools for teachers and leaders, K–12.* New York, NY: Teachers College Press.

Edwards, P. A., Pleasants, H. M., & Franklin, S. H. (1999). *A path to follow: Learning to listen to parents.* Portsmouth, NH: Heinemann.

Neuman, S. B., & Celano, D. (2001). Access to print in low-income and middle-income communities: An ecological study of four neighborhoods. *Reading Research Quarterly, 36*(1), 8.

ADDITIONAL RESOURCES

Dolly Parton's Imagination Library: imaginationlibrary.com

MODULE 23

Caregiver Empowerment:
Making Caregivers Feel Comfortable at School

SECTION 1: CASE SCENARIO

Context

Tamara is an African American female student at Heritage Elementary, which is located in a small southern town in the United States. Tamara's mother and father, Linda and John, both work full-time jobs, but their family is considered lower working class.

Ms. Hart, a middle-income, White female, has been teaching for 15 years. She has never quite felt successful in involving each of her students' families every year.

Scenario

Tamara is a shy, quiet student in Ms. Hart's 5th-grade class. Her work habits are strong, and she is eager to please teachers. Despite her efforts, her academic performance is consistently below grade-level standards according to district assessments. Tamara's parents, John and Linda, have attended Open House and parent–teacher meetings. They have expressed concern about Tamara's academic performance yet seem reluctant to open up to suggestions Ms. Hart has made for at-home support. When Ms. Hart mentioned a parent literacy education class presented by the district, Tamara's mother answered with an emphatic "No." She responded that she didn't get the help she needed from the district when she, herself, was a student so she didn't see the need to go to a class now. Ms. Hart would like to help Linda and John feel more comfortable at school, thus increasing chances for them to build a parent–teacher partnership to help Tamara, but Ms. Hart isn't sure how to proceed.

SECTION 2: EXPLORING CURRENT PERSPECTIVES

Complete Appendix A, Tasks for Section 2: Exploring Current Perspectives.

SECTION 3: GETTING ON THE SAME PAGE

Caregivers' own experiences as students can influence their perceptions of how they might be involved at their child's school. A caregiver who had a difficult schooling experience might feel reluctant to become involved. Also, caregivers who feel their child's schooling is inadequate or who don't know how to share their thoughts might not know how to become involved. Or, possibly, caregivers are unable to physically be involved at the school, so they feel they are not able to be involved at all. There are ways schools and teachers can work with caregivers to empower them to become involved at their child's school.

Invite Input

Caregivers' opinions of their children's schooling vary widely, even within one individual school. While some caregivers might feel content with how their child is being taught, others might resent the services rendered to their children. Often, schools offer little to no outlet for caregivers to provide feedback, which might fuel frustration. Sometimes caregivers might not know exactly how to assert themselves into being involved at the school. Caregivers might interact in ways that teachers perceive to be negative or ill-natured, which might discourage teachers from promoting caregiver engagement. Although school staff might not explicitly state their expectations for caregivers to be "positive" and "polite," this is the implicit standard for caregiver behavior in most schools (Lareau & Horvat, 1999). Caregivers who had difficult schooling experiences or perceive a difficult experience for their child might shy away from school involvement.

Schools might curtail potential avoidance of caregiver involvement by inviting caregivers to provide input about their child's schooling experience. Providing caregivers an outlet to share input allows them the opportunity to weigh in regarding their child's experience, thus giving them a feeling of empowerment. Schoolwide input is valuable, as well as caregivers providing input on individual teachers or grade levels. Teachers can help caregivers feel empowered by offering them chances to share their reflections on their child's schooling experiences. Encouraging surveys, installing a comment box, or holding a town hall event provides caregivers opportunities to provide feedback that could be constructive.

Share Stories

As discussed earlier, caregiver stories are a way for caregivers to feel understood, or heard, as well as a way to foster open lines of communication, leading to building trust in the school (Edwards, Pleasants, & Franklin, 1999). Teachers can invite caregivers to share stories about their family, and perhaps their own schooling experiences, giving them an opportunity to build fellowship within the school. When educators demonstrate an interest in getting to know their students' families, caregivers will feel more comfortable at school and might feel more empowered to be involved. By using students' caregivers' "funds of knowledge" (Moll, Amanti, Neff, & Gonzalez, 1992) as a foundation for student learning, teachers and schools demonstrate that all involvement from all caregivers is welcome and encouraged.

Differing Levels of Involvement

Schools and teachers can draft unique definitions of what it means for caregivers to be involved at their school. For example, some people may envision working at holiday parties or spending all day outside working at field day. Others may envision spending a few hours per week leading reading groups or science experiments. Caregiver involvement of this sort can be very helpful to teachers, but caregivers with little to no time outside of work and other daily routines might feel alienated. Before teachers send out caregiver volunteer sign-up sheets, they might consider alternative ways for caregivers with little extra time to become involved without being physically inside the school building.

Caregiver involvement can range from being physically present in the classroom to staying abreast of what is going on in a child's classroom and talking with them about it. Caregivers might stay involved through reading a weekly blog or finding ways to motivate and encourage their children's schooling. Teachers might consider having a parent–child interaction around academic content as part of a homework assignment. Teachers and schools can reiterate to caregivers that being involved is taking an interest in their child's education and setting the stage for academic success.

SECTION 4: LISTENING TO EXPAND PERSPECTIVES

 Complete Appendix B, Tasks for Section 4: Listening to Expand Perspectives.

SECTION 5: FIXING IT

 The following are suggestions for empowering caregivers. Complete Appendix C, Tasks for Section 5: Fixing It, for further reflection and analysis.

Invite Input

- Consider asking caregivers to fill out a brief survey at the beginning of the year. Ask them to share their goals for their child in the upcoming year.
- Consider offering a suggestion or comment box. Invite caregivers to share constructive comments that might help with developing a partnership with them.
- Respond to caregivers who provide feedback. Let them know they have been heard.

Learn Caregivers' Stories

- Ask caregivers to share their own schooling experiences either in a survey or at a parent conference. Ask them how they see their own schooling as compared to that of their child.
- Consider having children interview their caregivers about their own schooling experience and have them reflect together on goals for the school year.

Differing Levels of Involvement

- Share with caregivers how involvement can differ among differing families. Give them examples of how they might help, going beyond classroom parties. Consider that some caregivers work full time and their time is limited.
- Consider framing school involvement as having regular conversations with their child about school. Assign this as homework so that the children see their caregivers' continued investment in their schooling.

SECTION 6: REBUILDING THE CASE

This year, Ms. Hart put some measures in place to encourage caregiver involvement in the school. Each week, she sends home conversation-starters that relate to the work her students complete in class.[1] For example, as students were working on learning about character point of view, Ms. Hart suggested to caregivers, "Think of a movie that is familiar to your child. Ask them how the 'bad guy' might explain the situation differently." She also asked students to interview a member of their family and present the information in the form of a slide show.[2] She asked students to share photos of their chosen family member electronically or to bring them into the classroom. Tamara selected her mother, Linda, as the subject of her interview. Tamara talked to the class about how her mother had served in the National Guard. When Ms. Hart met with Tamara's parents at caregiver–teacher conference time, she made sure to mention specific points of Tamara's presentation. When Ms. Hart mentioned a parent literacy education class presented by the district, Tamara's mother replied that she would like to hear more about it. She responded that she didn't get the help she needed from school when she was young, but that she would like to see Tamara have a better experience than she had. Ms. Hart would like to help Linda and John feel more comfortable at school, thus increasing chances for them to build a caregiver–teacher partnership to help Tamara.

1. By providing conversation-starters with caregivers, Ms. Hart has given Tamara's parents the opportunity to be involved with Tamara's schooling, with little to no effort. They are tuned into what is going on in the classroom and also providing ways to apply Tamara's learning in new situations.

2. The interview project is one way to have caregivers share family stories, and to show them that their family backgrounds matter in the classroom.

When Ms. Hart met with Tamara's parents, they were likely more receptive to her feedback because she had taken opportunities to show she had a genuine interest in learning about Tamara and her family.

REFERENCES

Edwards, P. A., Pleasants, H. M., & Franklin, S. H. (1999). *A path to follow: Learning to listen to parents*. Portsmouth, NH: Heinemann.

Lareau, A., & Horvat, E. M. (1999). Moments of social inclusion and exclusion: Race, class, and cultural capital in family–school relationships. *Sociology of Education, 72*(1), 37.

Moll, L. C., Amanti, C., Neff, D., & Gonzalez, N. (1992). Funds of knowledge for teaching: Using a qualitative approach to connect homes and classrooms. *Theory into Practice, 31*(2), 132–141.

ADDITIONAL RESOURCES

Dell'Angelo, T. (2014, December 10). The beginners' guide to connecting home and school. *Edutopia*. Retrieved from www.edutopia.org/blog/beginners-guide-connecting-home-school-tabitha-dellangelo

Head Start Early Childhood Learning and Knowledge Center's Digital tools for engaging caregivers to support children's learning: eclkc.ohs.acf.hhs.gov/family-engagement/article/digital-tools-engaging-parents-support-childrens-learning

Michigan Department of Education's strategies for strong parent/caregiver and family engagement: www.michigan.gov/documents/mde/strategies_for_strong_parent_and_family_engagement_part_II_370142_7.pdf

Michigan Department of Education, examples of traditional and nontraditional parent/
    caregiver participation: www.michigan.gov/documents/mde/traditional_and
    _non-traditional_parent_participation_370139_7.pdf

MODULE 24
Technology and Literacy

SECTION 1: CASE SCENARIO

Context

Tatiana is a Latin American female at Lakeside Elementary, located in a rural community in southeastern United States. Tatiana's family is considered middle income.

Ms. Warren, Tatiana's teacher, is a White female who has taught elementary school for 25 years.

Scenario

It is a few months into the school year, and Ms. Warren notices that her 4th-grade students are not turning in reading logs as consistently as they were at the beginning of the year. Some students who turned them in regularly at the beginning of the year are either turning them in intermittently or not at all. Additionally, she has noticed that some students' logs indicate they are reading a fewer number of days and in fewer chunks of time. When Ms. Warren questions students, they tell her they don't have as much time to read as they did before. She decides to ask caregivers at upcoming caregiver–teacher conferences for ideas in helping students increase reading time at home.

At caregiver–teacher conferences, Ms. Warren polls caregivers about students' at-home reading times. Several caregivers tell her they have a difficult time getting their children to get off electronic devices and read a book. They report that their children are "obsessed" with using mobile devices such as smartphones and playing video games. Esme, Tatiana's mother, even tells Ms. Warren that she downloaded some reading games, but Tatiana lost interest in the games after only a few minutes. Esme asks Ms. Warren for help. After speaking with the majority of students' caregivers, Ms. Warren learns that most of them have tablets or smartphones and that these devices are holding students back from getting reading done at home. When the subject comes up at conferences, caregivers ask Ms. Warren if she has any solutions on how to balance electronics and books.

SECTION 2: EXPLORING CURRENT PERSPECTIVES

 Complete Appendix A, Tasks for Section 2: Exploring Current Perspectives.

SECTION 3: GETTING ON THE SAME PAGE

The prevalence of technology in students' everyday lives is emerging as a topic in early childhood educational research studies. Mobile technology has infiltrated children's educational experiences as well as their private lives at home. Teachers in many schools have incorporated tablets into literacy instruction. Tablets require users to read and manipulate what is on the screen. Researchers have found that reading digital texts has distinct similarities to reading printed texts, yet there are differences as well. For example, for both digital and printed texts, readers must be able to decode letter and sound systems as well as understand vocabulary (Coiro & Dobler, 2007). On the other hand, when readers encounter a digital text, they do not necessarily read from left to right, top to bottom. They may begin reading a box in the left corner and click on a link that takes them somewhere altogether different from where they started. Thus, the definition of literacy and what it means to be literate, among adults as well as children, is changing as a result of ubiquitous mobile device use in and out of schools. Scholars have noted that it is important to consider how digital literacy, which includes "literacy practices . . . enacted in digital spaces" (Marsh, Hannon, Lewis, & Ritchie, 2017, p. 47), affects a student's overall literacy development.

Tablets, smartphones, and other devices are becoming more affordable and easily accessible. They are often marketed as tools to assist in a child's education, but with little guidance and support from teachers and caregivers, children tend to use them primarily for entertainment. However, now that smartphones, tablets, and other devices have infiltrated homes and schools, teachers need to provide caregivers with information on how to help their children use these devices to enhance literacy development at home.

Consider Access

A first step is to survey students and caregivers to see what types of devices, if any, are accessible to them in their homes. Despite the prevalence of digital devices, some households may have no access. Before teachers send out information on how to use digital devices to enhance literacy, they must know precisely what tools their students can access. Students with little or no access at home might need to use school or library resources. Some libraries have a check-out system for mobile devices.

Digital Texts

There are a variety of digital texts freely available to children with mobile devices. Teachers can help caregivers use these devices to enhance their child's literacy development by giving them information on how to locate digital picture books. Many digital picture books offer animations to stories as a narrator reads aloud, which can be engaging for young students. Be sure to remind caregivers that the goal is *reading*, and that too many bells and whistles might distract young readers from engagement in reading. Also, digital picture books usually offer a range of ways for children to interact with the texts. One student might choose to listen to the text read aloud, while another might choose to read it themselves and turn the pages by tapping the screen when they are ready. Teachers can check if local libraries offer access to digital picture book applications as one way for families to gain free access to digital books. Also, websites are available that allow teachers to set up accounts for students and their families to use at home.

Digital picture books are not the only online texts available to students. Most children's novels, as well as many magazines, are accessible online. Most public libraries offer access to electronic books that can be downloaded for free. A library card is required, and there is usually a finite time period during which the book can be accessed, but once a student sets up an online account (for free), they can begin reading loads of books. Online magazines are another online reading option. Again, teachers should caution caregivers that games and advertisements might distract their children from reading. It's important for educators and caregivers to guide young readers as they begin to explore the digital world—otherwise, little actual reading will occur.

There's an App for That

Teachers can also explore mobile app stores for applications that might complement classroom learning. Many free apps are dedicated to enhancing literacy development for students of all ages. Investigating free apps helps to ensure that the chosen digital literacy practice can be accessed by all households with access to mobile devices. Teachers can "test drive" the apps to ensure they cover the skills necessary and that they are age, subject, skill, and grade appropriate. Some apps might claim to be educationally driven despite failing to address any specific educational goals. "Taking a test drive" will allow teachers to see if the app actually does what it claims or if it is simply designed to entertain.

Mobile Tools

Many mobile devices come with a lot of tools already installed that could be used in literacy instruction. Teachers should explore the types of tools and apps available, as new ones are always being created. Some tools might not be advertised as literacy instruction tools or educational apps, but teachers might discover that they inspire writing and reading. Photo- and video-making apps, voice-recording apps, bookmaking apps, and email and text apps can all provide avenues for literacy instruction. Students might take photos and write a story about their photo. They might do an interview activity in which they write questions and use a voice recorder to interview someone in their families. Teachers can use email and texting in literacy instruction by having children connect with each other or family members. The possibilities for using mobile tools to accompany literacy instruction appear to be limitless.

SECTION 4: LISTENING TO EXPAND PERSPECTIVES

 Complete Appendix B, Tasks for Section 4: Listening to Expand Perspectives.

SECTION 5: FIXING IT

Consider Access

Teachers should learn which devices are accessible to their students. Some students might be inundated with technology at home, and others might have little or no access. In order to do this, teachers can do the following:

- Survey families to find out which devices students use at home and what they use them for.
- Talk with caregivers at caregiver–teacher conferences and share ways that technology is incorporated in the classroom.
- Find out if the school or local organizations lend devices to families in need.
- Before recommending any apps or software, consider the cost. Obviously, apps that can be used at no charge will benefit more students.

Digital Texts

Public libraries often offer a collection of digital books for children to access. Additionally, some book collection apps, such as Epic, are freely available for educators and librarians to share with children.

Mobile Tools

Remind caregivers that literacy is more than sitting and reading a book. Talk with them about ways they can help their children use digital tools to tell or share stories. Suggest ways for them to help their children balance entertainment with educational activities.

SECTION 6: REBUILDING THE CASE

It is a few months into the school year and Ms. Warren notices that her 4th-grade students are not turning in reading logs as consistently as they were at the beginning of the year. Some students who turned them in regularly at the beginning of the year are either turning them in intermittently or not at all. Additionally, she has noticed that some students' logs indicate they are reading a fewer number of days and in fewer chunks of time. Ms. Warren questioned students and they say that they don't have as much time to read as they did before. She decides to ask caregivers at upcoming caregiver–teacher conferences to see how to help students increase reading time at home.

Ms. Warren decides to offer caregivers some electronic resources at upcoming caregiver–teacher conferences.[1] At Open House, Ms. Warren completes a short survey about children's access to digital devices at home.[2] She discovers that nearly all of her students—everyone but two—have access to either a smartphone or a tablet, such as an iPad. Ms. Warren signs up for an online reading repository, Epic, in which caregivers can receive free access. She shares the link at caregiver–teacher conferences and shows caregivers how they can access books online. For the two students with no access to digital devices at home, Ms. Warren informs their caregivers that the local library gives free access to tablets while visiting the branch. Using the library's website, she shows them online resources they can access while at the library. Esme, Tatiana's mother, tells Ms. Warren that she previously downloaded some reading games, but Tatiana lost interest in the games after only a few minutes. She says she wasn't aware of electronic books available for free and looks forward to trying out Epic.

Ms. Warren also assigns students to take some digital photos and to ask their caregivers to text or email the photos to her for use in the classroom. She asks students to choose one photo to write about in class. She works with the school librarian to allow her two students with no access to digital devices at home to check out an older digital camera. She asks the students to take the camera home to take photos of their families. She then helps these students download the photos and use them in the writing activity.

1. Teachers can explore which electronic resources may be easily accessible by families and then share ones they find helpful to their students."

2. "By surveying families, Ms. Warren is able to see who has access to mobile resources."

REFERENCES

Coiro, J., & Dobler, E. (2007). Exploring the online reading comprehension strategies used by sixth-grade skilled readers to search for and locate information on the Internet. *Reading Research Quarterly, 42*(2), 214–257.

Corbett, H. D., Wilson, B., & Webb, J. (1996). Visible differences and unseen commonalities: Viewing students as the connections between schools and communities. In J. G. Cibulka & W. J. Kritek (Eds.), *Coordination among schools, families, and communities: Prospects for educational reform* (pp. 27–48). Albany, NY: State University of New York Press.

Marsh, J., Hannon, P., Lewis, M., & Ritchie, L. (2017). Young children's initiation into family literacy practices in the digital age. *Journal of Early Childhood Research, 15*(1), 47–60.

ADDITIONAL RESOURCES

Family Media Plan: www.healthychildren.org/English/media/Pages/default.aspx

Epic: www.getepic.com

Library of Congress Center for the Book: read.gov/cfb/

Common Sense Media's tips for how to choose educational apps, games, and websites: www.commonsensemedia.org/guide/essential-school-tools/s/related-info/How%20to%20Choose%20Educational%20Apps%2C%20Games%2C%20and%20Websites

Tasks for Section 2: Exploring Current Perspectives

Task 1: Initial Reaction

Directions: Consider how you would react to the scenario if you were the student's teacher. The guiding questions below will support your thoughtful reflection. Jot down notes or bullet points that respond to each of the guiding questions.

1. After "experiencing" the scenario, what would your feelings and inner thoughts be?
2. How would you respond to this situation?
3. What do you know or did you learn about the student as a learner from this experience?
4. What do you know or did you learn about the student's family?

Task 2: Maslow's Hierarchy

Directions: Consider Maslow's (1943) Hierarchy of Needs (pictured below). Then complete Table 2, Mapping Individual Needs Onto Maslow's Hierarchy.

Self-
Actualization
Needs
(achieve potential,
self-fulfillment)

Esteem Needs
(achievement, adequacy,
independence, reputation, recognition)

Love/Affection and Belongingness Needs

Safety Needs
(security, health and wellness, knowing what to expect)

Physiological Needs (food, water, sleep)

Table 2. Mapping Individual Needs onto Maslow's Hierarchy

Individual	What are the individual's needs as described in the scenario?	Where do these needs fit on Maslow's Hierarchy of Needs?
The Student		
The Student's Caregiver(s)		
The Teacher		

Task 3: Probing Deeper

Directions: Consider issues of power, prestige, positioning, and access as defined in Chapter 2. Complete Table 3, Considerations of Power, Prestige, Positioning, and Access, based on the case scenario.

Table 3. Considerations of Power, Prestige, Positioning, and Access

| Individual | WHAT ARE THE THREATS (REAL OR PERCEIVED) TO THE INDIVIDUAL'S . . . | | | |
	Power?	Prestige?	Positioning?	Access?
The Student				
The Student's Caregiver(s)				
The Teacher				

Task 4: Summarizing

Directions: For each individual, compare what they need (Table 2) with what threats they are experiencing to their power, prestige, positioning, and access (Table 3). What overlaps exist between the two tables (Table 2 and Table 3)? Write down any overlapping needs and threats in Table 4, Summarizing Overlapping Needs and Threats.

Table 4. Summarizing Overlapping Needs and Threats

Individual	Overlapping Needs & Threats (Real or Perceived)
The Student	
The Student's Caregiver(s)	
The Teacher	

Tasks for Section 4: Listening to Expand Perspectives

Task 5: Probing Even Deeper

Directions: Let's probe this background information more deeply. What additional potential threats to the individual's power, prestige, positioning, and access were identified in the background information presented? List all potential threats in Table 5, Expanded Considerations of Power, Prestige, Positioning, and Access.

Table 5. Expanded Considerations of Power, Prestige, Positioning, and Access

Individual	BASED ON BACKGROUND INFORMATION, WHAT ARE ADDITIONAL POTENTIAL THREATS TO THE INDIVIDUAL'S . . .			
	Power?	**Prestige?**	**Positioning?**	**Access?**
The Student				
The Student's Caregiver(s)				
The Teacher				

Task 6: Integrating

Directions: After considering this background, revisit the Case Scenario. Review the information in Table 4 (Appendix A). Consider how the potential threats listed in Table 5 overlap or extend the needs and threats listed in Table 4.

For each individual, complete Table 6 by revising the needs and threats according to the information contained in Tables 4 (Appendix A) and 5 (Appendix B).

Table 6. Revised Needs and Threats

Individual	Revised Needs & Threats (Real or Perceived)
The Student	
The Student's Caregiver(s)	
The Teacher	

Tasks for Section 5: Fixing It

As noted in Chapter 2, we use the ABC (antecedent-behavior-conse-quence) model of behavior analysis (Pierce & Cheney, 2013) to extend our thinking about each case:

- *Antecedent:* Events and other behaviors that occur prior to the behavior of interest (i.e., the target behavior). Also, elements from the context in which the events or behaviors occur may be antecedents.
- *Behavior:* What the student, family, or teacher does that is of interest. This is referred to as the "target behavior." The target behavior is pivotal because it shapes the consequences or outcomes.
- *Consequence:* The outcome or what transpires as a result of the target behavior occurring.

Task 7: Analyzing

Directions: Complete Table 7, ABC Model, below. For each of the listed be-haviors, identify the antecedents. These can be either known antecedents identified in the Case Scenario or potential antecedents outlined in Getting on the Same Page. Next, identify consequences (either known or potential).

Use the following questions to guide your thinking as you complete Table 7. An example has been provided for you.

- What are the student's underlying needs? What are potential threats to the student's power, prestige, positioning, or access?
- What are the caregivers' underlying needs? What are potential threats to their power, prestige, positioning, or access?

Table 7. ABC Model

Antecedent	Behavior	Consequence
Ex. Caregivers' work schedules conflict with school start times.	*Ex. Arriving to school late*	*Ex. Student misses instruction.*

Task 8: Identifying Action Steps

Directions: After completing the ABC chart above, select the desired behavior(s) that you want to encourage. You will complete Table 8 for each identified target behavior. In the table below, phrase the desired behavior in positive terms (i.e., as something you want to happen).

Next, brainstorm ways to alter the antecedents and/or consequences so that the selected behaviors are more likely to occur. By reviewing the expanded perspectives described in Getting on the Same Page, you can identify antecedents/consequences that could contribute to increasing the desired behaviors.

A note about brainstorming ways to increase desired behaviors: proposed alterations to antecedents/consequences should address how personnel at the school (e.g., after-school care staff, teacher, support staff) and caretakers might be involved. Proposed alterations should *not* depend solely on the involvement and actions of the caretakers! Remember: The greatest success depends on collaboration among the school, caretakers, and the community.

Please use the following questions to guide your thinking as you identify altered antecedents and/or consequences.

- How would you respond to this situation in ways that meet the student's and the student's caregivers' underlying needs and preserve (and hopefully increase) their power, prestige, positioning, and access? Keep in mind that identified responses should be feasible, meet your needs as the teacher, and reflect an asset-based perspective.
- How do the potential responses you have identified affect the student's academic achievement and/or emotional well-being?

Table 8. Target Behaviors

Selected Target Behavior _____

Altered Antecedents	Behavior	Altered Consequences
Ex. Relatives or friends transport student to school. Identify additional backup drivers that parents could call if they are running late and relatives/friends are not available.	*Ex. Arriving to school on time*	*Ex. Student did not miss instruction.*

Index

About the Authors

Patricia A. Edwards, member of the Reading Hall of Fame and NCRLL (National Conference on Research in Language and Literacy) Distinguished Scholar, is a professor of language and literacy in the Department of Teacher Education at Michigan State University. She is a nationally and internationally recognized expert in parent involvement; home, school, and community partnerships; multicultural literacy; early literacy; and family/intergenerational literacy, especially among poor and minority children. She served as a member of the IRA board of directors (1998–2001), as the first African American president of the Literacy Research Association (formerly the National Reading Conference; 2006–2007), and as president of the International Reading Association (2010–2011). She has published articles in numerous highly refereed journals and authored two nationally acclaimed family literacy programs: *Parents as Partners in Reading: A Family Literacy Training Program* (1990, 1993) and *Talking Your Way to Literacy: A Program to Help Nonreading Parents Prepare Their Children for Reading* (1990). She is the coauthor of *A Path to Follow: Learning to Listen to Parents* (1999, with Heather M. Pleasants and Sarah H. Franklin), *Bridging Literacy and Equity: The Essential Guide to Social Equity Teaching* (2012, with Althier M. Lazar and Gwendolyn T. McMillon), and *Change Is Gonna Come: Transforming Literacy for African American Students* (2010, with Gwendolyn T. McMillon and Jennifer D. Turner). Dr. Edwards is also the author of *Tapping the Potential of Parents: A Strategic Guide to Boosting Student Achievement Through Family Involvement* (2009), *Children's Literacy Development: Making It Happen Through School, Family, and Community Involvement* (2004), and *New Ways to Engage Parents: Strategies and Tools for Teachers and Leaders* (2016), winner of the 2017 Delta Kappa Gamma Educators Book Award. Dr. Edwards is the recipient of the Literacy Research Association's Albert J. Kingston Service Award, the International Reading Association's 2014 IRA Jerry Johns Outstanding Teacher Educator in Reading Award, and the 2015 Michigan Reading Association's Outstanding Teacher Educator Award. More recently, Dr. Edwards was named as the 2017–2018 Jeanne S. Chall Visiting Researcher at the Harvard Graduate School of Education.

Rand J. Spiro is a professor of educational psychology and educational technology at Michigan State University. Before coming to MSU, Dr. Spiro was a distinguished senior scholar in the College of Education at the University of Illinois at Urbana-Champaign, where he was professor of educational psychology, psychology, and the Beckman Institute for Advanced Science and Technology. He has been a visiting scientist in psychology and in computer science at Yale University, where he worked in the Yale Artificial Intelligence Laboratory, and a visiting professor of education at Harvard University. He was a founding member and served for a time as co-director of the national Center for the Study of Reading at the University of Illinois. He also served as chair of the Department of Educational Psychology at Illinois. His books, with various collaborators, include *Schooling and the Acquisition of Knowledge; Theoretical Issues in Reading Comprehension; Cognition, Education, and Multimedia; Hypertext and Cognition;* and *Reading at a Crossroads.* Dr. Spiro has been quoted and his ideas discussed in such national media outlets as the *New York Times*, the *Washington Post*, and the *Wall Street Journal*, as well as on National Public Radio. Dr. Spiro is the co-originator of Cognitive Flexibility Theory, a theory of learning and instruction that, with the help of novel uses of technology, supports high-proficiency learning in complex knowledge domains and realms of real-world application (including practice in the professions), with an emphasis on the acceleration of advanced learning for situation-adaptive performance.

Lisa M. Domke was an elementary teacher for 8 years in Michigan, teaching not only a range of grades, but also in a Spanish immersion program. In addition, she worked 5 years in a summer migrant education program and has taught various undergraduate and master's literacy and language courses. Lisa is in the final semester of her PhD program at Michigan State University, specializing in literacy, language learning, and emergent bilinguals/English learners. Her research focuses on elementary students' biliteracy development, including the development of children's literacy skills in multiple languages.

Ann M. Castle is a former elementary classroom teacher, Reading Recovery® teacher, literacy coach, and professional development consultant in Michigan, with two decades of experience. She is currently an elementary internship coordinator, literacy course instructor, and PhD candidate at Michigan State University in curriculum, instruction, and teacher education, with a specialization in language and literacy education. As coordinator, she facilitates yearlong student teaching experiences between teacher candidates and partner schools in the Lansing, Michigan, area. In addition, she teaches undergraduate and master's literacy methods courses, many at local elementary schools, where teacher candidates and school partners work together to learn literacy methods for practice. Her research interests include early literacy instruction and teacher preparation, with a focus on scaffolding readers during small-group differentiated instruction. Castle holds master of arts degrees in child development and K–12 reading and literacy education.

Kristen L. White is a former classroom teacher with over a decade of experience working with grades K–8. Kristen has a PhD in curriculum, instruction, and teacher education with a language and literacy specialization from Michigan State University. She is an assistant professor of education at Northern Michigan University. Interested in how young children are labeled as particular "kinds of readers" and embody reading identities, Kristen's research interrogates how materials construct children's literate identity in early childhood classrooms.

Marliese R. Peltier was an elementary special education teacher for 5 years, providing both resource room and teacher consultant supports. During her time as an elementary special education teacher, she was awarded teaching fellowships with Chicago Public Schools and the Social Equity Venture (SEVEN) Fund. Marliese has served as an elected member of the board of directors of the Michigan Council for Exceptional Children. Marliese is a doctoral candidate in curriculum, instruction, and teacher education at Michigan State University, where she is pursuing a specialization in language and literacy. Her research examines how teachers learn to enact instructional practices that (dis)connect students' home and school literacy practices. Marliese was a co-principal investigator on a Spencer Foundation grant, which examined how to support teachers in their efforts to connect students' home and school literacies.

Tracy H. Donohue worked in early literacy for over a decade in North Carolina. She has experience teaching in a whole-class setting as well as providing literacy intervention for at-risk students. Tracy also worked as an instructional coach, providing literacy support to classroom teachers as well as families within the community. Tracy also worked as a literacy consultant with the Iowa Reading Research Center. As part of her work, Tracy reached out to families across Iowa via social media and blogs to share literacy practices that can be implemented in daily family life. Tracy is particularly interested in helping educators learn how to support families in early literacy practices, and these interests are demonstrated within Donohue's parent modules within this text. Tracy Donohue is currently pursuing a PhD in curriculum and instruction and teacher education at Michigan State University. Donohue's educational background and professional experiences have motivated her to understand more about family and school partnerships.